TOP TEN THEOLOGIANS

Timothy G. Kimberley

TOP TEN THEOLOGIANS

ISBN: 1517251672
EAN-13: 978-1517251673

Printed in the United States of America.

Plough Boy

ploughboy.org

In the 1500's WilliamTyndale was talking with a friend about the need for the Scriptures to be in English. At that time, because of the Oxford Constitutions enacted in the previous century, it was not legal to own a copy of the Bible in the English language. Tyndale's friend wasn't sure people needed to know the Scriptures. He thought it might be good enough for the Pope to know the Bible in Latin and then tell all the English speakers what it says.

To this Tyndale replied, "**I defy the Pope and all his laws, if God spare my life, I will make a boy that driveth the plough know more of the Scripture than thou dost.**"

On September 6th, 1536 Wiliam Tyndale was killed and then burned at the stake for his passion to see every person, even a plough boy, have access to all of God's truth.

Plough Boy resources exist to carry on the heart of Tyndale's prophetic idea. All people, even farm boys, should have as much access to the depths of our God as any well-educated, well-financed and well-connected intellectual.

Dedicated to my beloved children:

Hannah, Silas and Grace

I hope in these pages you'll one day meet some of daddy's friends and they'll become your friends too.

TABLE OF CONTENTS

10

TOP TEN THEOLOGIANS

INTRO

INTRODUCTION

TOP TEN THEOLOGIANS

Aim of this Book

The title of this book is self evident. My aim is to introduce you to the Top Ten Theologians of Church History. Yes, I will rank them in order. I will start with #10 and work my way down to the #1 person I believe to be the greatest theologian. My aim is wrought with danger. I am foolish to attempt ranking the ten greatest theologians. I will leave out some people you think should be in the top ten. I will have some people lower in the list than you might think. I will proceed, nonetheless, because these people need to be known by the Bride of Christ.

What is a Theologian?

What is a theologian? Or more appropriately the question should be asked, "*Who* is a theologian?" A theologian is most simply someone who thinks about God. Is an atheist, then, a theologian? Yes, an atheist thinks about God. Their thoughts led them to the conclusion there is no God, but the Atheist is a theologian. Everyone is a theologian.

Are there any Atheists on our Top Ten list? No. That leads me to the Criterion upon which led to the formulation of the Top Ten list.

Criterion

First, to make the Top Ten list you need to be a Christian theologian. I should have, technically, called this Top Ten Christian Theologians, but I simply opted for a shorter title. Have there been theologians beneficial to humanity who did not have Jesus as their Savior? Yes, but this list seeks a specific Christian purpose.

Second, to make it on the Top Ten list you must be a positive influence. Friedrich Schleiermacher was an incredibly influential "Christian" theologian, yet he had a negative influence on orthodox Christianity (what everyone has believed everywhere for all time). I would refer to Schleiermacher ultimately as a heretic. I know, harsh words, but my list of Top Ten Heretics and why each person should bear that title is for another series. Overall, each one of these Top Ten Theologians positively influenced the Church.

Third, each one of these theologians must have had a broad influence in how people understand God. Faithful pastors all over the world help their congregations, through God's Word, better understand and live for Jesus. The Top Ten Theologians influenced not only their immediate congregations but also positively influenced people all over the world for decades and centuries to come. A man like Charles Spurgeon was a wonderful pastor and biblical teacher but he will not be on the list. I love Spurgeon dearly but these ten men on the list influenced the church at a deeper and wider level than Spurgeon. Spurgeon's ministry stood on the shoulders of many of the men in this series.

The list does not purposefully exclude women. There are many amazing female theologians who have made an important impact on the Church. The top ten, however, all happen to be men.

We'll look at each of these Ten Theologians through a consistent grid:

Their World

First, in order to appreciate each of these Ten Theologians we must have a certain understanding of their world. Our understanding of *their influence in their world* will help us for the sake of *our world* today. Each chapter will contain enough background information to hopefully allow us to appreciate the setting within which these people lived.

Their Life

To appreciate the Top Ten Theologians we need to examine the life they lived. Many of the Top Ten Theologians experienced tremendous adversity. If you don't care about the details of their lives you will fail to appreciate what they accomplished through their circumstances.

Their Thoughts

Ultimately, it is their thoughts we are seeking to most understand and appreciate. Many of these people wrote volumes as they meditated upon Scripture. We will spend a considerable portion of every post getting an overview of their influential thoughts to hopefully deepen us in Jesus.

Their Influence

What has been the influence of each theologian? If their thoughts represent a rock falling into a lake, their influence looks at the ripples in the water spreading out from the impact. This is one of the key areas where these people will be set apart from many other people who could have been contenders for the Top Ten list. Why have the thoughts of these people influenced so many?

Their Foibles

A foible is defined as a minor weakness or eccentricity in someone's character: "they have to tolerate each other's little foibles". Only one person who has ever lived deserves worship: Jesus Christ. Each of these ten theologians would fully agree with the previous statement. If you ask any of these people, "Are you perfect?" "Should I worship you or should I worship Jesus?" They would all plead with us to worship the living God.

Each one of the theologians had aspects of their thought and of their lives which I would not recommend for you to follow. Some acted in ways which would even be criminal at certain times and places. Every human being, if you dig deep enough, will have parts of their lives which are not admirable. Every human being desperately needs a living Savior. We will spend time in each chapter discussing the foibles of every person on the Top Ten list.

Their Effect on Us

We will then spend time explicitly seeing areas where each one of the theologians should positively affect our life. By becoming friends with these theologians my hope and prayer is your thoughts about God and your life lived before God will be the better for the time spent hanging out with a bunch of dead people.

My list is set. If you made a list right now who would be on your Top Ten? Hint, do not add yourself, you will be automatically disqualified.

Buckle your seat belt, I now offer to you our #10 Theologian.

IRENAEUS

10

#10: IRENAEUS

TOP TEN THEOLOGIANS

Irenaeus' World

In order to appreciate the influential role Irenaeus played in the history of the Church, we need to have a working knowledge of three major elements that were significant factors in Irenaeus' world: 1) the persecution of Christians; 2) Gnosticism and 3) Marcionism.

Persecution of Christians

AMPHITHEATER IN LYONS

In 177 AD several old men were eaten by wild beasts while the crowd cheered their approval. What was the crime committed by Alexander, Attalus, Espagathus, Maturus, Sactius and Pothinus? They were Christians.

Under the Roman Emperor Marcus Aurelius (161-

180 AD), persecution of Christians broke out in a region called Gaul (modern day France). People from the two major cities in Gaul: Lyons and Vienne, wrote letters to other churches letting them know of the horrendous persecution in their land. These first-hand accounts were eventually preserved and published by the first great Church historian, Eusebius (263-339 AD). The letter states:

> "*The greatness, indeed, of the tribulation, and the extent of the madness exhibited by the heathen against the saints, and the sufferings which the martyrs endured in this country, we are not able fully to declare, nor is it, indeed, possible to describe them.*"[1]

The letters do, however, go on to describe the horrors of the persecution in Lyons. After enduring lengthy torture, which killed some of the oldest Christians, the rest were taken into the Amphitheater in Lyons and eventually killed by wild beasts.

The city of Lyons and the outbreak of persecution became a very important event for our tenth most important theologian: Irenaeus.

Gnosticism

Many people in the second century flocked to a new form of the Christian message known as Gnosticism. The Greek word *gnosis* simply means knowledge. Gnostics claim there's secret knowledge you need, *in addition to the Bible*, which will open your eyes to the real truth and make it possible to truly be a Christian. Would you like to know the secret of Gnosticism? I'm sure you do. Here's what they taught:

The ultimate God is an amazing God too great to know. In the Pleroma (think: heaven), God lives and has many sub-gods. One of these sub-gods, known as Sophia, grew impatient and wanted to be like the unknowable supreme God. Pride and arrogance led her to take matters into her own hands and birth a son known as **Demiurge**. He had all the traits of his mother: sinful, prideful, arrogant, and evil. Gnostics

1 Eusebius, Ecclesiastical History, 5.1.4

taught that Demiurge then created the world, and everything in the world was evil.

The ultimate God placed on the evil earth some good spirits, known as **Aeons**. These Aeons occupy evil bodies and give them the chance to escape the world and rise to be part of the Pleroma.

Quite a cast of characters, huh? You might know Demiurge through another name - Yahweh. **According to Gnostics, the Yahweh we read of in the Old Testament is evil, everything Yahweh created is evil, and his people, Jews, are especially evil since they worship an evil god.** So what is the secret that allows evil people to be saved from the evil world? Here is the way a Gnostic would explain the way to salvation:

You might have an Aeon inside you, which is a "seed of light" that needs to be turned on in order for your eyes to be opened to the truth. How does your "seed of light" get turned on? Well, let me quote a verse you probably already know: "*For God so loved the world, that he gave his only Son, that whoever believes in him should not perish but have eternal life.*" *(John 3:16)*

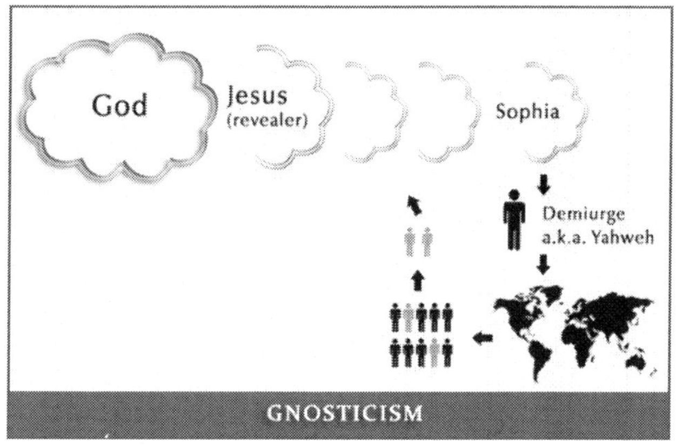

You see, the true God, not that evil Yahweh sub-god, sent another glorious sub-god named Christ to enlighten select Aeons. Christ had to join up with the evil body of a man named Jesus (luckily only for a little while) to give people the secret knowledge. A Gnostic would then ask you to believe in Jesus today as your Savior. He came for you to show you the way. He is the way, the truth and the life. No one comes to the unknowable God but through Him.

Gnostics would tell you that Jesus came to rescue you from the deceptions of the evil Yahweh and his people.

One of the leading Gnostics, who had a big following, was a man named Valentinus. He will become a huge part of Irenaeus' world. Valentinus gained so much popularity that he would become a leading candidate for the next Bishop of Rome.

Marcionism

I will not go into as much detail on Marcionism. Marcion had many of the same ideas as the Gnostics. However, he is known uniquely for his approach to the Bible. Marcion rejected The Old Testament. He saw these as the writings which spoke of an evil god. He only liked the New Testament. He didn't, however, like all of the New Testament. He only acknowledged one of the Gospels, the book of Luke. He came up with a list of 11 total books which he believed to be the Scripture for Christians. Irenaeus would interact directly with the ideas of Marcion.

This is the world into which Irenaeus was called to fulfill his role in history – a world filled with persecution, Gnosticism, and Marcionism. Iraneus would be called by God to contend with these three factors for the minds of the Christians he would influence.

Irenaeus' Life

Little is known of Irenaeus's life. He was born in Asia Minor (modern day Turkey) in 130AD. As a young man he saw and heard Polycarp of Smyrna.[2] It is unclear how much Polycarp may have mentored Irenaeus. Polycarp was a well-known lead pastor (bishop).

Polycarp is known for two things. First, he was directly discipled by John the Apostle. Yes, the same John who wrote the book of Revelation. How's that for an impressive résumé? Second, Polycarp is famous for how he died. When Irenaeus was 25 years old, the aged Polycarp was given an ultimatum: Worship the gods of Rome, reject Jesus, or you

---

2 Bettenson, Henry. The Early Christian Fathers. Page 12.

will die. Honoring Polycarp for his old age, the proconsul insisted if he would only curse Christ he would be free to go.

Here's Polycarp's response in the face of martyrdom, "*For eighty-six years I have served him, and he has done me no evil. How could I curse my king, who saved me?*"[3]

Polycarp was tied to a post and fires were lit to burn him alive. When the fire failed to touch him, he was then stabbed.[4] Irenaeus describes Polycarp as "*a man who was of much greater weight, and a more steadfast witness of truth, than Valentinus, and Marcion, and the rest of the heretics.*"[5]

Irenaeus watched his mentor die for a faith which Valentinus and Marcion were seeking to corrupt.

In 177 AD, Irenaeus was offered a new job. Pothinus had just been martyred for being the bishop of Lyons. There was now a job opening. When both your mentor and your predecessor have been killed for their faith, it's clear the health benefits of the job aren't that good. Would you accept the position? Irenaeus courageously accepted the position and became the bishop of Lyons. An important position in an important city.

Irenaeus spent his life doing two things: shepherding the flock given to him by God, and refuting the beliefs of the Gnostics and Marcionites.

---

3 Gonzalez, Justo. The Story of Christianity. Page 44.
4 The Martyrdom of Polycarp
5 Irenaeus, Against Heresies. III.3.4

Only two of his literary works survived: the *Demonstration of Apostolic Faith*, and the famous *On the Detection and Overthrow of the So-called Gnosis* – more popularly known by its Latin title *Adversus Haereses* ("Against Heresies").

IRENAEUS

Tradition places the death of Irenaeus (some say by martyrdom) in the first years of the next century (202 AD).[6] He survived for 25 years as the bishop of Lyons.

Irenaeus' Thoughts

Irenaeus may justly be called the first biblical theologian; for him the Bible is not a collection of proof-texts as it is for the church leaders who came before him, but a continuous record of God's self-disclosure and his dealings with man, reaching its culmination in the person and work of Christ.[7]

With Gnostics and Marcionites in mind, he upholds the importance of the entire Old and New Testaments. Jeffrey Bingham, Department Chair and Professor of Theological Studies at Dallas Theological Seminary, writes:

> *What distinguished Irenaeus from the heretics was his theme of unity and his commitment to interpreting Scripture within the parameters of the faith passed down from apostle to bishop. What has been entrusted from one faithful Christian to another always plays an important role in interpretation.*[8]

6 Bettenson. The Early Christian Fathers. Page 12.

7 Bettenson. P 13.

8 Bingham. Pocket History of the Church. P 42.

Irenaeus saw the Bible speaking to the importance of interpretive tradition:

> *Timothy, guard what has been entrusted to your care. Turn away from godless chatter and the opposing ideas of what is falsely called knowledge, which some have professed and in so doing have wandered from the faith. (1 Tim. 6:20-21)*

> *What you heard from me, keep as the pattern of sound teaching, with faith and love in Christ Jesus. Guard the good deposit that was entrusted to you – guard it with the help of the Holy Spirit who lives in us. (2 Tim. 1:13-14)*

> *The things you have heard me say in the presence of many witnesses entrust to reliable men who will also be qualified to teach others. (2 Tim 2:2)*

It is clear to Irenaeus that Gnosticism and Marcionism were never taught by Jesus, the apostles, nor the earliest followers of Christ. We do not need secret knowledge to unlock the Bible. There is no hidden layer of meaning that re-interprets the entire Bible. He declares:

> *All Scripture, given to us by God (2 Tim. 3:16), will be found consistent. The parables will agree with the clear statements and the clear passages will explain the parables. Through the polyphony of the texts a single harmonious melody will sound in us, praising in hymns the God who made everything.* [9]

No one can change the message of God. Irenaeus emphasizes this when he writes:

> *Nor will any one of the rulers in the Churches, however highly gifted he may be in point of eloquence, teach doctrines different from these (for no one is greater than the Master); nor, on the other hand, will he who is deficient in power of expression inflict injury on the tradition. For the faith being ever one and the*

9 Irenaeus. Against Heresies. 2.28.3

> *same, neither does one who is able at great length to discourse regarding it, make any addition to it, nor does one who can say but little diminish it.* [10]

Irenaeus became the first human to fully articulate the extent of the Word of God. He classifies as Scripture not only the entire Old Testament, but also most of the books known today as the New Testament. He quotes from 21 of the 27 New Testament books, while clearly excluding many Gnostic books which flourished in the 2nd century. Where Marcion only accepted a heavily edited form of Luke's gospel, Irenaeus asserted there were four Gospels: Matthew, Mark, Luke, and John. He states:

> *It is not possible that the Gospels can be either more or fewer in number than they are…he that sits on the churbim and holds all things together, when he was manifested to humanity, gave us the gospel under four forms but bound together by one spirit.* [11]

Irenaeus focused a great deal of his effort in refuting the Gnostic view of God (unknowable who is not Yahweh) and Christ (a sub-god sent to thwart Yahweh). He possessed an advanced view of the incarnation of Christ and of the Trinity.

He writes, "*The Father is Lord and the Son is Lord, and the Father is God and the Son is God; for that which is begotten of God is God.*" [12] This wording is not so clearly articulated at a wide level until the Council of Nicea 200 years later!

To make it clear the Trinitarian God, not the Demiurge, created the world, Irenaeus writes:

> *For always with him are his Word and Wisdom, the Son and the Spirit, through whom and in whom he made everything freely and independently, to whom he also speaks when he says, 'Let Us make man after our image and*

10 Ibid. 1.10.2

11 Irenaeus. Against Heresies. 3.11.8

12 Irenaeus. Demonstration. P 47

> *likeness' (1:26), taking the substance of the creatures from himself as well as the pattern of things he adorned.* [13]

Irenaeus wrote volumes, surrounded by persecution, articulating what he believes to be the biblical teaching on many topics being used by the Gnostics and Marcionites to confuse, mislead, and threaten the pure Bride of Christ.

Irenaeus' Influence

In a pivotal era where people are seeking to change the message of Jesus, Irenaeus is the distinct figure viewed as shaping orthodoxy (correct thought).[14] The bishop from Lyons, with a Bible in his hand and a heart to accurately shepherd his people in the Way effectively labored to keep the church from embracing Gnosticism and Marcionism.

His articulation of Scripture, which was not yet in canonical form throughout Christian communities, helped to show a certain collection of writings to be Scripture.[15]

His surprisingly advanced view of the Trinity, along with contemporaries like Tertullian, became the foundation upon which the Church would ultimately build the famous articulation all of church history at the Council of Nicea in 325 AD.

John Lawson applauds the talent behind his legacy by saying, "Irenaeus is a man of many-sided genius." [16]

Irenaeus' Foibles

If Irenaeus is removed from the 2nd century and the chaotic influence of Gnosticism and Marcion, his thoughts can be harmfully taken out of context. Some of his teachings could be misconstrued if not interpreted as a direct response to the Gnostic teachings.

---

13 Against Heresies. 4.20.1

14 Green. Shapers of Christian Orthodoxy. P 59.

15 Ibid., P 51.

16 Ibid., p 60.

For example, Irenaeus refutes the Gnostic belief that Jesus was not fully human by describing Christ as the second human Adam. In order to show the Gnostics the extent of Christ being human he depicts Mary as the second Eve. Christ must be fully human. His mother was fully human as well. However, in putting Mary and Jesus on the same level, some would charge Irenaeus with leading people into a heretical idea. This concept of equating Mary and Jesus is something that is today known in Roman Catholic circles of Mariology as the Co-Redemptrix (Mary as the co-redeemer of humanity).

This unfortunate metaphor that Irenaeus used in his teaching, not aware how it would be interpreted centuries later, is a small foible on his otherwise spotless record as a theologian. Irenaeus lived so long ago we do not know much about his personal life. Most of his foibles, therefore, are lost to history.

Irenaeus' Effect on Us

I hope Irenaeus' legacy will fill you with new courage to step into an unknown situation and do anything possible to shepherd those around you in the entire Word of God. Irenaeus helped to direct his people to Jesus through every page of Scripture. Jesus is not only the messenger, but the message of all Scripture.

I hope you will find a renewed passion for the importance of the Word of God, the importance of understanding and teaching the Trinity, and the importance of living for a Savior who is both completely like us and completely God. The world in which Irenaeus lived threatened to erase all of those ideas from humanity. Please let Irenaeus inspire you to courageously uphold and live out these important realities in the sphere of your world.

TURN TO PAGE
167
TO EXPERIENCE
IRENAEUS IN HIS
OWN WORDS

KARL BARTH

9

#9: KARL BARTH

In order to appreciate Barth, it is important to understand a couple people/movements playing a crucial role in Barth's world: The Enlightenment; Friedrich Schleiermacher and Adolf Hitler.

Barth's World

The Enlightenment

Imagine living in a world where you know more than your parents. Every teenager would respond, "That's easy to imagine! My parents are clueless." In the 1600's and 1700's, however, people genuinely knew more about life than those who came before them.

Guess what? The earth is actually round, not flat. For so many centuries we thought the earth was the center of our solar system. Not anymore. The sun, not the earth, is at the center of our little world.

A newly discovered land called America is being colonized across the

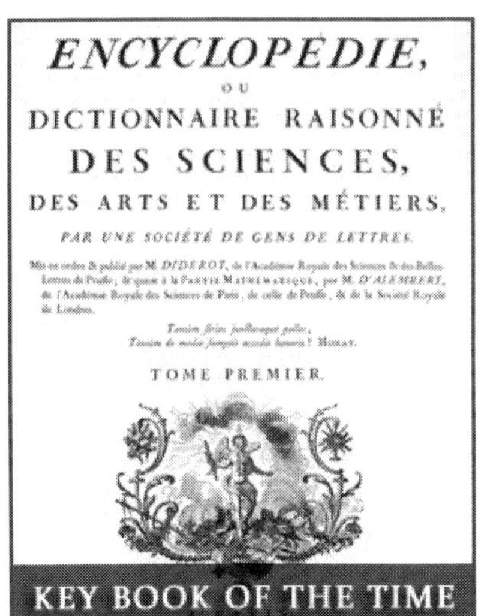

ENCYCLOPÉDIE,
OU
DICTIONNAIRE RAISONNÉ
DES SCIENCES,
DES ARTS ET DES MÉTIERS,
PAR UNE SOCIÉTÉ DE GENS DE LETTRES.

TOME PREMIER.

KEY BOOK OF THE TIME

Atlantic Ocean. The laws of the universe are being unlocked by Isaac Newton with the recent discovery of gravity. The Age of the Enlightenment, also known as the Age of Reason, is turning the world upside down. People felt they were emerging from centuries of darkness and ignorance into a new age enlightened by reason and science.

If our grandparents and great grandparents had been so naïve about our world, where else were they naïve? [Warning: the next sentence is a spoiler alert!] Imagine the whole world, for centuries, believing Santa Claus flew in his sleigh, came down your chimney, ate your cookies, drank your milk and left you a gift. For the first time the world collectively understands our dad is eating the cookies. We're not little kids anymore; we see the world with adult eyes.

We know there was a man named Saint Nicholas who lived a long time ago. Our research shows he was born in 270AD in modern-day Turkey. He was a gracious man who secretly gave gifts to people. Yes, he existed but I'm not so naïve any more to believe he drank my milk, in my house, on December 24th. The scientific method, coupled with reason, allows us unprecedented understanding. The Age of Reason now turns its suspicious eye to the Church.

Many end up surmising:

> *We know there was a man named Jesus who lived a long time ago. Our research shows he was born around 5BC in the city of Bethlehem. He was a holy man whom we greatly respect. Yes, he existed but I'm not so naïve any more to believe he walked on water, was the actual son of God, and he definitely didn't die for the sins of the entire world.*

Friedrich Schleiermacher

Could Christianity survive such inquiry? Would it crumble under the scientific method? Friedrich Schleiermacher came on the scene to save Christianity. He would become one of the most famous "Christians" of the last 400 years.

Schleiermacher loved the faith. Let's stay with our Christmas illustration. Just like everybody else, he didn't believe in Santa Claus anymore. Was he ready to cancel Christmas? **No way, are you kidding me? He loved Christmas.** He loved the warm fuzzy feeling of Christmas. It was such a marvelous season of the year. Spending time with people you love, eating wonderful food, the glow of the fire warming your soul. Waking up early on Christmas morning is so delightful. Schleiermacher would never dream of cancelling Christmas. He actually wanted everyone to love the feeling of Christmas.

SCHLEIERMACHER

Schleiermacher could care less about Christmas; my illustration is merely to show the approach he took in trying to save Christianity from the Enlightenment. Schleiermacher reduced Christianity to a single aspect: the romantic notion of *feeling*.[1] It didn't matter what you thought about God, the important response came from your feelings toward God. God is a powerful being, but He is not to be separated from the world. Think of it this way, Santa Claus really only exists within the atmosphere of Christmas. God does not exist in some objective sense; God exists within the feelings of the people. Why was Schleiermacher a Christian? Couldn't he have been a Buddhist? **He thought Jesus was**

1 Bingham. Pocket History of the Church. P.151

the all-time best at feeling God.

Jesus didn't have to be God, walk on water, or die for the sins of humanity. He believed we needed his example to show us how to best *feel* God. Schleiermacher was a follower of Christ because Christ was the most religious man who ever lived.[2] It is like Jesus had the greatest "Christmas Spirit" and those who follow Jesus closely will have the most "Christmas Spirit."

Friedrich Schleiermacher became the father of a movement called Theological Liberalism. Riding the wave of the Enlightenment seminaries from differing denominational backgrounds adopted Schleiermacher's thoughts. Princeton (Presbyterian), Harvard (Calvinist), Dartmouth (Congregationalist), Brown (Baptist), and Yale (Calvinist) all adopted much of Modern Theological Liberalism.

No one would stand toe-to-toe against Schleiermacher and theological liberalism as much as Karl Barth. In addition to standing against Schleiermacher, Barth also faced one of the most hated human beings to ever live. Instead of trying to "save" Christianity, Adolf Hitler looked to destroy the Church.

Adolf Hitler

Most of the men on our Top Ten list interacted with more than one "big time" issue during their lifetime. In addition to the rise of Theological Liberalism, Karl Barth lived in Germany during the rise of Adolf Hitler. Karl Barth was just 3 years older than Hitler. When Hitler became the leader of Germany in 1934, Barth was 48 years old.

Hitler capitalized on the shameful loss of World War I and the crushing Versailles Treaty to once again try to make Germany a great country. Without getting into all the events and theology of the Third Reich it is beneficial to mention a few things.

First, Hitler secretly wanted to destroy Christianity but realized he would become more politically powerful if he used Christianity for his own

---

2 Bingham. Pocket History of the Church. P.151

purposes. Hitler adopted a strategy "that suited his immediate political purposes."[3] He worked to unify the entire church of Germany under the "German Christian" movement. He used Christians as pawns all the while believing, "*We do not want any other god than Germany itself. It is essential to have fanatical faith and hope and love in and for Germany*"[4] He hoped to destroy Christianity in Germany once the war had ended.

ADOLF HITLER

Second, In *Mein Kampf*, Hitler refers to Martin Luther as a great warrior, a true statesman, and a great reformer.[5] Hitler tried to position himself as following in the footsteps of Martin Luther.

Third, in 1933 the total population of Germany was 65 million people. 45 million people were considered Protestant Christians. In 1933 Germany had 18,000 Protestant pastors. **15,000 (83%) of them would support Hitler during the war.**[6]

Karl Barth would play a crucial role in responding to Hitler.

Barth's Life

Karl Barth was born in Basel, Switzerland on May 10th, 1886. His family moved to Bern, Switzerland due to his father being a professor at the University of Bern. In 1904, at the age of 18, Karl enrolled at the University of Bern for theological studies.

---

3 Conway. The Nazi Persecution of the Churches 1933-1945. P 3.

4 Heiden. A history of National Socialism. p100.

5 Hitler. Mein Kampf. Section 7.

6 Shirer. The Rise and Fall of the Third Reich. pp234-240.

The University of Bern introduced him to Enlightenment thinker, Immanuel Kant, who's *Critique of Practical Reason* he called "the first book that really moved me as a student."[7]

KARL BARTH

Karl Barth then studied in Berlin, Germany. What you must understand is that Germany was the bastion of theological liberalism. In Berlin he would study under liberal theologian Adolf Van Harnack with unbounded enthusiasm.[8] Barth then continued his studies at the famous German Tübingen University before finally going to the oldest Protestant-founded school in the world, the University of Marburg in Marburg, Germany. Barth was drawn to Marburg in order to study under Wilhelm Herrmann. He states, "I absorbed Hermann through every pore."[9] Hermann was able to articulate a coherent account of Christianity which took Kant and Schleiermacher with full seriousness.

Here is the key: It would *appear* Barth was on the road to becoming the next great liberal theologian.

Barth went on to spend the next 11 years as a pastor back in Switzerland. While pastoring in Geneva, Barth plunged into Calvin's *Institutes* "with profound impact."[10] As Barth's studying of the Christian faith increased he started lecturing in Switzerland and Germany. By 1921 he was appointed an Honorary Professor of Reformed Theology at the University of Göttingen.

---

7 Barth, Bultmann. Letters 1922-1968. p157.

8 Webster. Cambridge Companion to Karl Barth. p2.

9 Ibid., p2.

10 Webster. Cambridge Companion to Karl Barth. p154.

In 1935 Barth was removed from his teaching position in Germany and sent to Switzerland. He would teach at the University of Basel for the rest of his professional life.

Barth is best known for writing his 13 volume *Church Dogmatics* (nearly 8,000 pages in the English Translation). Barth's thoughts, as we will see, greatly shaped the 20th century and beyond.

Barth's Thoughts

Karl Barth completely believes the liberal theology of Schleiermacher as he leaves the university and first enters the pastorate. In his first two years of sermons he makes statements such as, "*the greatest thing is what takes place in our hearts*"; "*Calvin's view of the authority of the Bible would be quite wrong for us*"; "*Sometimes they [the Ten Commandments] contain too much for our needs and sometimes too little.*" In one sermon he dismissed the orthodox understanding of Christ articulated in the Chalcedonian Definition, commenting that "*if Jesus were like this I would not be interested in him.*"[11]

August 1914

Everything changed for Barth with the outbreak of World War I in 1914. Barth writes:

> *One day in early August 1914 stands out in my personal memory as a black day. Ninety-three German intellectuals impressed public opinion by their proclamation in support of the war policy of Wilhelm II and his counselors. Among these intellectuals I discovered to my horror almost all of my theological teachers whom I had greatly venerated. In despair over what this indicated about the signs of the time I suddenly realized that I could not any longer follow either their ethics and dogmatics or their understanding of the Bible and of history. For me at least, 19th century theology no longer held any future.*[12]

11 Franke. Barth for Armchair Theologians. p22.
12 Barth. The Humanity of God. p.14

To continue with my Christmas illustration, **Karl Barth begins to recognize that if your faith is wrapped up in wanting to experience the warm fuzzy feelings of Christmas, you may one day kill people to ensure you get what you want to feel.**

Barth concluded such ideas were blasphemous and simply amounted to equating talk about humanity and human culture with talk about God.[13] He declares religion to be a human effort by which we seek to hide from God. Barth is quickly on the road to becoming one of liberal German scholarship's top ten heretics.

How you ask? First he recovers the doctrine of the Trinity from liberalism. God is not existing as part of human knowledge, as Schleiermacher thought, for Barth God exists through God's self-knowledge apart from human involvement.

As if this were not enough, he then makes moves back toward a traditional understanding of the inspiration of Scripture. Regarding the Bible he states, "*It is not right human thoughts about God that make up the content of the Bible, but rather right divine thoughts about human beings.*" This is a one-two punch in the face of his German mentors. God, who exists as Trinity, operates far outside the feelings of humans. The second person of the Trinity, Jesus, is far from Santa Claus. He is indeed "*two natures who met to be thy cure.*" Unless two natures had met in Christ "*without separation or division*" yet also "*without confusion or change*", neither reconciliation nor revelation, as Barth explained them, could have taken place. By 1916 Barth had fully rejected modern liberal theology.

Barth's Influence

The influence of Karl Barth is most clearly apparent in two areas. First, his thoughts are seen as dismantling the tidal wave of modern theological liberalism. Webster writes, "*The brilliance of Barth's account of the reality of Christ was enough to bring large parts of the edifice of 19th century liberalism crash-*

13 Franke. p.31.

ing to the ground."[14] Schleiermacher found his match in Barth.

Second, Barth's rejection of liberalism for an objective Christ-centered faith made it possible for him to clearly see the evil of Hitler. Barth wouldn't let Schleiermacher redefine Christianity and he wasn't going to let Hitler do it either. 15,000 pastors had already thrown their hat in with Hitler. Barth wrote the Barmen Declaration of 1934 which proclaimed:

the church cannot be run by Hitler because it is solely Christ's property, and that it lives and wants to live solely from his comfort and from his direction in the expectation of his appearance. Furthermore, the church cannot submit to Hitler, it only submits itself explicitly and radically to Holy Scripture as God's gracious Word.

Barth provided much of the theological foundation upon which 3,000 German pastors stood against Hitler, many of them at the cost of their very lives. Heroic men like Dietrich Bonheoffer were heavily influenced by and personally knew Barth.

BARTH IN 1956

Barth's Foibles

One of the complaints many people have about Barth is he didn't communicate clearly enough. Webster writes:

Reading Barth is no easy task. Because the corpus of his writing is so massive and complex, what he has to say cannot be neatly summarized. Moreover, his preferred method of exposition, especially in the Church Dogmatics, is frustrating for readers looking

14 Webster. Cambridge Companion to Karl Barth. p.12.

> *to follow a linear thread of argument. Commentators often note the musical structure of Barth's major writings: the announcement of a theme, and its further extension in a long series of developments and recapitulations, through which the reader is invited to consider the theme from a number of different angles and in a number of different relations.* [15]

By far the greatest foible conservative American Evangelicalism has charged Barth with is his seemingly liberal theology. However, when we understand the context of Barth's situation, what he was expected to accomplish (i.e. being the next great liberal theologian Germany was to produce), we should cut him more than a little slack. While Barth's theology would not be in line with some American evangelical theology, he, as many people have put it, "dropped a bombshell on the playground of theological liberalism". While his pendulum may not have swung back to the far right, his conservative stance on God, Christ, and the Scriptures would be a catalyst for the fall of the prominence, respect, and hope of liberal theology.

Finally, the most serious possible foible is connected to the possibility Barth had a long affair with his assistant Charlotte von Kirschbaum. Scholars struggle to understand exactly the nature of their relationship. Charlotte moved in with the Barth family and from that relationship Barth produced all of his famous works. Many say it was a clear affair, others disagree saying it was purely a working relationship although it was unwise for her to live in the same house with Nelly and the kids. More research is needed in this area to try to grasp the nature of the relationship and how that should affect Barth's influence on future generations.

Suzanne Selinger provides some insight into the complexity of the nature of Barth's relationship with his wife, Nelly, and with Charlotte:

> *We may well wonder also where Nelly Barth was in the midst of all this. There is undoubtedly much we will never know. But we do know that in her own way she never ceased to believe in her husband and his work. We know that the two*

15 Webster. Cambridge Companion to Karl Barth. p.12.

> *of them experienced a reconciliation after Charlotte departed the household, that she and Karl both visited her at the nursing home on Sundays, that she continued those visits after Karl died in 1968, and that when Charlotte herself died in 1975, Nelly honored Karl's wishes by having Charlotte buried in the Barth family grave. Nelly herself died in 1976. Visitors to the Basel Hörnli cemetery today can see the names ofall three together engraved one by one on the same stone.*[16]

Barth's Effect on Us

[17]First, Barth's theology intends to be comprehensive in its engagement with the Bible and the history of Christian theology. It is a theology which takes seriously Scripture and Tradition. We would do well to emulate.

Second, Barth helps us see that no matter how thorough and advanced your theology will become you will still merely be a human thinking about an infinite God who exists outside of your time, space and thoughts.

Third, Barth's theology understands itself to be bound at every point to God and to God's Self-revelation in Jesus Christ. It is a theology of submission to God and, as such, naturally leads to worship. It is not a science of culture or even of religion; it is christocentric dogmatics.

Fourth, Barth shows dogmatics and ethics belong together in the closest possible relation. You can't separate what you know from how you act.

Fifth, Barth's theology makes the proper subject of theological existence to be the congregation. What emerges from Barth's concentration on the congregation is a call for congregations to become more "mature" as

---

16 Suzanne Selinger, Charlotte von Kirschbaum and Karl Barth: A Study in Biography and the History of Theology

17 This section is heavily sourced from the great work, Studies in the Theology of Karl Barth, by Bruce L. McCormack from Baker Academic.

unified bodies, with pastors and laity engaging together in the work of ministry rather than leaving such work to a professional class.

TURN TO PAGE
185
TO EXPERIENCE
BARTH IN HIS
OWN WORDS

ANSELM

8

#8: ANSELM

TOP TEN THEOLOGIANS

In order to appreciate Anselm, #8 on our list of Top Ten Theologians, we must have a working knowledge of Anselm's world. Let's take a look at two events which need to be in our minds to appreciate him.

Anselm's World

Crowning of Charlemagne

CROWNING OF CHARLEMAGNE

If you were a citizen of Rome in 450AD life stunk. Most parents kissed their kids good-night thinking they all would be dead soon. One of the most feared men on the planet, Attila the Hun, is on his way to be your nightmare. His army, consisting of more than

300,000 soldiers, seeks to destroy everything you love. As Attila nears Rome an interesting strategy develops. Instead of sending out our army, let's do something different. Let's send out our head pastor, Leo, and see if he can get Attila to forget about destroying Rome. As Rome held its breath, Leo met Attila the Hun. Attila, remarkably, turned back from attacking Rome. Leo returned to Rome a hero. People started to see how powerful the church could be in preserving the state.

In 800AD the power of the church in relation to the state reached a whole new level. In order for Charlemagne to become the Emperor of Rome he had to be crowned by Pope Leo III. This was done on on Christmas day, 800AD. Imagine today if someone like Billy Graham needed to approve of any presidential candidate before they were sworn into office. Many of these church leaders did not seek such power. Understanding Leo's influence on Attila and Leo III's crowning of Charlemagne will allow you to see how Anselm could reluctantly become one of the most powerful men on the planet.

Rise of Islam

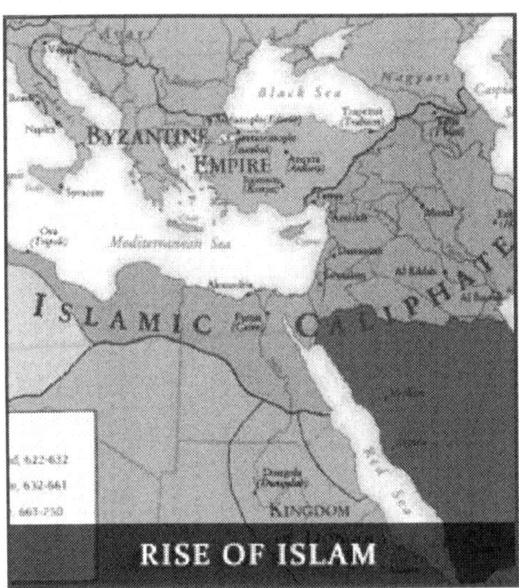

RISE OF ISLAM

The spread of Islam started shortly after the death of Muhammad in 632AD. Muslims do not see Muhammad as the creator of Islam, but instead regard him as the last messenger of God. Muhammad is seen as following in the footsteps of Adam, Abraham, Moses and Jesus. The Qur'an is believed to be the final revelation from God.

Conversions to Islam paralleled the rapid military expansion of the Arab Empire. Muslim dynasties were soon established in North Africa, West Africa, throughout the Middle East and in Iran. The Crusades were carried out as military responses from predominately Christian nations to the military expansion of Islam.

Islam carried something interesting into their conquered lands: **learning**. In the 10th and 11th century a great wave of intellectual sophistication swept through the Islamic world. There are several reasons for such intellectualism: [1]

First, the study of the Qur'an was encouraged for all Muslims. The Islamic world, therefore, had a very high literacy rate.

Second, classical texts from writers like Aristotle were lost to the Latin world with the fall of the Roman Empire, but were preserved (many times by Christians) in the Muslim world. Muslim countries had access to sophisticated thoughts which had become virtually unknown to the Western world.

Third, Islam had a positive view between the material and spiritual world. The material world is not at war with the spiritual world. This positive attitude led to greater openness toward science than in early medieval Europe. Our modern-day concept of science stems from the Islamic world.

Fourth, Muslims had schools of learning, called Madrasa, which were schools with resident students (precursors to the university). At this higher level, students would carry out formal logical disputations stating thesis, counter thesis, and conducting dialogue of objections and answers.

Christianity enjoyed nearly a thousand years without any major challenge from outside religions. Could the Christian faith withstand reasoned intellectual inquiry growing in the Islamic world? Anselm arrives to the scene to answer that question.

---

1 Outline taken from the course notes of Loyola University Chicago professor Leslie Dossey. Transmission of Islamic Learning and European Scholasticism

Anselm's Life

Anselm was born in Northern Italy around 1033AD. He was born into a comfortable noble family, owning considerable property.

At the age of 15, however, Anselm wanted to enter a monastery but could not obtain his father 's consent. His father thought it would be a waste of his noble life. Without his father's consent, the head of the monastery refused his entry. Anselm gave up his desire to study theology and lived a carefree life. His mother, however, soon died and his father's harshness became unbearable.

At the age of 23 Anselm left home, crossed the Alps and wandered through Burgundy and France.[2] It was common at this time, before universities, for there to be "wandering scholars" like Anselm who would seek out older, wiser people to learn from.

LANFRANC

After wandering around for three years Anselm made his way to the monastery of Bec in central Normandy, France. Anselm was attracted to Bec by a famous fellow Italian countryman named Lanfranc. Lanfranc was the primary teacher at the Bec monastery. Anselm's friend writes:

> *Lanfranc's lofty fame had resounded everywhere and had drawn to him the best clerks from all parts of the world. Anselm therefore came to him and recognized the outstanding wisdom which shone forth in him. He placed himself*

2 Charlesworth. St. Anselm's Proslogion. p9.

> *under his guidance and in a short time became the most intimate of his disciples.*[3]

Lanfranc's discipleship of Anselm would be profound:

> *When he got there, it was Lanfranc who started him on the course of religious and intellectual development which was to make him one of the outstanding figures in the history of Latin Christendom. He put himself entirely in Lanfranc's hands: 'So great was his influence over me' (Anselm later confided to his biographer) 'and so greatly did I trust his judgment, that if he had told me to go into the forest above Bec and never come out, I would have done it without hesitation.'*[4]

No longer to be content as just a student at Bec, at the age of 27, Anselm officially entered the monastery as a monk. He started out at the absolute bottom rung with the official title: Novice. Three years later, Anselm started to climb the ladder when Lanfranc was promoted to a different monastery. Lanfranc's promotion left Anselm as the primary teacher at Bec. **Anselm became very interested in training the minds of the monks in ways which would foster their spiritual as well as their intellectual development.**[5] After a short while Anselm's students begged him to write down his teachings. He wrote his first two works at this time: *Monologion* (Only Words) and *Proslogion* (First Words).

BEC MONASTERY (ORIGINAL DESTROYED IN THE 18th CENTURY DURING FRENCH REVOLUTION)

In 1078,

3 Davies. Anselm of Canterbury: The Major Works. VII
4 Stephen. Saint Anselm: A Portrait in a Landscape. p15.
5 Davies. Anselm of Canterbury: The Major Works. VII

at the age of 45, Anselm was promoted to the head (Abbot) of the monastery. By 1085, people were reading his *Monologion* and *Proslogion* in France, England, and probably in Rome. Anselm was gaining a reputation for himself which went well beyond the confines of his monastery.[6]

Much against his desires, Anselm was chosen in 1093 at the age of 60 to succeed Lanfranc as Archbishop of Canterbury. The Archbishop of Canterbury was the highest religious leader of all England. Since the church was seen in many ways as being above the state, Anselm had just become one of the most powerful men on the planet. What did he think about this new position? He wrote to a friend, "*I am so harassed in the archbishopric that if it were possible to do so without guilt, I would rather die than continue in it.*"[7]

Anselm's position required him to be involved in politics. For example, soon after becoming Archbishop, King William requested £1,000 from Anselm to finance an expedition to Normandy. Anselm felt the funds could be better spent relieving the hardships and helping to reform the morals of those in the church. William would eventually send Anselm into exile. He stayed away from England until after William's death in 1100AD. While Archbishop, Anselm wrote the works: *Why God Became Man; On the Virgin Conception and Original Sin; and On the Procession of the Holy Spirit.*

A new king led to some new disagreements and once again Anselm was exiled. He returned to England in 1106AD at the age of 73. His biographer wrote, "Anselm was received with great joy and honour by the Church and the King was heartily glad that he had made his peace with Anselm."[8] Anselm was writing his last major work *De Concordia* (On God's Foreknowledge and Predestination) when he died at the age of 76.

---

6 Davies. Anselm of Canterbury: The Major Works. VII

7 Ibid., VIII

8 Eadmer. The Life of St. Anselm. p138.

Anselm's Thoughts

ANSELM

Anselm wrote on many aspects of the faith, but he is best known for his thoughts in three areas: harmonizing faith and reason; his thoughts on the atonement; and his ontological argument for the existence of God.

Harmonizing Faith and Reason

Anselm asserted the harmony of faith and reason. Faith and reason are not enemies, they can exist together. He desired to apply reason to questions of faith. What he sought in doing this was not to prove something which he did not believe without such proof, but rather to understand more deeply what he already believed.[9] Anselm writes:

> *Lord I am not trying to make my way to your height, for my understanding is no way equal to that, but I do desire to understand a little of your truth which my heart already believes and loves. I do not seek to understand so that I may believe, but I believe so that I may understand; and what is more, I believe that unless I do believe I shall not understand.*[10]

Spirituality, life in the Spirit of God, was not to be viewed as a pious, hopeful wish in something basically irrational and unreasonable. Rather, spirituality involved thinking as much as feeling, pondering as much as sensing, brain work as much as willing, head as much as heart.[11]

---

9 Gonzalez. The Story of Christianity: Volume 1. p313

10 Anselm, Proslogion. 1.155-57, p244

11 Bingham. p92

Reason assists faith by helping us grasp its reasonableness and its significance. But reason never substitutes for revelation or faith.[12] Scripture remains the final authority for Anselm.

Doctrine of the Atonement

In his greatest work, *Cur Deus Homo* (The God-Man), Anselm undertakes to make plain, even to unbelievers, the rational necessity of the Christian mystery of the Atonement.[13] Most Christians, historically, viewed the death of Jesus on the cross as a ransom paid to Satan for the souls of mankind. Anselm's theory pointed people in a different direction.

Anselm explores the question of the reason for the incarnation, and offers an answer that would eventually become standard in western theology. The importance of a crime is measured in terms of the one against whom it is committed. Therefore, a crime against God, sin, is infinite in its import. But, on the other hand, only a human being can offer satisfaction for human sin. This is obviously impossible, for human beings are finite, and cannot offer the infinite satisfaction required by the majesty of God. For this reason, there is need for a divine-human, God incarnate, who through his suffering and death offers satisfaction for the sins of all humankind.[14]

In stunning beauty Anselm writes:

> *O hidden strength: a man hangs on a cross and lifts the load of eternal death from the human race; a man nailed to wood looses the bonds of everlasting death that hold fast the world. O hidden power: a man condemned with thieves saves men condemned with devils, a man stretched out on the gibbet draws all men to himself. O mysterious strength: one soul coming forth from torment draws countless souls with him out of hell, a man submits to the death of the body and destroys the death of souls...See, Christian soul, here is the strength of your*

12 Ibid. p92
13 Walsh, p75
14 Gonzalez. The Story of Christianity: Volume 1. p313.

> *salvation, here is the cause of your freedom, here is the price of your redemption. You were a slave and by this man you are free. By him you are brought back from exile, lost, you are restored, dead, you are raised.*[15]

Ontological Argument

Anselm seeks to prove, using pure reason, the existence of God. He starts with the idea that God would leave footprints in the minds of the rational creatures he had made to enable them to find their way to him by contemplation of their own deepest nature.[16]

In the Proslogion he develops what has come to be called "the ontological argument for the existence of God." Anselm's argument is that when one thinks of God, one is thinking of "that-than-which-no-greater-can-be-thought." For example: Is Tiger Woods God? No, I do not believe he is God. Why? I can imagine an older being. I can imagine a stronger being. I can imagine a more ethical being (I can say this about all people so I'm not throwing Tiger Woods under the bus). I can imagine, at least for the time being, even a better golfer. Tiger Woods is not god because I can think of a greater being. If I was wrong, and there was no greater being than Tiger Woods, than Tiger would be God. God is the One upon which there is no greater. Therefore, it is nonsensical and unreasonable to speak of a God who does not exist. Even if an Atheist is asked if he believes in God, the moment he ponders the existence of God, he has proven the existence of God.

Anselm's Influence

Anselm is called the founder of Scholasticism. He is the first person to provide a strong intellectual foundation for the faith while also maintaining the heart of the faith. He paved the way for the rise of the university to occur built upon these intellectual virtues. Bologna, Paris and Oxford numbered among the most famous early locations.[17]

---

15 Anselm, Meditation on Human Redemption, pp230-231, 234
16 Davies. Anselm of Canterbury: The Major Works. XI
17 Bingham, p94

Anselm's view of the work of Christ, which was by no means the generally accepted one in earlier centuries, soon gained such credence that most western Christians came to accept it as the only biblical one.[18] His ontological argument, additionally, is still pondered by philosophers and theologians to this day.

He touched the thought, the piety and the politics of the time at every important point; and whatever he touched looked different afterwards.[19]

Anselm's Foibles

The two greatest foibles I see in Anselm are as follows:

1. Anselm reasoned Mary must have been one of the purest human beings to be chosen as the mother of Christ. Anselm denied the Immaculate Conception, but Roman Catholics still look to Anselm as the one who invoked the ideas and laid the groundwork for the doctrine of Immaculate Conception.

2. Due to his affectionate letters to his friends and fellow-monks some authors accuse Anselm of being a homosexual. Author John Boswell in *Christianity, Social Tolerance and Homosexuality* makes this charge of Anselm. Most attribute his affectionate writing to a shared spiritual intimacy. This is similar to David's love for Jonathan. Some people accuse them of being lovers, most recognize however a strong bond that can form between very heterosexual men, think "band of brothers." Anselm even wrote, "It must be recognized that this sin of sodomy has become so common that hardly anyone even blushes for it, and many, being ignorant of its enormity, have abandoned themselves to it…they are warned that they are acting against God, and incurring damnation."

Anselm clearly refutes homosexuality.

---

18 Gonzalez. The Story of Christianity: Volume 1. p314.
19 Southern. Introduction.

Anselm's Effect on Us

We live in an age where Christians are generally seen as brain-washed lightweights. Atheists are the intellectuals and Christians are idiots who can't naturally cope with life. Christians, additionally, are seen as moral hypocrites. The pastorate is no longer viewed as a dignified position but more popularly seen as an incubator for power-corrupted immorality.

Anselm is a great example of someone who fully interacts intellectually with his culture, on their terms, but is still absolutely saturated with the Word of God. In him we see hardly any distinction between head and heart, doctrine and practical piety, knowledge and prayer.[20] Anselm's mind is disciplined for God and his affections are for Christ. He has all the power in the world but seeks to serve the lowest of people. He is a man worthy to follow as he follows Christ.

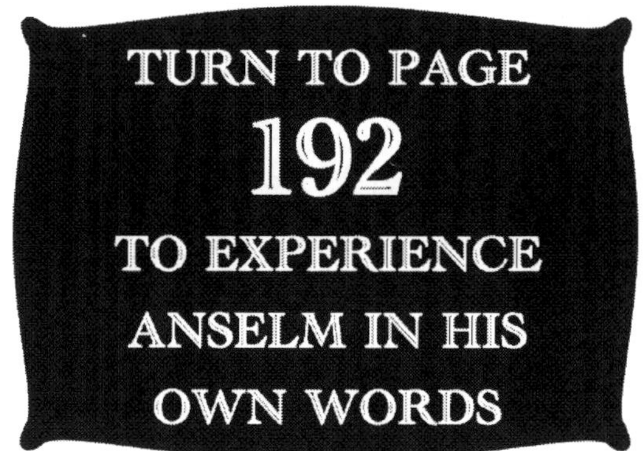

20 Bingham, p86

C.S. LEWIS

7

#7: C.S. LEWIS

TOP TEN THEOLOGIANS

Our count down of Top Ten Theologians continues with #7: C.S. Lewis. His inclusion on this list will be an obvious choice for some and a surprise for others. Yes, I completely agree it is risky and potentially short-sighted to have two 20th century people (Lewis and Barth) on the list. Time has not vetted these men as much as someone like Irenaeus or Anselm. Generations to come may downgrade the influence from any 20th century theologian. I am excited, nonetheless, to offer you C.S. Lewis.

Lewis's World

Michel Foucault

Michel Foucault (pronounced foo-ko) may be one of the most influential 20th century thinkers you've never heard of. He was interested in studying the development of ideas. How and why do we know what we know? He held a chair at Collège de France with the title, "History of Systems of Thought." He wrote several books on diverse subjects such

as: psychiatry; medicine; the human sciences; prison systems; as well as the history of human sexuality.

Foucault's observations and skepticism challenged many long-standing ideas. His first book wondered why some people are considered crazy? What if these "crazy" people lived at a different time in a completely different culture? Would they still be considered crazy?

How about, for example, John the Baptist? His clothes were nasty. He lived out in the desert eating bugs. He yelled at people to repent. They responded by letting John hold them under water. In first century Israel John was viewed as one of the greatest prophets who ever lived. Transfer John the Baptist to New York City and he'd be locked up in a mental hospital. Craziness is relative.

In Foucault's studies on sex he wondered why people seemed to possess differing ideas of sexual appropriateness. Why do women in certain developing countries walk around topless? Every person at that particular time and place believes topless women are normal. It is unimaginable to consider the same women walking around Victorian England. The sexual customs of these two cultures are worlds apart. Sexual morals appear to be relative.

Foucault believes periods of history have possessed specific underlying conditions of truth that constituted what he expresses as *discourse* (for example art, science, culture, etc.). Foucault argues that these conditions of discourse have changed over time, in major and relatively sudden shifts, from one period's knowledge to another.[1]

Different cultures have different ways of discussing and knowing reality. What is crazy? What is immoral? What is joy? Who is God? What is beautiful? Foucault shows how people answer these questions for themselves. There are no objective answers, knowing is relative to time and place.

Foucault's thoughts are very popular. Even though he died in 1984, he is currently the most cited author in the humanities.[2] For books published in 2007, for example, he was cited 2,521 times. During the same period, in comparison, Friedrich Nietzsche was only cited 501 times.[3]

Foucault is skeptical of ideas or realities which claim to exist for all people at all times. Christianity, however, claims a Savior who exists for all people at all times. C.S. Lewis will address Foucault head-on and become known as the "Apostle to the Skeptics."

Lewis's Life

Clive Staples Lewis was born in Belfast, Ireland on November 29, 1898. At the age of four, after the death of the beloved neighborhood dog "Jacksie," Lewis announced his new name would be "Jacksie." He eventually permitted friends and family to call him the shortened "Jack."

In 1905, at the age of seven, the family moved into a new home. Lewis writes:

> *The New House is almost a major character in my story. I am a product of long corridors, empty sunlit rooms, upstairs indoor silences, attics unexplored in solitude, distant noises of gurgling cisterns and pipes, and the noise of wind*

---

1 Robert, Holub. Crossing Borders. p57.
2 http://www.timeshighereducation.co.uk/story.asp?storyCode=405956 accessed
September of 2011
3 Lewis, Surprised by Joy. p10.

under the tiles. Also, of endless books.[4]

The "endless books" certainly shaped Lewis; he writes:

My father bought all the books he read and never got rid of any of them. There were books in the study, books in the drawing room, books in the cloak-room, books (two deep) in the great bookcase on the landing, books in a bedroom, books piled as high as my shoulder in the cistern attic, books of all kinds reflecting every transient stage of my parents' interest, books readable and unreadable, books suitable for a child and books most emphatically not. Nothing was forbidden me. In the seemingly endless rainy afternoons I took volume after volume from the shelves. I had always the same certainty of finding a book that was new to me as a man who walks into a field has of finding a new blade of grass.[5]

CHILDHOOD HOME

C.S. Lewis was well-read by the age of eight.[6] A complete list of the books he had read by the age of nine would be very long.[7] His diary entry of March 5, 1908: "I read *Paradise Lost*, reflections thereon."[8] The epic, *Paradise Lost*, contains over 10,000 individual lines of poetic verse!

4 Lewis, Surprised by Joy. p10.
5 Lewis. Surprised by Joy. p10.
6 Sayer. Jack: A Life of C.S. Lewis
7 Ibid.
8 Lewis. The Lewis Papers. 3:102

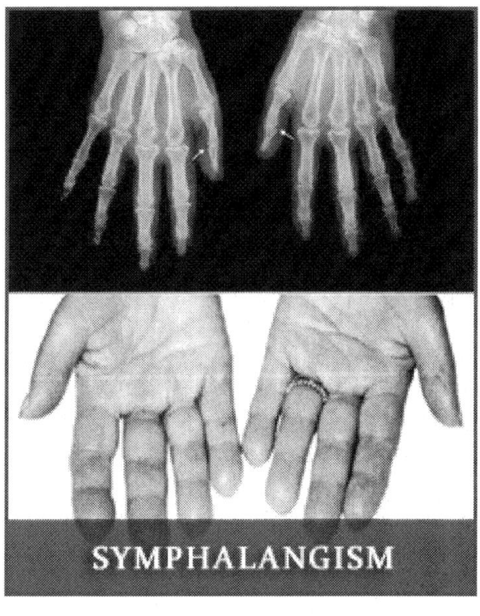

Lewis gravitated to not only reading but writing at an early age, due to a hereditary condition with his thumbs known as Symphalangism. He explains the condition:

> *What drove me to write was the extreme manual clumsiness from which I have always suffered. I attribute it to a physical defect which my brother and I both inherit from our father; we have only one joint in the thumb. The upper joint (that furthest from the nail) is visible, but it is a mere sham; we cannot bend it. But whatever the cause, nature laid on me from birth an utter incapacity to make anything. With pencil and pen I was handy enough, and I can still tie as good a bow as ever lay on a man's collar; but with a tool or a bat or a gun, a sleeve link or a corkscrew, I have always been unteachable. It was this that forced me to write. I longed to make things, ships, houses, engines. Many sheets of cardboard and pairs of scissors I spoiled, only to turn from my hopeless failures in tears. As a last resource, as a pis aller, I was driven to write stories instead.*[9]

Lewis was brought up in a Christian home. He states, "I was taught the usual things and made to say my prayers and in due time taken to church. I naturally accepted what I was told but I cannot remember feeling much interest in it."[10]

---

9 Lewis. Surprised by Joy. p12.
10 Ibid. p7.

Shortly after the death of his mother, in 1908, Lewis and his brother were sent to boarding school. The school Matron, Miss C., had been on a spiritual journey for truth and a way of life. Mysticism, Mythology and the Occult occupied a large part of her thoughts at this time. Lewis writes:

> *Nothing was further from her intention than to destroy my faith; she could not tell that the room into which she brought this candle (her ideas) was full of gunpowder.*

Lewis began to doubt many aspects of Christianity. Prayer became a ludicrous burden of false duties. He felt it strange for all religions to be considered wrong except for his Christianity. He called the truthfulness of Christianity, in light of seemingly incorrect paganism, a fortunate exception. He writes:

> *In addition to this, and equally working against my faith, there was in me a deeply ingrained pessimism; a pessimism, by that time, much more of intellect than of temper. I was now by no means unhappy; but I had very definitely formed the opinion that the universe was, in the main, a rather regrettable institution.*[11]

Lewis considered himself an atheist by the time he was fifteen. He resonated with Lucretius's atheistic argument:

> *Had God designed the world, it would not be;*
> *A world so frail and faulty as we see.*[12]

Lewis explains, "*And so, little by little, with fluctuations which I cannot now trace, I became an apostate, dropping my faith with no sense of loss but with the greatest relief.*"[13] Lewis viewed his Atheism in a very interesting way:

---

11 Lewis. Surprised by Joy. p63.
12 Ibid., p65
13 Ibid., p66

MAGDALEN COLLEGE: OXFORD

I was at this time living, like so many Atheists or Antitheists, in a whirl of contradictions. I maintained that God did not exist. I was also very angry with God for not existing. I was equally angry with Him for creating a world.[14]

In 1917, at the age of 18, Lewis left his studies to volunteer in the British Army. During World War I he was commissioned an officer in the Third Battalion. He arrived on the front lines and experienced trench warfare for the first time on his nineteenth birthday. On April 15th, Lewis was wounded and two of his friends were killed by friendly fire. He was discharged in December 1918, and soon returned to his studies.

Lewis began his academic career as an undergraduate student at Oxford; he excelled in every area he studied. He won a triple first, the highest honors in three areas of study.[15] By 1925, at the age of 27, Lewis began teaching at Magdalen College, a part of the University of Oxford. He taught at Oxford for most of his adult life and then spent the last several years as Professor of Medieval and Renaissance English at the University of Cambridge.

While teaching at Oxford, Lewis continued writing prolifically. In 1929, an informal group of literary friends from Oxford began meeting together on Tuesday mornings. The group named themselves the "Inklings." Members of the group included: J.R.R. Tolkien; Nevill Coghill; Lord David Cecil; Charles Williams; Owen Barfield; and Lewis's brother Warren. Concerning Tolkien, Lewis writes:

---

14 Ibid., p115

15 Nicholi. The Question of God. p4 Cf. Wikipedia

When I began teaching for the English Faculty, I made two other friends, both Christians (these queer people seemed now to pop up on every side) who were later to give me much help in getting over the last stile. They were H.V.V. Dyson… and J.R.R. Tolkien. Friendship with the latter marked the breakdown of two old prejudices. At my first coming into the world I had been (implicitly) warned never to trust a Papist (Roman Catholic), and at my first coming into the English Faculty (explicitly) never to trust a philologist (study of language in written historical sources). Tolkien was both.[16]

PUB WHERE INKLINGS MET

Lewis slowly re-embraced Christianity, influenced by arguments with Tolkien. He was also largely influenced by reading George MacDonald and G.K. Chesterton's *The Everlasting Man.* Lewis explains leaving Atheism:

You must picture me alone in that room in Magdalen, night after night, feeling, whenever my mind lifted even for a second from my work, the steady, unrelenting approach of Him whom I so earnestly desired not to meet. That which I greatly feared had at last come upon me. In 1929 I gave in, and admitted that God was God, and knelt and prayed: perhaps, that night, the most dejected and reluctant convert in all England. I did not then see what is now the most shining and obvious thing; the Divine humility which will accept a convert even

16 Lewis. Surprised by Joy. p216.

on such terms.[17]

Tolkien, upon Lewis's conversion, tried to get him to join the Roman Catholic Church. Lewis would be a committed Anglican (Church of England) for the rest of his life. He made a purposeful effort through his writings, however, to avoid promoting any one denomination.

Between 1929 and 1963 (34 years) Lewis wrote approximately 58 literary works. He wrote works in his academic field of Medieval and Renaissance English, as well as many books in the theological field of apologetics (defending the faith). He wrote in several genres including: non-fiction; fiction; science-fiction; and children's books.

Later in life Lewis corresponded with an American lady named Joy Gresham. She was a Communist and an Atheist who converted to Christianity mainly through the writings of Lewis. Lewis's brother writes, "For Jack the attraction was at first undoubtedly intellectual. Joy was the only woman whom he had met…who had a brain which matched his own in suppleness, in width of interest, and in analytical grasp, and above all in humor and a sense of fun."[18] Lewis agreed to enter into a civil marriage with Joy so she could live in the UK. Joy was diagnosed with terminal bone cancer and their relationship developed to the point that they sought a Christian marriage. They were married at the side of her hospital bed in 1957, Lewis was 59 years old.

YOUNG C.S. LEWIS

Joy's cancer thankfully went into remission and the two newlyweds were able to experience a couple years of "normal" married life. The cancer relapsed and she died in 1960. Lewis wrote the book *A Grief Observed* describing his experience

17 Lewis. Surprised by Joy. p228-229.

18 Haven, San Francisco Chronicle. December 31, 2005: 01-01

coping with the death of his wife. The book was so raw and personal he originally released it under the pseudonym N.W. Clerk to keep readers from knowing it was written by him. Ironically, many friends recommended the book to Lewis as a method for dealing with his own grief.[19] He allowed the book to reflect the name of the true author upon his death.

The last three years of his life Lewis struggled with health problems related to his kidneys. He eventually died in 1963, one week from his 65th birthday. Lewis is buried next to his brother at Holy Trinity Church in Oxford.

Lewis's Thoughts

The thoughts of C.S. Lewis place him at #7 on our list of Top Ten Theologians. Men like Michel Foucault were getting people to doubt the knowability of things. How do we really know what we know? Europe was transitioning at the time from being the center of Western Orthodox Christianity to being a post-Christian society. Lewis considers himself to be a layman, not a trained theologian. His expertise is in Medieval and Renaissance English. To the seeming embarrassment of many colleagues, Lewis continually returns to writing about his Christian faith. He was once one of the world's most skeptical skeptics. He is now a fully convinced believer in Jesus. One of the central themes of his life and faith is the concept of Joy.

Surprised by Joy

Lewis thinks about joy in a unique way. He explains:

> *I call it Joy, which is here a technical term and must be sharply distinguished both from Happiness and from Pleasure. Joy (in my sense) has indeed one characteristic, and one only, in common with them; the fact that any one who has experienced it will want it again. Apart from that, and considered only in its*

19 Lewis. A Grief Observed. Jacket Notes, Faber & Faber, London.

quality, it might almost equally well be called a particular kind of unhappiness or grief. But then it is the kind we want. I doubt whether anyone who has tasted it would ever, if both were in his power, exchange it for all the pleasures in the world. But then Joy is never in our power and pleasure often is.[20]

Think of Lewis's concept of joy similar to an echo. When you are a child you hear an echo that fills you with more joy than you ever imagined possible on earth. You live your entire life listening to hear the echo again. If you have ever heard the echo you will know there is nothing sweeter in the world than hearing the echo. Your pursuit of joy is almost a life of grief because you live most of your life not hearing the echo. You yearn for its return to your ears, if only for a moment. Many people, however, will turn to the pleasures offered in this world as a replacement for the echo because the echo is not in our power but seeking pleasure is possible at our whim. Lewis found he heard the echo most when reading Christian writers such as George MacDonald and G.K. Chesterton.

In *The Weight of Glory* (1949) Lewis writes:

C.S. LEWIS AT WORK

A man's physical hunger does not prove that that man will get any bread: he may die of starvation on a raft in the Atlantic. But surely a man's hunger does prove that he comes of a race which repairs its body by eating, and inhabits a world where eatable substances exist. In other words, If I find in myself a desire which no experience in this world can satisfy, the most probable explanation is that I was made for another world.

---

20 Lewis. Surprised by Joy. p18

Lewis understands the echo in a whole new way. He was wrong to yearn for the echo. When he heard the echo it would be gone as soon as he recognized its arrival. His famous Surprised by Joy moment is the realization that the echo has a source. The echo is no longer the center of Lewis's life; the echo comes from the voice of a person: Jesus Christ. He is the source of the joy.

Lewis, with strong intellectual moorings, asks a society heading toward post-Christianity and relative post-Modernism if they possess this joy? Lewis spends his life wordsmithing his way from book to book directing people to Joy found only in Christ.

Objective Reality of God

Lewis does not leave people to simply seek their own conception of Joy. He does not plead with people to listen for whatever echo works best for them. He explains:

> *There was no doubt that Joy was a desire…but a desire is turned not to itself but to its object…The form of the desired is in the desire. It is the object which makes the desire harsh or sweet, course or choice, 'high' or 'low.' It is the object that makes the desire itself desirable or hateful. I perceived (and this was a wonder of wonders) that just as I had been wrong in supposing that I really desired the Garden of the Hesperides, so also I have been equally wrong in supposing that I desired Joy itself. Joy itself, considered simply as an event in my own mind, turned out to be of no value at all. All the value lay in that of which Joy was the desiring. And that object, quite clearly, was no state of my own mind or body at all.*[21]

If you lose an objective God existing outside of your subjective thoughts, you lose Joy and can only hope for momentary pleasures. You can only hope for what you can control. We experience the most Joy, however, when we experience the most of God. Lewis writes, "The

21 Lewis. Surprised by Joy. p220

Scotch catechism says that man's chief end is 'to glorify god and enjoy Him forever'. But we shall then know that these are the same thing. Fully to enjoy is to glorify. *In commanding us to glorify Him, god is inviting us to enjoy Him.*"[22]

Lewis makes a crucial link between Joy and Truth. Foucault is saying Absolute Truth is actually relative. So you see what is at stake. The entire modern world – and even more so the postmodern world – were moving away from the conviction of an objective God. Liberal theology and emergent writers flowed with the world of subjectivism and relativism. Lewis stood against it with all his might.[23]

Lewis's Influence

C.S. Lewis was a serious skeptic, a serious Christian and an intellectual powerhouse able to speak clearly to ordinary people. His BBC radio broadcasts during World War II provided a theological depth to people trembling under the Nazi bombing of London. These broadcasts became his classic work *Mere Christianity.*

The great influence of Lewis lies in his apologetic abilities. He sought to show how a Christian can be fully involved in their faith emotionally as well as intellectually. He did not try to prove the faith, in typical evidentialist ways, but he instead removed barriers to belief and helped those who were weak in faith to see that they could reasonably embrace Christ and remain intellectually honest. One British historian called Lewis the single most effective person proclaiming the gospel in England in the 20th century.[24]

Lewis stands tall for anyone questioning a full intellectual embrace of the Gospel. Those who have spent time sitting at the feet of Lewis will walk away with a heart and mind more devoted to the Savior.

---

22 Lewis. Reflections on the Psalms. p97.

23 John Piper. Lessons from an Inconsolable Soul. 2010 Desiring God Pastors Conference

24 John H Armstrong. The Influence of C.S. Lewis on Head and Heart. http://johnharmstrong.typepad.com/john_h_armstrong_/2009/10/the-influence-of-c-s-lewis-on-head-and-heart.html Accessed in September 2011

Lewis's Foibles

John Piper succinctly communicates some of Lewis's theological foibles:

> *He doesn't believe in the inerrancy of Scripture*[25]*, and defaults to logical arguments more naturally than to biblical exegesis. He doesn't treat the Reformation with respect, but thinks it could have been avoided, and calls aspects of it farcical*[26]*. He steadfastly refused in public or in letters to explain why he was not a Roman Catholic but remained in the Church of England*[27]*. He makes room for at least some people to be saved through imperfect representations of Christ in other religions.*[28] *He made a strong logical, but I think unbiblical, case for free will to explain why there is suffering in the world.*[29] *He speaks of the atonement with reverence, but puts little significance on any of the explanations for how it actually saves sinners.*[30]

Piper, however, who disagrees with Lewis on so many theological points, still considers C.S. Lewis to be one of the two men outside of the Bible who have had the greatest influence on his life. The other man is Jonathan Edwards.[31] Piper writes:

> *So, in spite of all Lewis's flaws, the most fundamental reason why he has been so influential in my life, and so awakening to my own soul, is that he remained anchored as a Christian in the unfathomable rock-solid objectivity of God and*

25 C. S. Lewis: Essay Collection and Other Short Pieces (London: Harper Collins, 2000), p. 45.
26 C. S. Lewis, English Literature in the Sixteenth Century, Excluding Drama (Oxford: Oxford University Press, 1953), p. 37.
27 C. S. Lewis, Letters of C. S. Lewis, ed. W. H. Lewis and Walter Hooper (New York: Harcourt Brace Jovanovich, 1966), pp. 223, 230.
28 Ibid. p468.
29 C. S. Lewis, The Problem of Pain.
30 Letters of C. S. Lewis, 1966, pp.197–198.
31 Piper. Lessons from an Inconsolable Soul. http://www.desiringgod.org/resource-library/biographies/lessons-from-an-inconsolable-soul

> *his Truth and his gospel as infinitely Beautiful and infinitely Desirable and, therefore, as the unshakeable ground of unutterable and exalted Joy.*[32]

In response to people criticizing certain aspects of his theology, Lewis explains:

> *Most of my books are evangelistic, addressed to tous exo [those outside]. . . When I began, Christianity came before the great mass of my unbelieving fellow-countrymen either in the highly emotional form offered by revivalists or in the unintelligible language of highly cultured clergymen. Most men were reached by neither. My task was therefore simply that of a translator—one turning Christian doctrine, or what he believed to be such, into the vernacular, into language that unscholarly people would attend to and could understand. . . . Dr. Pittenger would be a more helpful critic if he advised a cure as well as asserting many diseases. How does he himself do such work? What methods, and with what success, does he employ when he is trying to convert the great mass of storekeepers, lawyers, realtors, morticians, policemen and artisans who surround him in his own city?'*[33]

Lewis's Effect on Us

As we seek to reach the great mass of storekeepers, lawyers, realtors, morticians, policemen and artisans who surround us in our own city we are fools if we do not spend time sitting at the feet of C.S. Lewis. He combines a feeling artist with an intellectual. He is able to lecture at Oxford and Cambridge while writing stories for children. He is fully aware of the newest ideas, yet does not neglect the wisdom of the ages. He once said, "Every third book you read should be outside your century."[34] Lewis encourages us to be anchored in the past, to stand intellectually tall in the present for the objective truth of God, while raising our hands joyfully in worship to the Savior.

---

32 Ibid.

33 C. S. Lewis. God in the Dock, pp, 181, 183.

34 C. S. Lewis. God in the Dock, pp, 201-202.

The works of C.S. Lewis are easily available. If you are looking to get your feet wet with the more serious side of Lewis (outside of his fiction) then I recommend starting with *Mere Christianity*. It sounds silly but I recommend you skip chapter 1 and read it last. Chapter 1 can be difficult for some to grasp and I don't want you to get scared away before you can appreciate this side of Lewis. Once you get used to the way he thinks and writes then Chapter 1 will be easy to follow.

6

#6: THOMAS AQUINAS

TOP TEN THEOLOGIANS

In order to appreciate the contribution of Thomas Aquinas, #6 on our list of Top Ten Theologians, it's important to place him within his world.

Aquinas's World

Averroes

AVERROES IN SCHOOL OF ATHENS BY RAFAEL

In the 1100's AD a great threat arrived at the doorstep of Christianity. Islam was spreading throughout the known world. The tide of Islam brought with it many new ideas (which we learned about in the Introduction to Anselm). A Muslim man named Averroes threatened to crumble Christianity.

Averroes rocked the western world beginning at the University of Paris. He did not wield a sword, instead he brought a new way of thinking that would challenge the way Christians had been thinking for a thousand years.

Have you ever heard a Christian use the terms "secular" and "sacred"? Did you know those concepts did not exactly come from the Bible? Thinking of the world in terms of dividing between what is spiritual and physical came mainly from the philosopher Plato. This view is known as dualism. Plato taught here are two parts of the world. The seen and the unseen. The perfect and the imperfect. The holy and the ordinary. Creator and Creation. Faith and Reason.

From the very beginning of Christianity, most theologians, especially those living in the West, had grown accustomed to what was essentially a Platonic philosophy.[1] Plato's philosophy seemed to fit well with the Bible. The flesh is evil while the spirit is good. The earth is not as it should be, heaven is as it should be. Anselm, our #8 theologian, was so influential because he ultimately paved the way for Christians to fully embrace faith and reason. The two do not war against each other.

Averroes introduced to the West a competing view of reality which had been lost to all but those in the far East. *His major bomb-shell on western Christianity was making Aristotle available to the Latin-speaking world.* Aristotle was a student of Plato but did not agree with his mentor. Averroes, along with others, brought Aristotle to a new and hungry audience. Several professors in the Arts Faculty of Paris embraced the new philosophical ideas with enthusiasm.[2]

Theologians encountering Aristotle for the first time found his thoughts disturbing. Aristotle insisted on the independence between reason/ philosophy and theology. Aristotle believed philosophy always trumped theology. Faith and reason do not exist side-by-side. Faith sits below reason. If reason ever came into conflict with theology, reason would

---

1 Elliot, Shapers of Christian Orthodoxy. p341.
2 Ibid., p316.

win. Theology has to accommodate reason.

Here's a silly example. I am able to discover, through reason, that touching an oven is hurtful every time. I run an experiment where touching an oven ten times results in 10 wounds. Philosophically it is clear ovens and humans do not mix together. When I read the Bible, however, Daniel's three friends are able to walk around in a superheated oven. Does the Bible correct my reasoning? Are ovens now safe? Aristotle would say no. Reason wins every time.

ARISTOTLE

Aristotle's followers, for example, used reason to determine matter must be eternal. Since there is something there must have always been something. Something cannot come from nothing. The Bible, however, contradicts reason by saying God created everything *ex nihilo* (from nothing). Followers of Aristotle would say Theologians, not Philosophers, have some explaining to do.

Thomas Aquinas became one of the greatest philosophers AND theologians to ever live. He stepped up to offer an amazing solution between Aristotelian philosophy and theology.

Aquinas's Life

Aquinas was born in 1224AD. His parents were wealthy aristocrats in the area of Naples, Italy. He lived in a unique environment. He lived in a castle. How would you like to grow up in a castle? Thomas really couldn't tell you what it was like. He wasn't able to grow up in the castle. His parents had a different plan. At the age of 5 he was sent to start ecclesiastical training. Yes, at 5 years old, his parents groomed him to be a successful church leader. High church offices led to substantial power and wealth.

The Benedictines who were educating this promising boy sent him to Naples for his liberal arts education.[3] While in Naples, Thomas was won over to the Dominican order of monks, instead of the Benedictine order. The Dominicans were passionate about teaching the Bible. Unlike the Benedictines, the Dominicans took a vow of poverty. Thomas's family did not like his vow of poverty. It was social humiliation for a nobleman to become a monk. They envisioned great power and wealth for this budding theologian.

What did his family do? **In 1244, at the age of 20, they kidnapped Thomas and locked him in the castle tower for over a year.** They even brought by prostitutes to try to tempt him away from following the Dominican order of Christians. If he fell into temptation and eventually got married he would have to leave the Dominicans. His family even offered to buy him the post of Archbishop of Naples.[4] Thomas ended up escaping from the castle tower and fled to the University of Paris. He would soon be learning from the epicenter of the new Aristotle way of thinking.

Thomas learned from those who explained the entire universe, following Aristotle, not by using Scripture, but simply by using powers of observation and logic.[5] The question of the age was, "Could an intellectual person who held to the reasonable new philosophies retain their faith?" The powerful intellect of Aquinas would lead the way.

Many who knew Thomas in his early years, however, failed to see the genius in him.[6] People actually thought he was an idiot. He was so tall and obese he earned the nickname, "The Dumb Ox." He was the object, not merely of mockery, but of pity.[7] G.K. Chesterton writes:

---

3 Elliot, Shapers of Christian Orthodoxy. p341.
4 Christian History Magazine. Issue 28.
5 Ibid.
6 Gonzalez. p317.
7 Chesterton. The Dumb Ox. p33.

> *St. Thomas was a huge heavy bull of a man, fat and slow and quiet; very mild and magnanimous but not very sociable; shy, even apart from the humility of holiness…He was so stolid that the scholars, in the schools which he attended regularly, thought he was a dunce. Indeed, he was the sort of schoolboy, not unknown, who would much rather be thought a dunce than have his own dreams invaded, by more active or animated dunces.*[8]

It doesn't appear to have bothered Aquinas for people to think of him as an idiot. The old saying goes, "Better to remain silent and be thought a fool than to open your mouth and remove all doubt." Instead, Aquinas seemed to think, "Better to remain silent and be thought a fool than to open my mouth and make others feel like fools." But slowly his intelligence broke through his silence, and the Dominican order acknowledged his intellectual gifts.[9] Chesterton writes of his love for books and learning:

> *It was the outstanding fact about Thomas that he loved books and lived on books; that he lived the very life of the clerk or scholar in The Canterbury Tales, who would rather have a hundred books of Aristotle and his philosophy than any wealth the world could give him. When asked for what he thanked God most, he answered simply, "I have understood every page I ever read."*[10]

Aquinas went on to spend most of his life in the academic circles of Paris. He grew to become a famous professor. His introverted passion continued his whole life. According to one story:

> *His thoughts consumed him. He was dining with Louis IX of France (soon to be named "Saint Louis"), but while others engaged in conversation, he stared off into the distance lost in thought. Suddenly, he slammed down his fist on the table and exclaimed, "Ah! There's an argument that will destroy the Manichees!"*[11]

8 Chesterton. The Dumb Ox. p4.
9 Gonzalez. p317.
10 Chesterton. p4.
11 Galli & Olsen. 131 Christians Everyone Should Know.

Aquinas wrote a prolific amount of works. His two most famous are *Summa Contra Gentiles* (A Summary Against the Gentiles) and *Summa Theologica* (A Summary of Theology).

He died in 1274, when he had barely turned just fifty years old.

Aquinas's Thoughts

As Christians were running away from Aristotle, Aquinas ran toward him. He explored the possibility that the new philosophy offered for a better understanding of the Christian faith. It made sense to break the world into philosophy and theology.

Philosophy operates on the basis of objective principles which can be known apart from any needed revelation from God. A great philosopher does not seek to prove what the mind cannot understand. Truth is discovered by a well-reasoned method.

The theologian, on the other hand, does set out from the basis of revealed truths which cannot be known by reason alone. This does not mean, according to Aquinas, that theological doctrines are less reliable. On the contrary, revealed data are always more certain than those of reason, which may have error.[12]

Aquinas writes volumes showing the limits of philosophy. He is not seeking to destroy philosophy. He simply acknowledges its limits. A philosopher who claims to prove the eternity of the world, and a phi-

12 This paragraph is a paraphrase of Justo Gonzalez's excellent section on Aquinas's thoughts in his The Story of Christianity. p318.

losopher who claims to prove its creation out of nothing, are both poor philosophers, for they ignore the limits of reason.[13]

It is in revealed theology, Aquinas writes, where mankind receives information about God and the world upon which we could not attain solely through reason. He writes, "*In order that men might have knowledge of God, free of doubt and uncertainty it was necessary for divine truth to be delivered to them by way of faith, being told to them as it were, by God himself who cannot lie.*"[14]

Aquinas realizes if we are to depend fully on our five senses to understand the universe then we would need to all be excellent scientists. If my understanding of God rests on my scientific method, an accurate understanding of God would be based on the highest of intelligence.

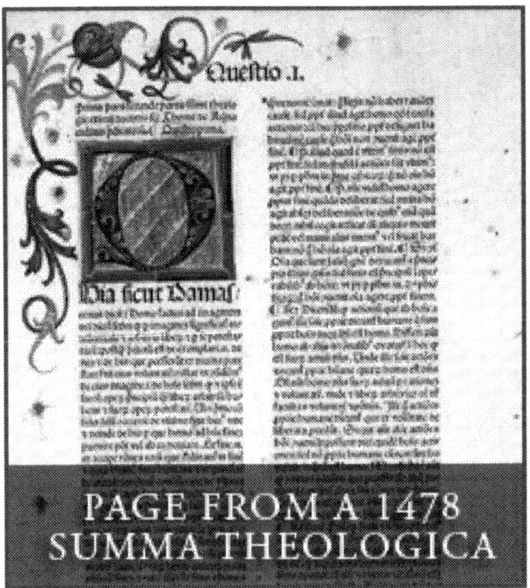

PAGE FROM A 1478 SUMMA THEOLOGICA

Aquinas beautifully articulates why the existence of God is a revealed theological truth. No one can plead lack of intelligence, even the most ignorant person can accept it on the basis of revealed truth from a trustworthy God. But this does not mean that the existence of God is a truth beyond the reach of reason. In this case, reason can prove what faith accepts. Therefore, the existence of God is a proper subject for both philosophy and theology, although each arrives at it following its own method.[15]

For example, someone looking at nature could tell by their senses that an intelligent creator exists. But that person would have no idea whether

13This paragraph is a paraphrase of Justo Gonzalez's excellent section on Aquinas's thoughts in his The Story of Christianity. p318.

14 Aquinas. Summa Theologica. p2149.

15 This paragraph is a paraphrase of Justo Gonzalez's excellent section on Aquinas's thoughts in his The Story of Christianity. p318.

the creator was good or if he might work in history. Philosophy and Theology are both needed.

Theologians like Anselm, whose thinking more aligned to Plato, did not trust the senses. Anselm wrote volumes combining pure reasoned ideas with faith. Aquinas took the opposite approach. He trusted the senses. He started with information known from the senses to learn as much about the universe as possible. When reason could take him no further, revelation would fill in the rest of the gaps.

Aquinas's Influence

Noted Boston College philosopher Peter Kreeft regards Thomas Aquinas as the greatest philosopher to have ever lived.[16] He gives eight reasons to support the claim: truth, common sense, practicality, clarity, profundity, orthodoxy, medievalism, and modernity.

Many people of his day considered Aristotle a threat to the faith. The reading and teaching of Aristotelianism was often forbidden. Therefore, Aquinas's sympathetic writings were at first seen by many as a threat to Christianity.

The old Platonic bias had helped Christianity through many early struggles with paganism, for it spoke of an invisible Supreme Being, of a higher world that senses cannot perceive, and of an immortal soul. Yet, Platonism also had its dangers. It was easy for Christians to undervalue the world which God had created. It was also possible to devalue the incarnation of Christ, for Platonism was not interested in temporary realities. There was a danger that theologians would pay less attention to Jesus Christ as a historical figure, and more to the eternal Word of God.[17]

Over time Aquinas's influence grew. Aquinas's work was of great significance for the further development of theology. He influenced the history of Christianity by joining traditional doctrine with the new

16 Kreeft, Peter. Summa of the Summa. II

17 This paragraph is a paraphrase of Justo Gonzalez's excellent section on Aquinas's thoughts in his The Story of Christianity. p319.

philosophical outlook. He used Aristotle to bring balance back from too much Platonic bias.

Aquinas did not reconcile Christ to Aristotle, he reconciled Aristotle to Christ.[18]

Aquinas's Foibles

Apart from his struggles with eating, Aquinas seemed to live a godly life. He believed only those following Christ were truly able to live virtuous lives.

For several hundred years, as Chesterton claims, people believed Aquinas had the ability to levitate. This claim is additionally interesting when considering his large size. Chesterton writes, "His experiences included well-attested cases of levitation in ecstasy; and the Blessed Virgin appeared to him, comforting him with the welcome news that he would never be a Bishop." Levitation and direct conversation with Mary are not foibles, but interesting tidbits we are left to only ponder.

Protestants will especially struggle with Aquinas's view of Purgatory. He provided one of the most scholarly justifications for purgatory which the Roman Catholic church later developed into their official doctrine. Aquinas writes:

> *It does at times happen that such purification is not entirely perfected in this life; one remains a debtor for the punishment, whether by reason of some negligence, or business, or even because a man is overtaken by death. Nevertheless, he is not entirely cut off from his reward…They must, then, be purged after this life before they achieve the final reward…And this is the reason we hold that there is a purgatory.*[19]

While the Roman Catholic church adopted Aquinas's teaching on purgatory, the reformers rejected it, believing it undermined the gospel of

18 Chesterton. p8.
19 Lewis. Aquinas, Rationes Fidei

salvation as a free gift.

Aquinas's Effect on Us

Thomas Aquinas is important for us today in several areas.[20] First, he brought together science and faith. As our world continues to see biblical faith as the inferior neighbor to science, Aquinas mastered both. Aquinas was the culmination of the greatest MIT scholar and the greatest orthodox theologian. He did not do it by separating science and faith but became great through bringing them both together.

Second, Aquinas was able to be clear and profound. We oftentimes think we have to jettison depth for the sake of clarity. All people need to know the depths of God through clear communication. We do not hold back God's revelation for the sake of thinking it is beyond the comprehension of God's people. It is precisely for the masses God gave His revelation. Aquinas joined the Dominicans in forsaking fame and wealth in order to simply teach people the revelation of God. A refreshing example for us today.

Third, Aquinas is full of common sense yet able to match anyone with technical sophistication. It's easy for us to prefer one over the other. One will say, "*I preach in a way that people can practically apply the Bible for today.*" Another will say, "*I preach the Word of God with technical sophistication with no need to mention application, the Spirit will apply it for me.*" Aquinas reminds us of the need to know the "what" and the "how."

Finally, Aquinas shows us how to have a "big picture" united view of God's universe, and then also how to carefully sort out all the smaller distinctions. He majors on the majors but does not neglect the minor aspects of the faith. Theology is not an ivory tower exercise for Aquinas. The focus of his thought is His living God. He maintains the focus on His God while also pondering all the smaller details. He writes thousands of pages in order to be as exhaustive as He can of what God has communicated to us through our 5 senses and through His Word.

His industrious passion for Jesus should encourage us all to "go all in"

20 Outline from Peter Kreeft, Summa of the Summa, p13.

living our lives for Jesus.

TURN TO PAGE
202
TO EXPERIENCE
AQUINAS IN HIS
OWN WORDS

JONATHAN EDWARDS

5

#5: JONATHAN EDWARDS

TOP TEN THEOLOGIANS

In order to appreciate the contribution of Jonathan Edwards, #5 on our list of Top Ten Theologians, it's important to place him within his world. A world full of lessons you can learn to change your world today.

Edwards's World

Puritans

JOHN OWEN

In the early 1560's a term was coined to explain some "hypocrites". The name "Puritan" was used to speak of some prudish, conceited, "holier than thou", odd and ugly people trying to "purify" the Church of England. These Puritans lived in both England and the new American colonies. Unlike the Mayflower riding Pilgrims who had left the Anglican church, the Puritans sought to make reforms by remaining inside the Church of England.

Puritans have been demonized during much of the last 300 years. Over the last 50 years, however, scholars have started to see the true heart of the Puritans. Puritans were not wild men, fierce and freaky, religious fanatics and social extremists, but sober, conscientious, and cultured citizens: persons of principle, devoted, determined and disciplined.[1]

These Puritans, encapsulated by men like John Owen, believed the Church of England stopped short of allowing the Reformation to fully purify the church. The Puritans at first, however, were not that successful. J.I. Packer writes:

> *The Puritans lost, more or less, every public battle that they fought. Those who stayed in England did not change the Church of England as they hoped to do, nor did they revive more than a minority of its adherents, and eventually they were driven out of Anglicanism (the Church of England) by calculated pressure on their consciences. Those who crossed the Atlantic failed to establish new Jerusalem in New England; for the first fifty years their little colonies barely survived. They hung on by the skin of their teeth. But the moral and spiritual victories that the Puritans won by keeping sweet, peaceful, patient, obedient, and hopeful under sustained and seemingly intolerable pressures and frustrations give them a place of high honour in the believer's hall of fame, where Hebrews 11 is the first gallery. It was out of this constant furnace-experience that their maturity was wrought and their wisdom concerning discipleship*

JOHN BUNYAN

1 Packer. A Quest for Godliness. p22.

was refined.[2]

A Puritan man like John Bunyan lived under the "sustained and seemingly intolerable pressures" of which Packer speaks. Bunyan was put in prison more than once for preaching. His blind daughter had to move into his prison cell so she would have someone to care for her life.

During his 12-year term in prison Bunyan wrote one of the greatest Christian books of all time. His Pilgrim's Progress has been in print for over 300 years. It has been translated into 200 languages.

It was their lack of apparent success, however, that fueled their unforeseen influence. George Whitefield, the famous evangelist, writes of the Puritans:

> *Ministers never write or preach so well as when under the cross; the Spirit of Christ and of glory then rests upon them. It was this, no doubt, that made the Puritans…such burning and shining lights. When cast out by the black Bartholomew-act [the 1662 Act of Uniformity] and driven from their respective charges to preach in barns and fields, in the highways and hedges, they in an especial manner wrote and preached as men having authority. Though dead, by their writings they yet speak; a peculiar unction attends them to this very hour.*[3]

The hardships experienced by the Puritans led them to uniquely live out the Christian life. Packer explains their significance:

> *They were great souls serving a great God. In them clear-headed passion and warm-hearted compassion combined. Visionary and practical, idealistic and realistic too, goal-oriented and methodical, they were great believers, great hopers, great doers and great sufferers. But their sufferings, both sides of the ocean (in old England from the authorities and in New England from the elements),*

2 Ibid.
3 Whitefield. Works. IV:306f.

> *seasoned and ripened them till they gained a stature that was nothing short of heroic. Ease and luxury, such as our affluence brings us today, do not make for maturity; hardship and struggle however do, and the Puritans' battles against the spiritual and climatic wildernesses in which God set them produced a virility of character, undaunted and unsinkable, rising above discouragement and fears.*[4]

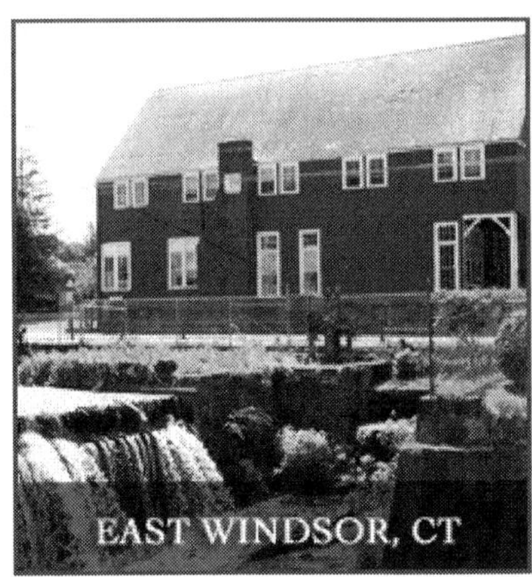

Jonathan Edwards would rise up, as one of the last great Puritans, to make an unmistakable mark on his and our world.

Edwards's Life

Jonathan Edwards was born in East Windsor, Connecticut on October 5, 1703. Edwards was the only son among ten daughters! He was born into one of the most respected families in all of Colonial America. His father was a Harvard-trained pastor who served his congregation faithfully for more than sixty years. His mother came from one of the most well-known families in all of New England.

Edwards's mother was the daughter of Solomon Stoddard, one of the most popular preachers in all of the Colonies. Stoddard pastored his Northhampton, Massachusetts congregation for 59 years.

Edwards showed intelligence as a young man. His father, Timothy, was his teacher. In addition to a general education, Timothy groomed him for ministry by teaching him the Scriptures, the Westminster Shorter Catechism, and theology. The entrance exams at Harvard and Yale tested proficiency in Latin, New Testament Greek and biblical Hebrew, the classical languages on which the college curriculum was based.[5] At the age of thirteen, Edwards was accepted and enrolled in the new Collegiate School of Connecticut, later to be named Yale College.

4 Packer. The Quest for Godliness. p22.

5 Sweeney, Jonathan Edwards and the Ministry of the Word. p34.

He received a broad liberal-arts eduction, studying grammar, rhetoric, logic, ancient history, arithmetic, geometry, astronomy, metaphysics, ethics, natural science, Greek, Hebrew, Christian theology, natural philosophy, and classical literature.[6] He graduated at the head of his class with a bachelor of arts degree in 1720 and delivered the valedictory address.[7] At the age of 16, immediately following his graduation, Edwards began the master's program at Yale.

Although Edwards appeared from the outside to be a believer since he was a little boy, he wrote to a friend, "*in process of time, my convictions and affections wore off; and I entirely lost all those affections and delights, and left off secret prayer, at least as to any constant performance of it; and returned like a dog to his vomit, and went on in ways of sin.*"[8]

During his second year of the master's program, however, he was converted to Jesus Christ. As he read 1 Timothy 1:17, "Now unto the King eternal, immortal, invisible, the only wise God, be honor and glory for ever and ever. Amen." He explains:

> *As I read these words, there came into my soul, and was as it were diffused through it, a sense of the glory of the divine being; a new sense, quite different from anything I ever experienced before. Never any words of Scripture seemed to me as these words did. I thought with myself, how excellent a Being that was; and how happy I should be, if I might enjoy that God, and be wrapt up to God in*

6 Lawson, The Unwavering Resolve of Jonathan Edwards. p6.
7 Ibid.
8 Edwards Letters and Personal Writings. p790-791.

> *heaven, and be as it were swallowed up in him.*[9]

He would preach years later:

> *There is a difference between having an opinion that God is holy and gracious, and having a sense of the loveliness and beauty of that holiness and grace. There is a difference between having a rational judgement that honey is sweet, and having a sense of its sweetness. A man may have the former, that knows not how honey tastes; but a man can't have the latter, unless he has an idea of the taste of honey in his mind. So there is a difference between believing that a person is beautiful, and having a sense of his beauty. The former may be obtained by hearsay, but the latter only by seeing the countenance. There is a wide difference between mere speculative, rational judging anything to be excellent, and having a sense of its sweetness, and beauty.*[10]

Edwards had finally tasted the sweetness of the Lord. He would never recover. From 1720 to 1726 he wrote in his diary his famous *Resolutions for living a passionate life for God.*

He started out in full-time ministry as co-Pastor of one of the most popular and fashionable churches in all of America. He pastored alongside his grandfather, Solomon Stoddard, in Northampton, New Hampshire. He was a scholar-pastor, not a shepherding pastor. He was required to spend thirteen hours a day studying. In the same year, 1727, Edwards married Sarah Pierpont. Jonathan was 24 years old, Sarah was 17. Like Edwards, she was also from a well-known religious family. Her father, James Pierpont, was the founder of Yale. Sarah's walk with God was well-known to Edwards. He first spoke of her great piety when she was just 13 years old.[11]

Two years later, with the death of his grandfather, Edwards became the Head Pastor at Northampton. He had been preaching for several years,

---

9 Edwards. Letters and Personal Writings. p792.

10 Edwards. The Sermons of Jonathan Edwards: A Reader. p127-128.

11 Marsden. Jonathan Edwards: A Life. p93-95.

with average results, when his preaching began evoking a response that surprised him.[12] From 1734-35 people responded to his sermons with emotional outbursts, remarkable life change, and with increased attention to their devotional lives. A few years later Edwards invited a well-known preacher from another denomination, George Whitefield, to speak at his church. It is said that while the visiting pastor preached, Edwards wept.[13] The awakening had renewed momentum. In a remarkably short time, the movement spread beyond his church into many areas of the colonies. It became known as *The Great Awakening.*

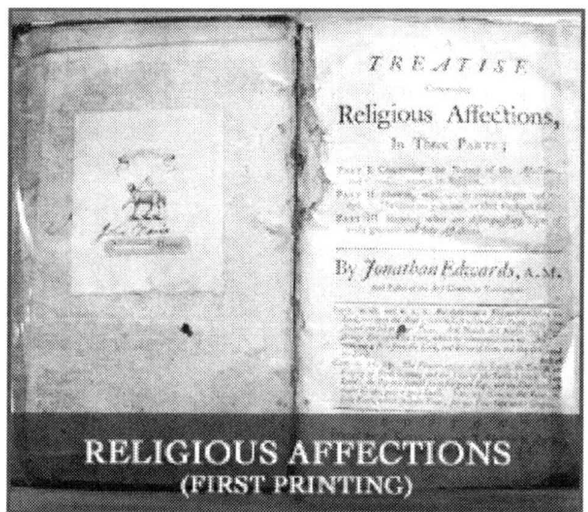
TREATISE
Religious Affections,
By Jonathan Edwards, A.M.

RELIGIOUS AFFECTIONS
(FIRST PRINTING)

From 1742 to 1743 he preached a series of messages under the title *Religious Affections.* This famous work, published in 1746, was Edwards's way of explaining how conversion to Christianity happens. A few years later, in 1749, he published a biography of a young man named David Brainerd who had lived for several months with his family before dying in 1747. Young Brainerd had been a missionary and it was rumored he was to marry one of Edwards's daughters. His biography has become a source of inspiration and encouragement to many Christians.

From 1743, however, Edwards was for various reasons at trouble with his church, and in 1750 he was dismissed from the pastorate.[14] How comforting for those who labor in ministry to know one of the greatest pastors from church history was himself fired from his church after serving for 21 years!

Edwards then, at the age of 47, moved his family to be missionaries to the Native Americans. They moved to the frontier mission station of

---

12 Gonzalez. The Story of Christianity: Volume 2. p228.
13 Ibid.
14 Packer. p309.

Stockbridge, Massachusetts. Yes, western Massachusetts, not western Nevada, was considered the Wild West. It was an extreme outpost during these early years of the American Colonies. From Stockbridge he wrote two of his greatest works *The Freedom of the Will* and *Original Sin.*

In 1757, at the age of 54, Edwards became the president of Princeton College. Immediately after becoming president, he decided to get inoculated against small pox in order to encourage the students to do the same. Never in great health, he unfortunately died of the inoculation on March 22, 1758. Edwards had three sons and eight daughters.

Edwards's Thoughts

Since The Great Awakening was characterized by an emotional experience leading people to be converted to Christ, it was accused of substituting emotion for study and devotion. Interestingly, however, Edwards was not a very charismatic person, he was more of a scholar. The goal of the movement was not worship services marked by continual shows of emotion, but rather a single experience that would lead each believer to greater devotion and more conscious study of Scripture.[15]

Regarding the Word of God Edwards writes, "*Be assiduous in reading the Holy Scriptures. This is the fountain whence all knowledge in divinity must be derived. Therefore let not this treasure lie by you neglected.*"[16]

Edwards devoted himself and those he led to living a God-entranced, Scripture Saturated, Passionately Practical, Thoughtful life. His passion

15 Gonzalez. p229.
16 Works, II, 162

was: pursuing the glory of God; forsaking sin; making proper use of God-allotted Time; living with all his being for he Lord; pursuing humility and love; and making frequent self-examination. He writes:

> *Seek not to grow in knowledge chiefly for the sake of applause, and to enable you to dispute with others; but seek it for the benefit of your souls, and in order to practice . . . Practice according to what knowledge you have. This will be the way to know more. . . . [According to Psalm 119:100] "I understand more than the ancients, because I keep thy precepts."*[17]

Similar to C.S. Lewis, Joy is a central focus for Edwards, he says:

> *So God glorifies Himself toward the creatures in two ways: 1. By appearing to . . . their understanding. 2. In communicating Himself to their hearts, and in their rejoicing and delighting in, and enjoying, the manifestations which He makes of Himself. . . . God is glorified not only by His glory's being seen, but by its being rejoiced in. When those that see it delight in it, God is more glorified than if they only see it. His glory is then received by the whole soul, both by the understanding and by the heart.*

The enjoyment of God is the only happiness with which our souls can be satisfied. To go to heaven, fully to enjoy God, is infinitely better than the most pleasant accommodations here. Fathers and mothers, husbands, wives, or children, or the company of earthly friends, are but shadows; but God is the substance. These are but scattered beams, but God is the sun. These are but streams. But God is the ocean.[18]

Edwards's sermons are not emotional tricks, but careful expositions of profound theological matters. Edwards believed that emotion was important. But such emotion, including the high experience of conversion, should not eclipse the need for right doctrine and rational worship.[19]

---

17 Works, II, 162f
18 Works, II, 244
19 Gonzalez. p229.

Edwards's Influence

Edwards was at the center of the first major spiritual awakening in the American Colonies. This movement influenced many by showing the power when someone clearly communicates the profound truths of God. People do not need a light show, they need the light of the World.

The Great Awakening brought together Congregationalists, Presbyterians, Anglicans, Baptists and Methodists. The Awakening fueled a major connection between the Colonies. This was the first movement that embraced the thirteen colonies that would eventually become the United States. A sense of commonality began developing among the various colonies which would produce momentous events in 1776.[20]

Edwards greatly influenced the modern missionary movement. Men like William Carey and Jim Elliot speak of Edwards's biography of David Brainerd as one of the main influences leading them to become missionaries.

Those who have sat most at the feet of Edwards will testify to what the Puritans called "logic on fire." Edwards brings together his mind and his heart to burn brightly for his God. As people are influenced by Edwards their view of God, passion for God, and knowledge of God grow.

This is why Dr. Martyn Lloyd-Jones says, "I am tempted, perhaps foolish, to compare the Puritans to the Alps, Luther and Calvin to the Himalayas, and Jonathan Edwards to Mount Everest! He has always seemed to me the man most like the Apostle Paul."[21]

Edwards's Foibles

Edwards had a few foibles we would do well to stay away from. First, he could spend up to 13 hours a day in his study. He welcomed people to his study for conversation, and he frequently taught private meetings

20 Gonzalez. p230.
21 Lloyd-Jones. The Puritans: Their Origins and Successors. p355.

in various neighborhoods as well as catechizing the young people in his home. As John Piper states, "In this pattern of pastoral labor we probably should not follow him."[22]

Second, Edwards is usually negatively characterized as a hell-loving wrathful fire and brimstone preacher in his most famous sermon, "Sinners in the Hands of An Angry God." Edwards, however, simply sought to communicate to his people the entire counsel of God. Including the wrathful side of God. When Scripture speaks of the wrath of God, Edwards felt compelled to make sure his people understood this side of God. Ignoring a message like, "Sinners in the Hands of An Angry God", would show a lack of love for his people. His people were aware of the gospel message, Edwards sought to make them aware of the necessity for them to fully respond. There are consequences for those who don't respond to the love of Christ on their behalf.

The greatest foible is the reality that Jonathan Edwards owned several slaves. In 1731 Edwards travelled to Newport, Rhode Island to purchase a slave named Venus. Edwards, during his lifetime, did not view slavery as wrong. His main focus was on the treatment of slaves. He writes,

"*We are made of the same human race. In these two things are contained the most forceable reasons against the master's abuse of his servant, viz. That both have one Maker, and that their Maker made 'em alike with the same nature.*"

Edwards's Effect on Us

Jonathan Edwards's effect on us is what mainly propels him forward to #5 on the list of Top Ten Theologians. Jonathan Edwards is the model needed for church leaders in post-Christian America and Europe.

He brings together many components needed in our world today: a theologically grounded pastor who leads their church to be attractional; missional; loving God with their entire being; devotionally loving Scripture; and bringing other churches/denominations to do the same.

---

22 http://www.desiringgod.org/resource-library/biographies/the-pastor-as-theologian

Edwards provides us with one word, "maturity." J.I. Packer explains:

> *Maturity is a compound of wisdom, goodwill, resilience, and creativity. The Puritans exemplified maturity; we don't. We are spiritual dwarfs. A much-travelled leader has declared that he finds North American Protestantism, man-centered, manipulative, success-oriented, self-indulgent and sentimental, as it blatantly is, to be 3,000 miles wide and half an inch deep. The Puritans, by contrast, are a body of giants.*[23]

Our churches and our world need church leaders of today to be more like Edwards. We need to be theologically grounded and fully consumed with God.

John Piper states, "**Our people need a God-besotted man. Even if they criticize the fact that you are not available at the dinner on Saturday night because you must be with God, they need at least one man in their life who is radically and totally focused on God and the pursuit of the knowledge of God, and the ministry of the word of God.**"[24]

Edwards leads us to radical singlemindedness in our occupation with spiritual things. He shows us to work like dogs to earnestly know the Scriptures. He pleads with us to redeem the time. Put down our Netflix streaming iPads and work with all our might for the Kingdom of God. The theological work of Edwards begs us to study for the sake of heart-felt worship and for practical obedience. Our lives and our world will be better by spending time with Jonathan Edwards.[25]

---

23 Packer. The Quest for Godliness. p22.
24 http://www.desiringgod.org/resource-library/biographies/the-pastor-as-theologian
25 Ibid. Paragraph modified version of Piper's great suggestions.

TURN TO PAGE
206
TO EXPERIENCE
EDWARDS IN HIS
OWN WORDS

ATHANASIUS

4

#4: ATHANASIUS

TOP TEN THEOLOGIANS

"If Christian theology had superheroes," scholar Kevin VanHoozer writes, "Athanasius would perhaps lead the list."[1] Athanasius is relatively unknown to most Christians today. In order for us to begin appreciating the significance of his life, we need to understand the world from which this little man stood tall.

Athanasius's World

Diocletian

In 302 A.D., when Athansius was only 6 years old, two men sought an audience with the god Apollo. These weren't ordinary men, they were two of the most power-

1 Back cover comment on the book: Leithart, Peter J. Athanasius. Baker Academic

ful people on the planet. Diocletian and Galerius were both Roman Emperors. They wanted Apollo to help settle an argument for them.

Christianity had been spreading like a virus. They knew the Roman gods weren't happy with so many Romans becoming Christians. Dicoletian and Galerius wanted Rome, with help from the gods, to be greater than ever. How could they accomplish their wishes?

Diocletian thought the gods would be happy if Christians were prevented from positions of influence. Galerius, however, thought the gods wanted more. Galerius thought the gods would want Christians exterminated. The best way to settle the argument? Why don't we just ask the head god and see what he wants? The two men asked their questions through the oracle of Apollo at Didyma (modern-day Didim, Turkey).[2]

The oracle told the two men the "impious" on the Earth were making it hard for Apollo to even provide advice. Diocletian and Galerius agreed; Christians needed to be exterminated. On February 23, 303AD Diocletian ordered the newly built church in his city to be leveled. Life was hell for many Christians. The horrendous ways Christians were persecuted and killed during this time period are only for the strongest of stomachs. The executions continued until at least April 24, 303AD when six people, including the lead pastor of a prominent city, were decapitated.[3]

Constantine

While the Diocletian persecutions were still fresh in everyone's mind, a man named Constantine became Emperor of Rome. The new emperor, shortly after taking office, faced a coup. Maxentius, a military leader, organized a huge force to defeat Constantine. The two forces met on October 28th, 312AD at

2 Barnes. Constantine and Eusebius. p21.
3 Ibid. p24.

Milvian Bridge, just north of Rome. Maxentius's army was twice the size of Constantine's. The night before, however, Constantine had a dream. He was advised in the dream to, "mark the heavenly sign of God on the shields of his soldiers...by means of a slanted letter X with the top of its head bent round."[4] Eusebius describes the sign as Chi (x) traversed by Rho (P), a symbol representing the first two letters of the Greek spelling of the word Christos or Christ.[5]

The battle was brief. Constantine's cavalry and infantry decimated the larger force. The mob of fleeing soldiers pushed Maxentius into the Tiber river where he drowned. Constantine's seemingly supernatural vision and victory would significantly change the way Christians were treated. Truth is stranger than fiction. No one who endured the Diocletian persecutions could have imagined such a drastic turn-around. Constantine credited his victory, not to Pagan gods, but to the Christian God who only decades before was seen as an enemy to Rome.

Just a few months after The Battle of Milvian Bridge, Constantine issued the Edict of Milan proclaiming religious tolerance for all religions throughout the empire. The edict had special benefits for Christians, it legalized the religion and granted restoration for all property seized during Diocletian's persecution.

ARIUS

The newfound Christian freedom made it possible for everything Athanasius is famous for to transpire.

Arius

Arius was 63 years old when Constantine issued the Edict of Milan. Arius led a church in Alexandria, Egypt. Alexandria was one of the most influential cities

4 Lactantius, De Mortibus Persecutorum 44.4–6, tr. J.L. Creed, Lactantius: De Mortibus Persecutorum (Oxford: Oxford University Press, 1984)

5 Barnes. Constantine and Eusebius. p306.

of the entire Roman Empire. Arius was one of the most prestigious and popular pastors of the city.[6] Arius started preaching something that would shake the Christian world and dominate almost the entirety of Athanasius's life. Jeffrey Bingham explains:

> *Arius was preaching from the Bible, with Proverbs 8:22 as a central verse, that the Son is not eternal with the Father but is created by the Father. That verse reads: "The LORD brought me forth as the first of his works, before his deeds of old." Arius and his followers argued their doctrine from this verse, which speaks of the creation of wisdom, and from the common early Christian understanding of Christ as "wisdom" (1 Cor. 1:24, 30). These verses…subordinate Christ, the Son, to the Father, who alone is God and who had begotten – that is, created – a Son. Other passages they pointed to in support of their view were Psalm 45:7-8 and Isaiah 1:2 and the words "only begotten" in John 1:14, 18. Thus, according to Arius, it was not true to say "Always God, always Son" or "At the same time Father at the same time Son," meaning that God the Father and God the Son are co-eternal and both possess the quality of deity. Rather, Arius proclaimed that "before [the Son] was begotten or created or defined or established, he was not for he was not unbegotten" and that "the Son has a beginning, but God is without beginning." For Arius, the Son is a creature and is not eternal.*[7]

Is Jesus the Creator or is He a creature? Did Jesus have a beginning? Is Jesus truly God? These are some of the most important questions in the universe. Athanasius would spend most of his life, sometimes standing alone, answering these questions.

---

6 Gonzalez. The Story of Christianity. p161.
7 Bingham, Jeffrey. Pocket History of the Church. p46.

Athanasius's Life

Early Years

Athanasius was born around 296AD. Little is known of his early life. A 10th century biographer, the Arabic speaking Severus, spoke about Athanasius's mother as having worshipped idols and having been wealthy.[8]

Sometime during his youth Athanasius and his mother were baptized as Christians. He was then discipled by Alexander, the head of the Alexandrian church. It was from Alexander that Athanasius obtained not only his cursory knowledge of contemporary philosophy, but also his thorough understanding of Scripture.[9]

Gregory of Nazianzus tells us:

> *He was brought up, from the first, in religious habits and practices, after a brief study of literature and philosophy, so that he might not be utterly unskilled in such subjects, or ignorant in matters which he had determined to despise…[rather] from meditating on every book of the Old and New Testament, with a depth such as none else has applied even to one of them, he grew in contemplation, rich in splendour of life, combining them in wondrous sort by that golden bond which few can weave; using life as the guide of contemplation, contemplation as the seal of life.*[10]

It was now time for Athanasius to step toward the spotlight.

---

8 Severus Ibn al-Muqaffa. History of the Patriarchs of Alexandria.
9 Weinandy. Athanasius: A Theological Introduction. p1.
10 Gregory of Nazianzus. Oration. 21,6 quoted in Weinandy p1.

With Alexander at Nicea

The entire Christian world pondered the ideas of Arius. Is Jesus a creature? The greatest creature ever created? Arius believed Jesus predated coming to earth; he even believed Jesus predated the earth itself. The phrase that eventually became the Arian motto, "there was when He was not," aptly focuses on the point at issue.[11]

Athanasius's mentor, Alexander, made the first move. Arius was a pastor under the authority of Alexander. Alexander, claiming his authority and his responsibility as bishop, condemned the teachings of Arius. Arius did not accept this judgment. He wrote to church leaders all over the world. Soon there were popular demonstrations in Alexandria, with people marching through the streets chanting Arius' theological teachings.[12] The local disagreement in Alexandria spread beyond Egypt and threatened to divide the church.

In 325 AD, Constantine decided to intervene. He called a great assembly of Christian bishops from all parts of the empire to meet him at Nicea (modern-day Iznik, Turkey). Constantine paid the travel expenses for all involved. Athanasius, only 29 years old at the time, travelled to the Council of Nicea as the personal assistant to his mentor Alexander.

Athanasius, as he arrived with Alexander, would have seen a spectacular sight. This was the first time in human history that it was safe for the leaders of the Christian Church to get together. It would have been foolish for them all to previously assemble in one location before the time of Constantine. All the leadership could have been wiped out in one strategic swoop.

The more than 300 bishops who walked through those doors at Nicea were true heroes of the faith. In order to understand what Athansius saw, it is necessary to remember that several of those attending the great assembly had recently been imprisoned, tortured, or exiled, and

---

11 Gonzalez. The Story of Christianity. p161.
12 Ibid. p162.

that some bore on their bodies the physical marks of their faithfulness.[13] Davis writes:

> *As confessors of the faith, some of the bishops bore the signs of the recent persecution on their persons: Paul of Neo-Caesarea had lost the use of his hands because of torture, the half blind and hamstrung Paphnutius of Egypt was kissed by Constantine himself in a touching diplomatic gesture.*[14]

Eusebius of Caesarea, who was present, describes the amazing scene:

> *There were gathered the most distinguished ministers of God, from the many churches in Europe, Libya [i.e., Africa] and Asia. A single house of prayer, as if enlarged by God, sheltered Syrians and Cilicians, Phoenicians and Arabs, delegates from Palestine and from Egypt, Thebans and Libyans, together with those from Mesopotamia. There was also a Persian bishop, and a Scythian was not lacking. Pontus, Galatia, Pamphylia, Cappadocia, Asia, and Phrygia sent their most outstanding bishops, jointly with those from the remotest areas of Thrace, Macedonia, Achaia, and Epirus. Even from Spain, there was a man of great fame [Hosius of Cordova] who sat as a member of the great assembly. The bishop of the Imperial city [Rome] could not attend due to his advanced age; but he was represented by his presbyters. Constantine is the first ruler of all time to have gathered such a garland in the bond of peace, and to have presented it to his Savior as an offering of gratitude for the victories he had won over all his enemies.*[15]

Did you know even Santa Claus was at Nicea? Yes, that's right! Saint Nicholas, bishop of Myra (modern day Demre, Turkey) was a voting bishop at the Council of Nicea.

---

13 Ibid. p162.
14 Leo Donald Davis. The First Seven Ecumenical Councils (325-787). p58.
15 Eusebius of Caesarea. Life of Constantine. 3.7.

For about two months, the bishops discussed the issue raised by Arius. The two sides argued and debated, with each side appealing to Scripture to justify their respective positions. It is unclear exactly how much influence Athanasius, as a non-voting member, had during the meetings.

Eusebius of Nicomedia, holding the same view as Arius, was convinced that a clear statement of his doctrine was all that was needed to convince the assembly. The reaction from the bishops was not what Eusebius expected. The assertion that the Word or Son was no more than a creature, no matter how high a creature, provoked angry reactions from many of the bishops: "You lie!" "Blashpemy!" "Heresy!"[16] Eusebius of Nicomedia was shouted down, and we are told that his speech was snatched from his hand, torn to shreds, and trampled underfoot.[17] According to many accounts, debate became so heated that at one point Arius was slapped in the face by Saint Nicholas![18]

The assembly finally decided the best way to articulate the Bible's teaching on the Trinity was through a creed. Eventually, the assembly agreed on the following creed:

> *We believe in one God, the Father Almighty, maker of all things visible and invisible.*
>
> *And in one Lord Jesus Christ, the Son of God, the only-begotten of the Father, that is, from the substance of the Father, God of God, light of light, true God of true God, not made, of one substance [homoousios] with the Father, through whom all things were made, both in heaven and on earth, who for us humans and for our salvation descended and became incarnate, becoming human, suffered and rose again on the third day, ascended to the heavens, and will come to judge the living and the dead. And in the Holy Spirit.*

16 Gonzalez.p164.

17 Ibid. p164.

18 Bishop Nicholas Loses His Cool at the Council of Nicea. From the St. Nicholas center. See also St. Nicholas the Wonderworker, from the website of the Orthodox Church in America.

But those who say there was when He was not, and that before being begotten He was not, or that He came from that which is not, or that the Son of God is of a different substance [hypostasis] or essence [ousia], or that He is created, or mutable, these the catholic church anathematizes.

The Nicene Creed clearly rejected Arianism. Arius and Eusebius of Nicomedia were both sent into exile. As the bishops all returned to their parts of the world, they hoped the Council of Nicea would end the controversy.

Defending Nicea as Bishop

Only three years after the Council, Alexander having died, Athanasius became Bishop of Alexandria on April 17th, 328AD. Athanasius became shepherd of one of the most vibrant cities within the Roman Empire.[19] Athanasius would now become the champion for the Nicene cause.[20] He would soon be swimming against the tide. Constantine, being won over to Arianism by Eusebius of Nicomedia, revoked the banishment of Arius in 328AD.

Eusebius of Nicomedia, Arius, and other Arian leaders knew Athanasius was their strongest enemy. They soon plotted his downfall by circulating rumors that he dabbled in magic. They also claimed Athanasius had killed a bishop named Arsenius, and cut off his hand to use it in rites of magic.

Constantine summoned him to appear before a judge and answer to the serious charges brought against him. Here's what happened during his murder trial:

Athanasius brought into the courtroom a man covered in a cloak. After making sure that several of those present had known Arsenius, he uncovered the face of the hooded man, and his accusers were confounded when they realized it was

---

19 Weinandy. p2.
20 Gonzalez. p166.

> *Athanasius' supposed victim. Then someone who had been convinced by the rumors circulating against the bishop of Alexandria suggested that perhaps Athanasius had not killed Arsenius, but had cut off his hand. Athanasius waited until the assembly insisted on proof that the man's hand had not been cut. He then uncovered one of Arsenius' hands. "It was the other hand!" shouted some of those who had been convinced by the rumors. Then Athanasius uncovered the man's other hand and demanded: "What kind of a monster did you think Arsenius was? One with three hands?" Laughter broke out through the assembly, while others were enraged that the Arians had fooled them.*

The murder charges were dropped and Athanasius was able to go back to shepherding the people of Alexandria. His freedom, however, would be short lived. Eusebius of Nicomedia had convinced Constantine that Athanasius was dangerous. Constantine sent Athanasius into exile. By this time most of the Nicene leaders were also banished. When Constantine asked for baptism, on his deathbed, he received the sacrament from the Arian Eusebius of Nicomedia.[21]

All exiled bishops, including Athanasius, were allowed to go back to their homes after Constantine's death.

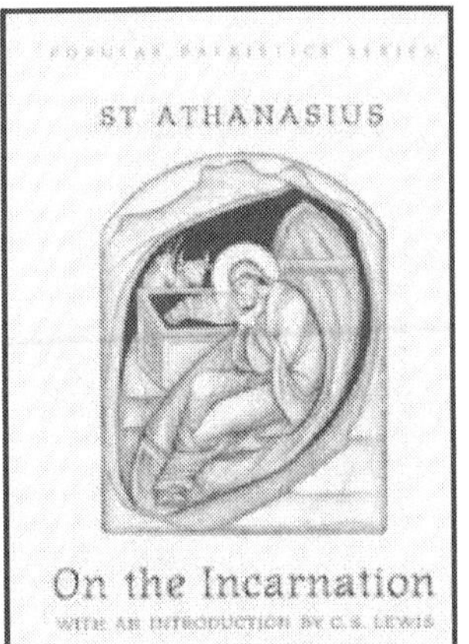

Exiles

Yet Athanasius' return to Alexandria was not the end, but rather the beginning of a long period of struggle and repeated exiles[22] For almost thirty years Athanasius would be considered a hero under one emperor and then have to flee to live with monks in the desert to survive the next emperor. It was at this time that Jerome said, "*the entire world woke from a deep slumber and discovered that it had become Arian.*"

21 Gonzalez. p166.
22 Ibid. p176.

Athanasius continued to speak, teach and write against Arianism. Although Athanasius never saw the final victory of the cause to which he devoted his life, his writings clearly show that he was convinced that in the end Arianism would be defeated. As he approached his old age, he saw emerge around himself a new generation of theologians devoted to the same cause.[23] Death claimed him in 373AD at the age of 77.

Athanasius's Thoughts

Shortly after the Council of Nicea, it is believed Athanasius wrote his first works – *Contra Gentes* (Against the Gentiles) and *De Incarnatione* (On the Incarnation). These works articulated what he considered the true faith in a climate of growing theological and political tension.[24]

The presence of God in history was the central element in the faith and thoughts of Athanasius.[25] Athanasius fully believed God himself had visited our planet. The visit from God in Jesus Christ made it possible for us to be free beings capable of living in communion with the divine.

He beautifully writes, "*For the human race would have perished utterly had not the Lord and Savior of all, the Son of God, come among us to put an end to death.*"[26] He then continues:

> *There were thus two things which the Savior did for us by becoming Man. He banished death from us and made us anew; and, invisible and imperceptible as in Himself He is, He became visible through His works and revealed Himself as the Word of the Father, the Ruler and King of the whole creation.*[27]

We see the depth, elegance and developed thoughts of Athanasius speak-

23 Ibid. p180.
24 Weinandy. p3.
25 Gonzalez. p175.
26 Athanasius. On the Incarnation. Section 9.
27 Ibid. Section 16.

ing of the power of Christ:

> *The marvelous truth is, that being the Word, so far from being Himself contained by anything, He actually contained all things Himself…A man cannot transport things from one place to another, for instance, merely by thinking about them; nor can you or I move the sun and the stars just by sitting at home and looking at them. With the Word of God in His human nature, however, it was otherwise. His body was for Him not a limitation, but an instrument, so that He was both in it and in all things, and outside all things, resting in the Father alone. At one and the same time – this is the wonder – as Man He was living a human life, and as Word He was sustaining the life of the universe.*[28]

The Arian controversy, for Athanasius, is not a matter of theological subtleties with little or no relevance. In it, the very core of the Christian message and the very core of Jesus is at stake.

Athanasius's Influence

C.S. Lewis conveys some of the Influence of Athanasius by saying:

> *He stood for the Trinitarian doctrine, "whole and undefiled," when it looked as if all the civilized world was slipping back from Christianity into the religion of Arius – into one of those "sensible" synthetic religions which are so strongly recommended to-day and which, then as now, included among their devotees many highly cultivated clergymen. It is his glory that he did not move with the times; it is his reward that he now remains when those times, as all times do, have moved away.*[29]

The anti-Trinitarian world had grown very dark around Athanasius. He himself was a very small dark African. He was nicknamed in his day,

28 Ibid. Section 17.

29 Athanasius. On the Incarnation. C.S. Lewis Introduction. p9.

"the black dwarf." This black dwarf stood tall with a bright light and almost single-handedly kept defending Nicene orthodoxy until reinforcements eventually arrived. Men like the Great Cappadocians were soon to arrive on the scene and continue re-awakening the world to the full beauty and power of the God-Man.

Athanasius's Foibles

Historically, Athanasius is known for his godly life. Gonzalez writes, "His monastic discipline, his roots among the people, his fiery spirit, and his profound and unshakable conviction made him invincible."[30] Additionally, Weinandy writes, "He was extolled through the centuries as a holy and selfless man of steadfast and fearless faith, of long suffering patience, and of zealous passion for the truth of the Gospel."[31]

In the early 20th century, however, many contemporary scholars portrayed Athanasius as very sinister[32] T.D. Barnes states, "Like a modern gangster, he evoked widespread mistrust, proclaimed total innocence – and usually succeeded in evading conviction on specific charges."[33] Barnes goes on to explain why most people haven't heard of this side of him:

> *If the violence of Athanasius leaves fewer traces in the surviving sources…[the reason is] that he exercised power more efficiently and that he was successful in presenting himself to posterity as an innocent in power, as an honest, sincere and straightforward 'man of God.'*

Barnes makes an argument from silence. In order to survive and even win the day Athanasius surely needed to be a wise, resourceful and clever man. The fact that he ultimately bested his opponents in no way implies that he was more evil than they.[34]

---

30 Gonzalez. p174.
31 Weinandy. p8. 31
32 Ibid. p8.
33 Barnes. Constantine and Eusebius. p230.
34 Weinandy. p9.

Athanasius's Effect on Us

The most obvious effect Athanasius has on our life is with our view of the Trinity. Is a correct understanding of the Trinity (one in essence, three in persons) important for you? So many Christians look at the Trinity like a bad shallow dating relationship, "I want to date you, have the warm fuzzy romantic dinners, but I really don't want to know too much about you. Let's spend an hour together each week but don't require me to learn about you. I like what we've got going on, let's not ruin it with information."

As we spend our lives singing about God, listening to sermons about God, talking about God it seems like we should know who we're talking about. Athanasius teaches us how vitally important it is to have an orthodox understanding of the Trinity.

Athanasius, additionally, helps us to realize we do not live by public opinion polls. Athanasius was right, he was reading the Bible correctly, but the world around him had gone mad. He had the courage and conviction to proclaim the central truths of God when it was most unfashionable. We need thousands of people like Athanasius. People who love God and love people enough to tell them what they need to hear, not necessarily what they want to hear.

TURN TO PAGE
216
TO EXPERIENCE
ATHANASIUS IN HIS
OWN WORDS

JOHN CALVIN

3

#3: JOHN CALVIN

TOP TEN THEOLOGIANS

Wow, we've now arrived to the top three in our Top Ten Theologians. Whether you consider yourself a 5-point Calvinist, 4-point Calvinist, Arminian or something else; John Calvin should be a hero in your life. In order to appreciate Calvin we need to have a working knowledge of his world.

Calvin's World

A Post-Reformation World

The world was forever changed on October 31st, 1517AD. While John Calvin was only 8 years old, a 33 year old German priest posted 95 grievances he had with his church. No human being could have anticipated the result stemming from one monk, Martin Luther, who wanted to reform his church.

MARTIN LUTHER

All people will agree the 15th century church needed reformation. The church of the day started to contradict itself in many areas. A crack had been developing for quite some time.

Martin Luther was a brilliant troubled man. He excelled scholastically but found no relief for his soul. Much like Bunyan's character "Christian" in Pilgrim's Progress, Luther had a burden of sin he couldn't unload. Getting rid of his burden became the occupying passion of his life.

Luther tried over and over to attain righteousness. There were many religious ways in the 15th century to supposedly attain righteousness from sin. Luther tried them all to no avail. He eventually discovered how to be righteous. Only one way could remove his burden of sin. He realized
righteousness was not earned. It could not be attained. It only came as a gift through faith in Christ. Luther was now a free man.

The institutionalized church made a drastic error one day when they sent a guy to raise money from Luther's congregation. They were told money given to the church in Rome would quicken the time their dead relatives would spend in the pain of Purgatory. Do you want your grandma in heaven? They would ask. Then give $1,000. If you give me just $100 it will help, but if you want your grandma in heaven faster give me $1,000.

PEASANT REVOLT LEADER BURNED AT STAKE

The sale of these indulgences absolutely infuriated Luther. His congregation couldn't afford what they gave. Their hearts were in the right place, but they were simply led astray. Luther knew their money made no difference. Luther's 95 theses on the door of the Wittenberg castle were 95 reasons why the sale of indulgences was an idiotic scheme from a church in dire need of money and reform.

The twenty years following October 31st, 1517 were unexpected by all. It was as if Luther's 95 theses was a spark which set the world on fire.

Luther's fear of God and of unwarranted innovation were such that he had hesitated to take the concrete steps that would follow from his doctrine.[1] With Luther hidden in a castle to prevent his death by the church, Luther's thoughts were quickly taken to an extreme by others. In 1524, a peasant rebellion broke out in Germany under the name of Luther and the Reformation. The peasants wanted religious reform, but they equally sought economic reform. The motives and actions of everyone involved cannot be known. The aftermath is known. More than 100,000 peasants were killed in Germany.

In 1527, right after these events, troops from Spain and Germany sacked the city of Rome. Since many of these troops were part of the reformation the sack of Rome took on a heavily religious tone. How would the church survive? All over Europe reforms were taking place. Some reforms took place inside of the church, many outside of the traditional church. The Protestant church was being born. What would the church look like?

Luther brought great reform but still held to beliefs which other reformers thought unbiblical. Erasmus wanted great reform but didn't want to leave the church. Zwingli wanted to wipe the slate clean and start over from scratch. Zwingli and Luther met to try to bring unity. They couldn't agree on a unified Reformed church. Other reformers from all over Europe were leading people into many differing directions. Had we lost true North? Could all the various Protestant teachings be brought into a cohesive whole? Would the Reformation die from a lack of unity?

John Calvin arrived to provide the much needed theological stability and unity for the Reformed church. While Luther was the trumpet call of the Reformation, Calvin provided the symphony.

---

1 Gonzalez, The Story of Christianity: Volume 2, p39.

Calvin's Life

Early Years

John Calvin was born in Noyon, France on July 10, 1509. Calvin's mother, sadly, died a few years after his birth from a breast disease. His father held a prosperous administrative position working at the cathedral. His father, initially, desired for all his sons to join the priesthood. His connections allowed much of Calvin's schooling to be paid by the Noyon church.

By age 12, Calvin was studying Latin about 70 miles north of his home town from one of its great teachers at the University of Paris.[2] Upon completing his studies in Latin he became a philosophy student.

Around 1526, at the age of 17, his dad pulled him away from a path of theological studies to study law. This was possibly due to a conflict between the priests at Noyon and Calvin's father.[3] His father believed his academically gifted son would make more money through a career in law.[4]

Calvin entered the University of Bourges. Bourges is a French town 200 miles north of Noyon. Here he would learn from humanists who stressed classical studies. He would also become familiar with the thoughts of pre-reformers Wycliffe, Huss and also Luther.[5] Of this time he later declared, "I was stubbornly tied to the superstitions of the

2 Cottret. Calvin: A Biography. p17.

3 Ibid. p20.

4 Parker. John Calvin. P15.

5 Gonzalez. p62.

papacy."[6] Calvin would learn Greek at Bourges, equipping him to study the New Testament for himself in its original language.[7]

In 1533, at the age of 24, Calvin experienced a religious conversion. He writes about it in his Commentary on the Book of Psalms:

> *God by a sudden conversion subdued and brought my mind to a teachable frame, which was more hardened in such matters than might have been expected from one at my early period of life. Having thus received some taste and knowledge of true godliness, I was immediately inflamed with so intense a desire to make progress therein, that although I did not altogether leave off other studies, yet I pursued them with less ardour.*[8]

Calvin's conversion experience corresponded with a distinct break from the Roman Catholic Church. On May 4th, 1534 he resigned from the clerical benefits that had been provided for him during his childhood, which officially broke off relations with the unreformed church and clergy.[9] From this time forward, he would never cease from tireless work in support of the Reformed Church.[10]

On the Run

BASEL, SWITZERLAND

The atmosphere of France had changed by 1535. The country was not safe for leaders of the new Reformed movement. At the age of 26, Calvin decided to leave his country behind. He traveled 360 miles southeast to Basel, Switzerland looking for a safe retreat where he could devote his life to study. Gonzalez explains, "What he sought was not to become one of the leaders of the Reformation, but rather to settle in a calm environment where

6 Preface to the Commentary on the Book of Psalms

7 Cottret. p24.

8 Introduction to his Commentary on the Book of Psalms. ppxl-xli

9 Introduction to Institutes of the Christian Religion. Edited by McNeill pxxx.

10 Ibid.

he could study Scripture and write about his faith."[11]

Institutes of the Christian Religion

While in Basel, Calvin heard of horrific events transpiring back home in France. Reports reached him of the "many burnings" taking place in France and the perverse explanations given for these. What was being burned? People were being burned alive; people who led the Reformation. These people's views were being terribly misrepresented. Calvin sensed more horror would come if he didn't do something. McNeill explains:

> *Calvin decided that silence on his part would entail a just charge of cowardice and treachery. He could not be silent while those who had suffered death for their faith, and whom he regarded as faithful and "holy martyrs" were so grossly misrepresented, and while many still living were similarly imperiled. Some of the sufferers were his personal friends, notably the Paris merchant, Etienne de la Forge...who was burned alive February 15, 1535. He felt bound, as he says, to "vindicate from undeserved insult my brethren whose death was precious in the sight of the Lord."*[12]

John Calvin, as his friends literally burned at the stake in his home country sat down and wrote. He certainly wrote with a lump in his throat and a heart on fire to redeem those paying the ultimate price. To show everyone these people were living out the true Christian faith. The reformation was not a newly invented heresy; it was orthodox biblical Christianity rooted in the ancient church. Although he most likely had already been working on his book, he labored intensely from January until August of 1535. The work was published in Basel in March of 1536. Calvin was only 26 years old when his masterpiece was completed.

The 16th century did not care about short pithy titles. The Latin title of

11 Gonzalez. p63.

12 Introduction to Institutes of the Christian Religion. Edited by McNeill pxxxii.

his first edition can be translated:

> *The Institute of the Christian Religion, Containing almost the Whole Sum of Piety and Whatever It is Necessary to Know in the Doctrine of Salvation. A Work Very Well Worth Reading by All Persons Zealous for Piety, and Lately Published. A Preface to the Most Christian King of France, in Which this Book is Presented to Him as a Confession of Faith. Author, John Calvin, of Noyon. Basel, MDXXXVI*[13]

His work was presented to the King of France to convince him to stop the burning of his reformed friends. Hopefully the Institutes would provide the badly needed systematic defense of the reformed faith.

Until the publication of Calvin's *Institutes of the Christian Religion* most Protestant literature had dealt exclusively with specific points of discussion. Most literature said little regarding the Trinity, the Incarnation, and many other important doctrines. Calvin sought to fill this vacuum with his "short manual".[14] The first edition consisted of only six chapters totaling 516 pages. Gonzalez explains the book's reception:

> *The book enjoyed immediate and surprising success. The first edition, which was in Latin and therefore could be read in different countries, was sold out in nine months.*[15]

Calvin would continue updating his Institutes for the rest of his life. The 6 chapters would grow to 80. The entire work shows a profound knowledge, not only of Scripture, but also of Christian literature – particularly the works of Augustine – and of the theological controversies of the sixteenth century.[16]

---

13 Introduction to Institutes of the Christian Religion. Edited by McNeill pxxxiii.
14 Gonzalez. p63.
15 Ibid.
16 Ibid. p64.

While Calvin respected the leaders of the Reformation, he was convinced his gifts were not that of the pastor or the leader, but rather those of the scholar and author.[17] Calvin made a decision in 1536, shortly after the publication of the Institutes, which would drastically change his plans. He decided a move to Strasbourg, Switzerland would help his study and writing. In order to get to Strasbourg, Calvin would pass through the city of Geneva.

WILLIAM FAREL

Geneva

Calvin arrived at Geneva in 1536 planning simply to stop there for no more than a day, and then continue on his journey. A 47 year old man named William Farel happened to hear the author of the Institutes was in town. Here's what happened:

> *Farel, who "burned with a marvelous zeal for the advancement of the gospel," presented Calvin with several reasons why his presence was needed in Geneva. Calvin listened respectfully to the other man, some fifteen years older. But he refused to heed Farel's plea, telling him that he had planned certain studies, and that these would not be possible in the confused situation Farel was describing. When Farel had exhausted his arguments, and failed to convince the young theologian, he appealed to their common Lord, and challenged Calvin with a dire threat: "May God condemn your repose, and the calm you seek for study, if before such a great need you withdraw and refuse to help." Calvin responds: "these words shocked and broke me, and I desisted from the journey I*

17 Ibid.

had begun."[18]

It's not every day someone threatens God's condemnation on your soul if you don't do what they want. Farel probably wanted Calvin to become minister in the church of Geneva right way, but Calvin was unwilling to do that even though he had agreed to stay.[19] Calvin's biblical knowledge, theological insight, legal training, and his zeal for reform quickly made him the leader of the Reformation in Geneva. Farel gladly became the number two guy.

The City Council ran into an issue with Calvin. Calvin wanted the church to be able to discipline its members, if necessary. The city council, however, wanted to retain the ultimate right to excommunicate someone from the church. Calvin was not suggesting the church should be in control of the state. He was simply asking that the church be in charge of the church and not under the state when relating to the church's own particular responsibilities.[20] Calvin's issue with the City Council did not go how Farel and Calvin anticipated. After just twenty-one months Calvin was fired as pastor. He was twenty-eight years old and apparently a pastoral failure.[21] Calvin went back to his initial plans and moved to Strasbourg.

OLDER JOHN CALVIN

Marriage

While in Strasbourg, Calvin preached or taught every day as well as two sermons on Sunday. He published his second edition of the Institutes in 1539 and published his Commentary on Romans in 1540. Around this time Calvin's friends pressured him to get married. Calvin reluctantly agreed to marry a young noble lady on the one condition that she learned

18 Gonzalez. p65.
19 Godfrey. John Calvin. p37
20 Godfrey. John Calvin. p41
21 Ibid. p42.

French. The wedding was planned for March. He later wrote that he would never think of marrying her, "unless the Lord had entirely bereft me of my wits."[22] Instead, in August, he married Idelette de Bure, a widow with two children from her first marriage.[23]

Return to Geneva

In September of 1540, one month after getting married, the Geneva city council voted to invite Calvin back to pastor. Calvin's first reaction, "**Rather would I submit to death a hundred times than to that cross on which I had to perish daily a thousand times over.**"[24] Farel came once again to the rescue for Geneva. Farel convinced Calvin to return. Calvin did not hurry. It took him a year to arrange his affairs, but in August 1541 he arrived back in Geneva.[25] Godfrey writes, "In 1541 Calvin was a more mature and patient man than he had been in 1538. Although he was still only thirty-two, he had learned the value of waiting and determined to try to work with those who had opposed him."[26]

Calvin would spend the rest of his life with his family in Geneva. He would reform Geneva to be what he considered an ideal Reformation city. He would preach sermons every day with three on Sunday.

TITLE PAGE OF FINAL EDITION OF INSTITUTES

Final Years

Calvin's health began to fail after 1559. Farel paid his friend a last visit. Calvin died on May 27, 1564 at the age of 55.

---

22 Parker. p87.
23 Cottrett. p142.
24 Parker. p105.
25 Godfrey. p58.
26 Ibid.

Calvin's Thoughts

A great asset to all Christians coming after Calvin is the depth, breadth, passion and clarity we find through his writing.

The Word of God is central to the vast thoughts of Calvin. The medieval church treasured the Bible as the very Word of God. It believed the Bible was true and invested much time and manpower in copying the Bible by hand. **But the medieval church had no confidence that the Bible could be understood by those who read it.** Calvin rejected the medieval church's approach to the Bible where it was honored, kissed, and carried in procession but was seldom opened or read by the people.[27]

Calvin clearly saw the Word of God as the lifeblood for every believer. He writes:

> *For, if we consider the mutability of the human mind, how easy its fall into forgetfulness of God; how great its propensity to errors of every kind; how violent its rage for the perpetual fashioning of new and false religions, it will be easy to perceive the necessity of heavenly doctrine being committed to writing, that it might not be lost in oblivion, or evaporate in error, or be corrupted by the presumption of men."*[28]

Furthermore, he artfully states, "A soul, therefore, when deprived of the Word of God, is given up unarmed to the devil for destruction."[29]

David Mathis explains the unique thoughts of Calvin:

> *Led by Scriptures, he rethought as much of reality as he was able, consciously appropriating God's revelation of himself in the Bible and in the person of his Son. In a day when many saw human reason and divine revelation as equals,*

27 Ibid. p169-170.
28 Calvin. Institutes. I,6,3
29 Calvin. Reply to Sodelto.

> *the Reformation principle of sola Scriptura – not Scripture as the only authority, but Scripture as the only ultimate authority – changed everything for Calvin. It captured him as a reality so massive that it would take more than a few weeks and a quiet place of study to work out its implications.(Mathis, With Calvin in the Theater of God, p21-22)*

Calvin lived and wrote as a man constantly aware of a big sovereign God.[30] He made sure the person interacting with his thoughts on God would only continue reading if the thoughts were leading to appropriate worship and obedience. The secret of his mental energy lies in his piety; its product is his theology, which is his piety described at length.[31] The piety and mental energy of Calvin has had incredible influence.

Calvin's Influence

Karl Barth dramatically explains the influence of John Calvin by saying:

> *Calvin is a cataract, a primeval forest, a demonic power, something directly down from the Himalayas, absolutely Chinese, strange, mythological; I lack completely the means, the suction cups, even to assimilate this phenomenon, not to speak of presenting it adequately…I could gladly and profitably set myself down and spend all the rest of my life just with Calvin.* [32]

Biographer Steven J. Lawson writes:

> *Towering over the centuries of church history, there stands one figure of such monumental importance that he still commands attention and arouses intrigue, even five hundred years after his appearance on the world stage. Called "one of the truly great men of all time," he was a driving force so significant that his*

---

30 McNeill. Introduction to the Institutes. pli.

31 Ibid.

32 Karl Barth to Eduard Thurneysen. June 8, 1922. Quoted in front page of Piper, With Calvin in the Theater of God.

> *influence shaped the church and Western culture beyond that of any other theologian or pastor. His masterful expositions of Scripture laid down the doctrinal distinctive of the Protestant Reformation, making him arguably the leading architect of the Protestant cause.*[33]

He moved millions not through the power of his personality but through the power of his biblical ideas and words.[34]

Calvin's Foibles

Michael Servetus

The greatest foible consistently brought up in the life of John Calvin is his involvement in the death of Michael Servetus. Servetus was a notable Spanish doctor. He was also interested in theology and wrote a number of works. He argued, among other provocative things, that the Council of Nicea had offended God.

Servetus had recently escaped from the prisons of the Catholic Inquisition in France, where he was being tried for heresy, and was passing through Geneva when he was recognized.[35] Calvin wrote up a list of 38 accusations against him. The city government asked the advice of leaders throughout Switzerland, all agreed that Servetus was a heretic, not only by Catholic standards, but also by Protestant ones. The laws at the time were for heretics to be burned at the stake. Calvin argued for a less cruel death, but without having any formal governmental power Calvin was overruled and Michael Servetus was burned to death in Geneva.

It is important to note Calvin was operating in a lenient way compared with the atmosphere of his day. All Christian leaders of 16th century Europe (Roman Catholic and Protestant) would have burned Servetus at the stake.

---

33 Lawson. The Expository Genius of John Calvin. p1-2.
34 Godfrey. p9.
35 Gonzalez. p67.

Calvin's Effect on Us

Those who spend time with Calvin walk away with a big God. We are told to make sure we live a holy life while meditating on our holy God. We are kept from seeking our salvation in any form of works. We have our hearts stirred to receive the entirety of God's revelation.

As heirs to the Reformation, do our churches today have the same confidence in the truthfulness and authority of God's Word?[36] We have the Word of God on our shelves, computers, our phones, our iPads, but do we have it in our hearts and in our churches? Calvin scholar Robert Godfrey laments:

> *The worship of the church has become a feel-good experience, rather than a meeting with the holy God of the universe. Exciting music has become the new sacrament mediating the presence of God and his grace. Sermons have become pop psychology, moralistic exercises in self-help.*[37]

Mathis writes:

> *Calvin's big, biblical vision of God changes everyday life. If you really want to be practical, don't reach for gimmicks, checklists, and self-helps, but come with Calvin to the Bible and get to know the most important realities in the universe: God, creation, sin, heaven, hell, Jesus, his cross and resurrection, the Holy Spirit. The biblical vision of the glory of God in Christ is the most practical reality in the universe. (Mathis, With Calvin in the Theater of God, p21-22)*

The 21st century church is in great need of depth; a stirring of the head and heart. The sheep have been fed a steady diet of junk food for too long. John Calvin must be allowed to play an important role mentoring new shepherds in leading the church back to greener pastures for the glory of God.

---

36 Piper. p37.
37 Piper. p37.

TURN TO PAGE
230
TO EXPERIENCE
CALVIN IN HIS
OWN WORDS

MARTIN LUTHER

2

#2: MARTIN LUTHER

TOP TEN THEOLOGIANS

To have an understanding of Martin Luther it's important to have a working knowledge of his multi-faceted world.

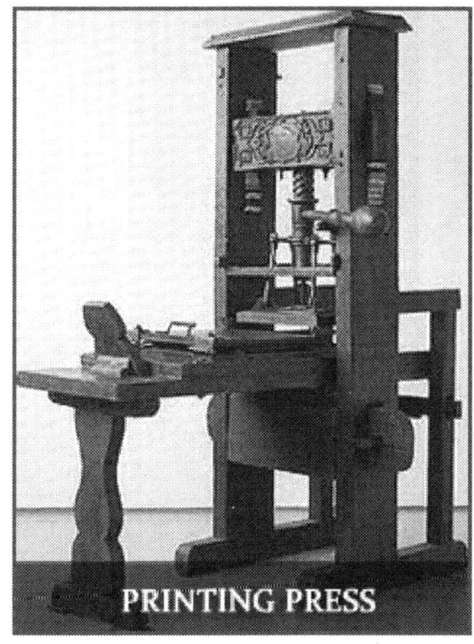
PRINTING PRESS

Luther's World

Gutenberg Printing Press

It's hard for us to imagine life without mass produced books. Throughout most of humankind, however, every single book was hand copied. I'll say it again just in case it didn't stick: before 1440 AD, every book on the planet was hand produced.

In 1440, Johannes Gutenberg invented the printing press. The invention was so earth shaking it led Time Magazine to rank it as the most important invention of the last 1,000 years. Four hundred years before Gutenberg, a man from China named Bi Sheng came up with the concept of moveable type. Bi Sheng's clay letters were fragile and not able to handle widespread use.

Gutenberg came up with many improvements to make mass-produced books a reality. First, he came up with a process for making durable metallic moveable type. Second, he used an ink easy enough to come by and economical enough for widespread usage. Third, he used a wooden printing press similar to agricultural screw presses of the day. Gutenberg engineered these elements together into a practical system for the mass production of printed books that were economically viable for printers and readers alike.[1]

The Gutenberg press allowed ideas to spread at a pace and a breadth previously unknown to humankind. Living through the development of the Internet can help us appreciate the invention of Gutenberg's Printing Press. What the Internet did to open up the spread of information in our day, the printing press did for the 15th century and beyond.

Without the printing press we may have never known Martin Luther.

St. Peters Basilica

ST. PETERS BASILICA

In 1506 construction began on St. Peters Basilica. Construction of the immense church in Rome would end up costing the equivalent of more than $2 billion dollars. The Basilica has the largest interior of any Christian church in the world. Construction would be tricky. Why?

It was believed to be a desecration for a church building to not continually stand in Rome. How can you build a new church on the exact same location

1 http://en.wikipedia.org/wiki/Johannes_Gutenberg

without first tearing down the old building? The solution was creative.

St. Peters is so colossal it was built surrounding the previous church. The entire old church, still standing, fit inside the main sanctuary of the new St. Peters. Once St. Peters was finished the older church was dismantled and carried out the front door!

How does the church of the day afford such opulent spending? The creative solution came from the selling of indulgences. An indulgence was a certificate providing someone a speedy trip through Purgatory. The sale of Indulgences would result from a conversation like this:

> *"Do you want your grandma to suffer less and make it to heaven? The Pope can help you out if you pay up. Haven't you heard it said, "When a coin in the coffer rings, a soul from Purgatory springs"? Giving us $100 will help your grandmother a little bit: $1,000 will more quickly ease her suffering. Do you love your church? Do you love your grandmother? Help us help you. You are one Indulgence away from the Pope easing the burden of your loved one."*

The Pope sent priests like Johann Tetzel throughout the western world selling indulgences. Was this a good way to finance the church of the day? Martin Luther had a few things to say (95 to be precise) about the sale of Indulgences.

A World Prepared for Change

In the hundred years before Martin Luther the world was preparing for massive change.

The office of Pope was in utter turmoil. For hundreds of years the Pope had been the most powerful person on the planet. In 1309, the new Pope refused to move to Rome. He stayed in France. For the next seven Popes, France was called home and immorality was rampant. The Papacy went to the highest bidder. A new Pope finally moved back to Rome and tried to clean up the position.

The leader in France liked being Pope so he refused to acknowledge the new guy in Rome. In 1409, both Popes were declared illegitimate and a third Pope was elected. The previous two Popes refused to step down so there were now three Popes at the same time! People were quickly losing respect for the Papacy.

Surrounding the Papal degradation, the Black Death was devestating Europe. Between 1347-1351, more than one out of every three people died from the Bubonic Plague. Outbreaks continued for the next 120 years. Death surrounded every person. By 1450, Europe's population was down seventy-percent. It felt like the world outside the church had been turned upside down. In addition to such uncertainty outside the church, two men stood up inside the church calling for massive change.

BLACK DEATH

Beloved Oxford professor **John Wycliffe** (1329-1384) believed the Bible to be the ultimate authority of the church, not the decisions of the Pope. The common people of his day did not have access to a Bible. Wycliffe broke the law when he translated the New Testament into English. The thoughts of Wycliffe laid a foundation for reform. He made it possible for people to start learning about God on their own. Church leaders, who thought it was too dangerous for a layman to read and interpret the Bible, were so upset with Wycliffe's influence that years after his death they dug up his body and burned his bones, throwing his ashes into the nearest river.

John Huss (1373-1415) also heavily criticized the practices of the institutional church. He stated Christ, not the Pope, was the head of the church. He was disgusted by the lives of the clergy and thought it immoral for people to buy church positions. The name Huss in Czech means Goose. Have you ever heard the saying, "Your goose is cooked?"

That saying comes from John Huss. For taking a stand against some of the church beliefs and practices of the day, Huss was burned at the stake. The queen was notified of his death by being told, "Your goose is cooked."

Huss prophetically made this statement before his death, "They will roast a goose now, but after a hundred years they will hear a swan sing, whom you will be unable to silence." Martin Luther stepped onto the scene almost exactly 100 years later. We now turn to the swan.

Luther's Life

Early Years

Martin Luther was born around 1483 in Eisleben, Germany. Luther's birth was a matter of such insignificance that he and his friends later debated the exact year.

BIRTHPLACE OF LUTHER IN EISLEBEN, GERMANY

His father, Hans, was a peasant farmer. Local inheritance laws specified that family lands would pass intact to the youngest son. Hans, as the older brother, was forced to leave the family farm shortly before Martin was born.[2] Eager for a way to support his family, Hans eventually found work as a copper miner. Martin's early life was a tough time for the Luther family. Remembering these years, Luther recalled that his mother had once beaten him until his hands bled merely for taking a nut from the kitchen table.[3]

Copper mining was a tough, dangerous job in the 15th century. While

2 Kittelson. Luther the Reformer. p.31

3 Ibid. p.33.

LUTHER'S PARENTS

many people died in the mines, Hans thrived. Within seven years he would own his own copper business.[4] Hans and Margaretta were determined for their children to have better lives.

Martin was sent, at an early age, to some of the best German schools. At **the age of four** he entered a school whose sole purpose was to teach Latin, which would prepare him for future studies. The school used barbaric practices to force the students to learn Latin. Kittelson explains Luther's early Latin education:

> *Any child caught speaking German was beaten with a rod. The one who had done least well in the morning was required to wear a dunce's cap and was addressed as an "ass" all afternoon.*[5]

Luther recalled being beaten with a rod 15 times in just one morning. Fortunately for Luther, he eventually excelled in school. By the time he was 17 years old his teachers recommended continuing his studies at the university. It was rare for the son of a peasant to have a university education. Luther's arrival at the University of Erfurt opened the doors for him to obtain a career in the church, in law, or in medicine.[6]

Not long after New Year's Day 1505, Martin Luther became Master Martin.[7] Getting his Masters degree was a huge deal. Kittelson writes:

> *Father Hans was enormously proud of his son and regarded the M.A. degree as just the beginning. Master Martin (as even his father now referred to him) was*

4 Kittelson. Luther the Reformer. p.33.
5 Ibid. p.37.
6 Ibid. p.39.
7 Ibid. p.49.

to become a lawyer.[8]

Just one month into his law studies Luther took a strange leave of absence. He travelled home to discuss something with his family and friends. No one knows exactly what happened during the infamous trip back home. On July 2, 1505 Luther was traveling back to the university. He was caught outside in a violent thunderstorm. The lightning grew so close it actually knocked him on the ground. Fearing for his life he cried out, "Help me, St. Anne, and I will become a monk." Luther saw the thunderstorm as a direct message from God to leave his career in law for the monastery.

Hans questioned whether the thunderstorm was truly from God. As a Lawyer, Luther would have been able to support his parents in their retirement years. Luther was their Social Security, Medicare and 401k all rolled into one. Luther turned his back on the guaranteed financial stability he could provide for his entire family for what he believed to be obedience to God.

Monk

Martin's room in the monastery was just three feet wide by seven feet long.[9] The monks attended seven worship services a day. The first service started at 2:00 A.M. Most of Luther's time was spent in worship, prayer and meditation.[10] Of this time Luther stated, "If anyone could have gained heaven as a monk, then I would indeed have been among them."[11] After just one year Luther had passed the rigorous physical, mental and spiritual tests to become a priest.

Martin's family was certainly proud of his religious achievements, but they were still upset with him for not becoming a lawyer. A great banquet was held to celebrate Luther's first mass as a priest. He asked his father during the feast if it wasn't better for him to be a priest than a lawyer. His father's response was a hurtful one that would stay with Luther his

---

8 Kittelson. Luther the Reformer. p.49.
9 Ibid. p.52.
10 Ibid. p.53.
11 Ibid. p.53.

entire life. His father said, "Have you not heard the commandment to honor your father and mother?"[12]

Dark Night of the Soul

Although Luther had boldly chosen to follow the priesthood against the wishes of his family, he was not looking for an easy life. Oberman explains:

> *Luther did not seek the monastery as a place of meditation and study to exercise a faith he had once lacked. Nor was he looking for a sanctuary of strict morals to protect him from the immorality of the world outside. He was driven by his desire to find the merciful God... Searching for the merciful God was a crucial part of the monastic life and was by no means a unique expression of Luther's hunger for salvation, out of step with the Community of Brethren.*[13]

In order to be saved from the wrath of God, people believed you must make use of all the means of grace offered by the church.[14] Luther dove deep into trying to rid his body from sin. Long periods with neither food nor drink, nights without sleep, bone-chilling cold with neither coat nor blanket to warm him – and self-flagellation – were common and even expected in the lives of serious monks.[15]

Out of all the ways the church of the day recommended for Luther to be saved, it was confession that Martin came to despise. Confession was a crucial part of the monastic life. In this sacrament, the "religious," sought to purge themselves of their sins almost as quickly as they committed them.

Bainton explains:

> *Luther endeavored unremittingly to avail himself to [Confession]. With-*

12 Luther's Works. Volume 44. p.712.
13 Heiko A. Oberman. Luther: Man between God and the Devil. p.127.
14 Gonzalez. The Story of Christianity: volume 2. p.16.
15 Kittelson. p.55.

> *out confession, he testified, the Devil would have devoured him long ago. He confessed frequently, often daily, and for as long as six hours on a single occasion. Every sin in order to be absolved was to be confessed... Luther would repeat a confession and, to be sure of including everything, would review his entire life...*[16]

With Luther finding no rest for his troubled soul, his superior, Johann von Staupitz, took a bold step. This young man on the verge of collapse over religious problems and emotional instability was to be commissioned as a teacher, preacher, and counselor to sick souls! Staupitz was practically saying, "Physician, cure thyself by curing others."[17] Luther, therefore, was ordered much against his expectations to prepare to teach Scripture at the new University of Wittenberg.[18]

Salvation by Faith Alone

MARTIN LUTHER

When Luther found himself forced to prepare lectures on the Bible, he began seeing new meanings in the Scripture, and the possibility that such meanings would provide an answer to his spiritual quest.[19] In 1515, Luther taught through the book of Romans. Then throughout 1516-1517 he taught through the book of Galatians.

The great discovery that would change Martin Luther and rock the world came from a simple daily reading of Romans 1:16-17.

16 Bainton. p.35.
17 Ibid. p.42.
18 Gonzalez. p.18.
19 Ibid. p.19.

He read that, *"For I am not ashamed of the gospel, for it is the power of God for salvation to everyone who believes, to the Jew first and also to the Greek. For in it the righteousness of God is revealed from faith for faith, as it is written, 'The righteous shall live by faith.'"*

Luther was greatly bothered by these verses. He thought, "How is this gospel really good news? Isn't it actually bad news that God seeks justice and righteousness?" Luther found God's justice to be unbearable. He wished God did not demand righteousness. He wished God was not just. He pondered how it was possible for "the righteous to live by faith."

Luther had been taught that God's justice, His righteousness, is a punishment to sinners. Since God is righteous, and we are not, God punishes us for our lack of righteousness.

God, however, allowed the eyes of Luther to open. **Luther famously came to the conclusion that God's righteousness is something which is possessed by God AND given to those who walk by faith.** Martin Luther had finally found freedom for his troubled soul. Faith in Jesus alone resulted in him *receiving* the righteousness of God. Indeed, God did not require him to produce his own righeousness, but to freely recieve an alien righteousness by faith. Faith and justification are the work of God, given as a free gift to sinners. The mediator between God and man is not your works, the Pope, the church, nor the Priest, but only Jesus.

Luther tells us, *"I felt that I had been born anew and that the gates of heaven had been opened. The whole of Scripture gained a new meaning. And from that point on the phrase 'the justice of God' no longer filled me with hatred, but rather became unspeakably sweet by virtue of a great love."*

While Luther is basking in his new found freedom, from the perspective of the institutional church of the day, the wrong man is about to show up to the wrong town at the wrong time.

Johann Tetzel

JOHANN TETZEL

While Luther's eyes are being opened to freedom found only in Christ, Johann Tetzel arrived in Wittenberg. Tetzel was sent by the pope to raise money for the church. He sold indulgences to people in Luther's church. Tetzel's famous saying was, "When a coin in the coffer rings, a soul from purgatory springs."

Luther watched poor people from his church give money they didn't have to try to pay freedom for their dead relatives. Luther saw the sale of indulgences as completely worthless. Luther reacted strongly against the sale of indulgences.

95 Theses

A huge collection of supposed relics accumulated in Wittenberg. There was supposedly a thorn from the crown of Jesus. They had a tooth from St. Jerome. You could see four hairs from the Virgin Mary. Those who viewed the thousands of relics in Wittenberg on All Saints Day (October 31st) and paid the necessary amount in indulgences might receive from the Pope 1,902,202 years and 270 days of reduction in Purgatory.

The arrival of Tetzel pushed Luther over the edge; he had enough. On October 31, 1517 Martin Luther nailed 95 complaints against indulgences to the church doors in Wittenberg. Thesis 82 captures the essence of Luther's complaints:

> *Why does not the pope liberate everyone from purgatory for the sake of love (a most holy thing) and because of the supreme necessity of their souls? This would be morally the best of all reasons. Meanwhile he redeems innumerable souls for money, a most perishable thing, with which to build St. Peter's church, a very*

minor purpose.

Luther's reasoning is insightful. If the Pope is able to set everyone free from purgatory, why does he need money? Shouldn't he just free everyone automatically out of his love for them? Why would such eternal matters be contingent on raising enough money to build a temporary building?

NAILING 95 THESIS

The printing press went into action. Without the permission of Luther, printers soon spread copies of the Ninety-Five Theses throughout Germany. Copies were printed in the original Latin and also for the masses in a German translation.

Troubled Times

Luther's life forever changed after nailing those 95 theses. The pope initially requested the radical monk be dealt with locally. He was called to the next chapter meeting in Heidelberg. He went in fear for his life, for he expected to be condemned and burned as a heretic.[20] To his surprise most of the people there agreed with Luther. Afterwards his friend Martin Bucer wrote, "*Luther responds with magnificent grace and listens with insurmountable patience. He presents an argument with the insight of the apostle Paul.*"[21]

By the summer of 1518, 35-year old Luther had provoked powerful opponents. Luther's life was in danger. Luther writes of this time, "*I know that whoever wants to bring the Word of Christ into the world must, like the apostles, leave behind and renounce everything, and expect death at any moment. If any other*

20 Gonzalez. p.23.
21 Kittelson. p.112.

situation prevailed, it would not be the Word of Christ."[22]

Luther is summoned to meet in Augsburg with Cardinal Cajetan so he can retract his writings and recant. Luther remembered saying as he set out: "*Now you must die…Oh, what a shame I have become to my parents!*"[23] Cajetan was prepared and intellectually capable to debate with Luther but was charged by the Pope not to debate with Luther, but simply to get him to say one word revoco (I recant). They couldn't help themselves, the two men got into a heated debate. Cajetan urged Luther that he had to submit to the authority of the Pope, Luther replied that he couldn't submit to something contrary to Scripture. He insisted the sale of indulgences were no more than a scheme to raise money. Luther appealed to Rome. Due to the protection of Frederick the Wise of Saxony, Luther was able to leave Augsburg alive.

On June 15, 1520 Pope Leo X issued a statement against Luther called *Exsurge Domine* where he declared that a wild boar had entered the Lord's vineyard. He ordered all books by Martin Luther to be burned and he gave him sixty days to submit to his authority.

In October Luther wrote his book, *On the Babylonian Captivity of the Church.* The captivity of which Luther complained was the priest's hold on the sacraments and the insistence that Christians must perform good works in order to gain salvation.

Luther was summoned to stand before the Emperor in 1521 at the Diet of Worms. Luther was now famous. Two-thousand people met him outside the city to escort him inside. His many books were sprawled out before him. He was asked if he would like to recant of his works. It was a hard time for Luther. To dare oppose the entire church and the emperor, whose

DIET OF WORMS

22 Kittelson. p.116.
23 Ibid. p.121.

authority had been ordained by God, was a dreadful act.[24] Given the chance to recant Luther eventually made his famous response. He spoke in German instead of using the more traditional theological debate language of Latin. Luther responded by saying:

> *Unless I can be instructed and convinced with evidence from the Holy Scriptures or with open, clear, and distinct grounds and reasoning – and my conscience is captive to the Word of God – then I cannot and will not recant, because it is neither safe nor wise to act against conscience. Here I stand. I can do no other. God help me! Amen.*

Luther was once again able to leave with his life intact. On his way back home, however, some armed horseman kidnapped Luther. Many believed Luther was killed He was fortunately taken by his friends who staged his attack, secretly hiding him away in the tower of Wartburg castle.

Like a man possessed, Luther translated the entire New Testament into German within 11 weeks.[25] This was an astounding rate of more than 1500 words per day. Luther translated the New Testament, "to free the ordinary person from false, albeit familiar, ideas, to lead him onto the straight path, and to give him some instruction."[26] He would go on to translate the Old Testament as well into German and write many more works instructing people to the central importance of the Gospel. Salvation is solely found by faith in Jesus Christ.

Marriage

On June 13th, 1525 Luther married Katherine von Bora. Katherine was 26 years old, Luther was 41 years old. Katherine had been a former nun. Luther helped her and 11 other nuns escape their convent. They amazingly escaped by hiding in herring barrels. Martin and Katherine ended up having six children and seemed to have a good marriage.

---

24 Gonzalez. p.28.
25 Kittelson. p.175.
26 Ibid.

A great deal more can be written about Luther's fascinating life. We now turn to his revolutionary thoughts.

Luther's Thoughts

The man who previously called upon a saint to save him was later to repudiate the cult of saints. The man who vowed to become a monk was later to renounce monasticism. A loyal son of the Catholic Church, he was later to shatter the structure of medieval Catholicism. A devoted servant of the pope, he was later to identify the popes with Antichrist.[27] Luther's thoughts are a game changer. He sought to awaken a church that had been asleep for quite some time. He had personally been awakened; he sought to wake up everyone else.

Payton helps us understand the overarching thoughts of Luther:

> *He declared time and time again, "It was not I that did it, but the Word of God." With this he expressed genuine humility: Luther urged repeatedly that he himself was insignificant, but that the gospel was great, and that what he had accomplished was not his work but God's.*
>
> *Even so, Luther was sure that God himself had entrusted him with this message. God had proclaimed the gospel anew through Luther; since that was the case, then all others should listen and heed.*
>
> *He often upbraided people and called them to a careful defense of and alertness to justification by faith alone. If they did not heed his advice, he could quite readily, if they continued to disagree with him, denounce them as servants as Satan, as those in league with the wicked one, seeking to divert people from the*

27 Bainton. p.1.

truth of the gospel.[28]

The absolute centrality of Luther's thought is focused on sola fide (salvation by faith alone). It is through faith in the risen Christ, not through any works we do, that we are justified and declared righteous. Jesus is the message and the messenger. Luther calls the church back to learning about the Word through the Word of God (sola Scriptura). We know of Jesus not from councils, Popes nor teachers, but through His Word.

Luther's Influence

In most big libraries, books by and about Martin Luther occupy more shelf room than those concerned with any other human being except Jesus of Nazareth.[29] Luther's influence in his day was immense. Kittelson explains:

> *Luther was a "media personality," the first such in three thousand years of western history. "We have become a spectacle," he once remarked of himself and his colleagues. He and his followers have been termed "obedient rebels." Others called him a seven-headed devil. At least one of his closest colleagues insisted he was a prophet – perhaps even Elijah – sent by God himself. He was the subject of controversy then just as he is now.*[30]

Among other monumental influences, Luther sparked a reawakening in his day around the purity of the Gospel and the authority of the Word of God. Many of his influences, however, were unintended. We now turn to the many foibles of Martin Luther.

28 James R. Payton Jr. Getting the Reformation Wrong. pp.107-109
29 Todd. Luther: A Life. xvi
30 Kittelson. p.9.

Luther's Foibles

Peasant Revolt

The most important thing on the planet for Luther, as we have seen, was justification by faith. He clearly sought major reform in the church to make justification by faith the renewed central focus of the church.

Many people who had been inspired by Luther did not share the same priorities. Some wanted serious political reform. Others sought major economic reform among the peasant class. All people saw Luther as their leader.

In 1524, a peasant rebellion broke out. Gonzalez explains:

> *For decades the conditions of the German peasantry had been worsening...One of the elements making this rebellion particularly virulent was that it took on religious overtones, for many among the peasantry believed that the teachings of the reformers supported their economic demands.*

Luther refused to support the peasants. Luther wanted the focus to remain on Christ. Many others wanted to take the reformation much further. Luther saw the demands of the peasants as justifiable, but disagreed with their methods. When the peasant revolt turned violent Luther turned on them. He instructed the nobility to suppress the movement. It is believed more than 100,000 people were killed.

The peasants blamed Luther for turning on them. While I admire Luther for wanting to keep the Gospel the central focus of the reform, he could have done much more to prevent the deaths of so many people. Luther's harsh words would continue to result in many deaths.

Anti-Semitism

Adolf Hitler, a fellow German arriving 400 years later, thought he was simply following out the heart of Martin Luther by killing 6 million Jews. Luther argued that the Jews were no longer the chosen people of God, but rather "the Devil's people." Three years before his death Luther wrote a 60,000 word book called *On the Jews and their Lies.*

Luther spoke harshly against the Jews. This is without question. Luther should not have spoken so harsh against the Jews. As a leader of millions of people, he should have been more careful with his words. From another perspective, however, Luther saw the hand of Satan in anything that denied Christ. If any people kept others from the freedom found in Jesus, Luther would unashamedly attribute their actions to the kingdom of darkness.

If given the chance, Luther would remove Judaism from the planet. It kept people from seeing Christ. Luther did not, however, advocate the killing of all Jewish people. Destroying a religion and destroying an ethnic group are two vastly different perspectives. Most biographers will say Luther wanted to destroy the former while Hitler focused on the latter.

Luther's Effect on Us

Moralistic therapeutic deism is a term introduced in the book *Soul Searching: The Religious and Spiritual Lives of American Teenagers* (2005) by Christian Smith and Melinda Lundquist Denton. The term has been accepted by many as an accurate view of the 21st century church. The mindset is: Go to church to be moral, get free therapy, and wait for God to come back from vacation.

We need thousands upon thousands of people to wake up from their moralistic therapeutic deism slumber. We need Luther to be our mentor. Luther cries out for us to wake up our world as he woke up his. Our greatest need and our greatest hope are the same: Jesus. We need Jesus more than we need Dave Ramsey to get us out of debt. We need Jesus more than we need to have good marriages. We need Jesus more than we need to be nice to each other. The temptation of the ages is to cloud Jesus over with good things. Luther reminds us of the utmost importance to never replace the eternal freedom found in Christ with lesser alternatives.

Similarly, we live in an age where the Bible is all around us. At no time in human history has the Bible been so accessible. The Bible, unfortunately, is everywhere except in the hearts of God's people. Luther leads us to not take such an immense treasure for granted.

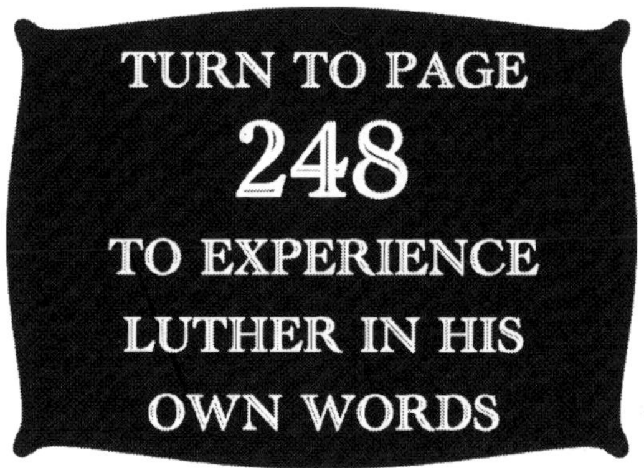

AUGUSTINE & MOM

1

#1: AUGUSTINE

TOP TEN THEOLOGIANS

People living within the Roman Empire during the 4th and 5th centuries embraced some ideas which would largely seem foreign to us today. These ideas are relatively unknown to us in the 21st century, but they played a large role in the life of our Top Theologian: Augustine. In order to appreciate Augustine, we need to appreciate his world.

Augustine's World

Cicero

CICERO

Cicero (106-43BC) was one of the greatest of the Roman orators. Many of his works are today lost to history. We know one of his books named Hortensius was popular during the time of Augustine. Cicero offered to the Romans a worldview.

Cicero wrote about happiness. He said everyone seeks happiness. In the life-long quest for happiness he observed most people tried to find pleasure through food, drink and sex.

Cicero believed, however, that happiness is not found in a self-indulgent life of pleasure, which merely destroys both self-respect and true friendships.[1] He observed people seeking happiness through indulgent pleasures ended up with a miserable life. Most people in his world, he observed, ended up with a miserable life. Cicero thought this misery possibly came from some sort of divine judgment.

Cicero, through refreshingly plain language, advocated a different way to seek happiness. To find happiness one should live a highly principled and aesthetically pleasing life. Happiness will come through a rigorous program of self-discipline and self-improvement. The wise man was someone who trained his head to rule his heart and physical passions in order to live a humble and objective life.[2]

Humility, discipline and selflessness replaced the Roman dream of self indulgence. *The thoughts of Cicero would rock Augustine's world.*

Mani

Along with the thoughts of Cicero, a new flavor of Christianity spread through the Roman world during the time of Augustine. Its founder, Mani, also offered the Romans a worldview.

MANI

Mani was born around 216AD in the area of modern-day Iran. He called himself an "Apostle of Jesus Christ." He claimed to have unique secret information about the nature of God, humanity and the universe. In actuality, Manichaeism was a Persian adaptation of Christianity, which added in Gnosti-

1 Chadwick. Augustine: A Very Short Introduction. p.11.
2 Knowles. Augustine and His World. p.48

cism, Zoroastrianism, speculative philosophy and superstition.[3]

According to Mani, the human predicament is the presence in each of us of two principles. One, which he calls "light," is spiritual. The other, "darkness," is matter.[4] The kingdom of darkness has been fighting to defeat the light. In every human being these two principles have mixed together. Every human is so mixed with these principles that everything from the waist down is considered part of the kingdom of darkness. Everything from the waist up is the kingdom of light. Sex is not allowed for a Mani. It only contributes to the furthering of the kingdom of darkness.

Salvation consists in separating the two elements, and in preparing our spirit for its return to the realm of pure light, in which it will be absorbed.[5] According to Mani, this doctrine had been revealed in various fashions to a long series of prophets, including Buddha, Zoroaster, Jesus and Mani himself.[6]

A great deal of Romans jumped on board with the ideas of Mani. Followers of Mani lived lives of extreme self-denial. Mani would have a large influence in the life and world of Augustine.

Plotinus

A third popular person of the day offering the Romans a worldview was a man named Plotinus. Plotinus (205-270AD) started a school of philosophy in Rome which became a hub of intellectual activity. Knowles talks about this fascinating man:

> *Plotinus lived an ascetic life with very little food or sleep. He ate only vegetables and never took a bath. His own body and person seem to have been of little interest to him, as though he were living as independently of them as possible.*[7]

---

3 Knowles. Augustine and His World. p.51

4 Gonzalez. The Story of Christianity: Volume 1. p.208.

5 Ibid.

6 Ibid.

7 Knowles. Augustine and His World. p.68.

Plotinus rediscovered the teachings of Plato. Many actually believed him to be a reincarnation of Plato. He is known as the father of a movement of ideas called Neo-Platonism. Neoplatonism was very popular at the time of Augustine.

PLOTINUS

Neoplatonism disagreed with the worldview of Mani. It taught there was only one principle in the universe. There is not a kingdom of light and a kingdom of darkness. There is, so to speak, only one kingdom. This kingdom is ruled by the One, the source of all things.

Reality is like the concentric circles that appear on the surface of the water when hit by a pebble. The realities of life that are closer to the One, the center, are superior. Evil then does not originate from a different source, but consists simply in moving away from the One.[8] The miserable life described by Cicero is seen by the Neo-Platonists as people living in the outer circles away from the One.

Gonzalez explains the pursuit of the Neoplatonist:

> *Through a combination of study, discipline, and mystical contemplation, it sought to reach the ineffable One, the source of all being. The goal of the Neo-platonist was the ecstasy that one experienced when lost in such contemplation.*[9]

Neoplatonists found great pleasure in their contemplation. Augustine would spend a great deal of time contemplating their contemplations. We now turn to #1 on our list of Top Ten Theologians.

8 Gonzalez. The Story of Christianity: Volume 1. p.210.
9 Ibid.

Augustine's Life

Early Years with Monica

Augustine was born in 354AD in the little town of Thagaste, in North Africa. His father worked for the Roman government. His father followed traditional North African pagan religions. His mother Monica, however, was a passionate believer in Jesus.

Thagaste, now in modern-day Algeria, was in the middle of a North African boom during the early years of Augustine. Life was good. An inscription has been discovered explaining the indulgent life there, "The hunt, the baths, play and laughter: that's the life for me!"[10]

Augustine grew up around this indulgent life but his family had lesser means. It was clear to his parents, however, that Augustine had unusual intellectual abilities. His family would sacrifice greatly to allow Augustine the best of educations. To that end they sent him to the nearby town of Madaura, and later to Carthage.[11] Augustine was 17 years old when he arrived in Carthage. While he did not neglect his studies, he set out to indulge in the full offerings of the city. In fairly a short time he had a girl living with him. She would end up living with him for the next fifteen years. Shortly later, Augustine and his girlfriend had a son. They named him Adeodatus – meaning 'given by God.'

All the students of his day preparing for careers inside government or as lawyers became students of Rhetoric. It was a crucial skill during this age to be able to speak and write in an elegant and convincing way. Truth wasn't that important in his studies. It was more valuable to speak convincingly than to speak truthfully.

Studying Cicero

During this time Augustine started to study one of the masters of Roman rhetoric: Cicero. Cicero began to shake Augustine's world. He saw

10 Brown. Augustine of Hippo. p.7.
11 Gonzalez. The Story of Christianity: Volume 1. p.208.

the masterful communication of Cicero, but Augustine would not allow himself to stop merely at Cicero's style. He began to read the content of his works. Rhetoric, without truth, could lead someone like Augustine to become a rich man able to fulfill every indulgent desire.

AUGUSTINE & MOM

Cicero's writings let Augustine know his life of indulgence will end in misery. Augustine, instead needs to pursue truth above rhetoric.

Augustine's response to the writings of Cicero are majestic:

Suddenly, all empty hope for my career lost its appeal; and I was left with an unbelievable fire in my heart, desiring the deathless qualities of Wisdom, and I made a start to rise up and return to Thee...I was on fire, my God, on fire to fly away from earthly things to Thee.[12]

Augustine becomes a Manichee

One of the fascinating aspects of Augustine's life is his journey of faith. With the influence of Cicero propelling Augustine forward, he went looking for a new worldview. He threw himself completely into the teachings of Mani.

Manicheism claimed to be the belief system of the intelligent. Its teachings were supported by astronomical observations. They ridiculed Christianity, and the Bible, as being too focused on the flesh and too barbaric in the writing of the Bible.

12 Brown. Augustine of Hippo. p.29.

The issue of evil became a big focus for Augustine. His mother had always taught him that there was only one God. If there was only one God then why would he allow or create evil? In Manicheism he found a worldview where evil is an equal opposite to the kingdom of light. Since they have no relation to each other the kingdom of light cannot be blamed for the kingdom of darkness.

Augustine's mother, Monica, was not happy with him becoming a Manichee. Monica was so opposed to his Manichee views she would not allow him in the house![13] During this time Augustine led several of his friends to become Manichees. Although Mani taught a strict self-denial, Augustine continued to live an indulgent lifestyle. Throughout this time, however, he continued to have questions and doubts about Manichee beliefs.

During Manichee gatherings Augustine started to vent his doubts. Gonzalez explains Augustine's last days as a Manichee:

> *He was told his questions were very profound, and that there was a great Manichean teacher, a certain Faustus, who could answer them. When the much announced Faustus finally arrived, he turned out to be no better than the other Manichean teachers. Disappointed, Augustine decided to carryon his quest in different directions.*[14]

On to Neoplatonism

Augustine at this time had become a professor in rhetoric. After unsuccessful attempts to teach in Thagaste and Carthage, he moved on in 384AD, at the age of 30, to a teaching position in Milan. In Milan he encountered the teachings of Plotinus and became a Neoplatonist. His nagging question about the origin of evil seemed to be answered.

In Neoplatonism you can have a single being, of infinite goodness, as

---

13 Knowles. Augustine and His World. p.54.

14 Gonzalez. The Story of Christianity: Volume 1. p.210.

the source of all things. Evil exists but it is not a "thing." This is a huge realization for Augustine. Evil is real, but it is not a "thing." It is rather a direction away from the goodness of the One. Neoplatonism helped to open the door for Augustine to become a Christian. He was still, however, disturbed by the Bible. He had come to see the Bible as sloppy rhetoric. Its language was crude and at times violent. How could this be the Word of God?

Ambrose

While in Milan, Monica convinced her son to go listen to the Bishop of Milan. Ambrose had been bishop for 11 years. Ambrose was the most famous speaker in all Milan. As a professor of rhetoric Augustine was interested to go hear the bishop. Initially, Augustine didn't care about what Ambrose said, just how he said it. Eventually, however, Augustine stopped listening as a critic and listened to Ambrose as a seeker of truth.

Augustine had long looked at the Bible as a second-rate work. Through the teaching of Ambrose, however, he saw how the Bible could be the Word of God. His major intellectual objections had melted away, yet there was still a big hurdle in his path.

AMBROSE OF MILAN

If Augustine were to accept the faith of his mother, he would be all-in: 100%. He was convinced that, were he to become a Christian, he must give up his career in rhetoric, as well as all his ambitions and every physical pleasure.[15] It was this last aspect he struggled with the most. By this time Augustine's initial girlfriend was out of the picture, but he was engaged to a second woman and sleeping with a third. During this time he famously would pray, "Give me chastity…but not too soon."

15 Gonzalez. The Story of Christianity. p.211.

Early Tragedy

After reading a biography of Athanasius (our #4 theologian) and hearing of several other people becoming Christians, Augustine gave his life fully to God. He and his now teenage son were then baptized by Ambrose.

Augustine resigned from his teaching position and decided to return to North Africa. On the way, tragically, his mother became ill and died. After several months of grieving in Rome he finally reached his hometown of Thagaste when another tragedy rocked Augustine. His son, Adeodatus, also died.

Leader and Bishop

Augustine's plan was to sell most of his possessions, move to nearby Cassiacum, and devote himself to contemplation and writing. From these early writings, Augustine's fame began to grow as his sharp mind and newfound life in Christ found expression. He was eager to write against all the worldviews he had been swept into that claimed truth but left the adherent empty.

Augustine's life was about to go in a totally different unexpected direction. He simply traveled to the city of Hippo to invite a friend to join him at Cassiacum. During a church service the bishop, Valerius, noticed Augustine sitting in the congregation. He spontaneously changed his message asking the congregation to seek God if someone in their midst might have been sent to be their minister! Augustine, much against his will, was ordained to serve with Valerius in Hippo.[16] Within four years Augustine was the bishop of Hippo.

He would never return to a life of solitude and writing. All his most famous writings, including his monumental interactions with Pelagius, would be done under the stress of daily pastoral responsibilities. It's these writings, his thoughts which made Augustine the #1 Theologian of Church History and which we now examine.

---

16 Gonzalez. p.211.

Augustine's Thoughts

Freedom of the Will

Since Augustine led many friends to become Manichees, many of his first works were written to refute their teachings. These early works dealt mainly with the divine authority of Scripture, the origin of evil and the freedom of the will. At such an early time in the history of Christianity Augustine goes on to develop a robust view of the freedom of the will. This was important to solve the difficulties having to do with the origin of evil.[17]

Influenced by Neoplatonism, Augustine sees in Scripture the fact that evil is never a substance. God did not create a substance called evil. He instead creates humans and angels with a good will. Humans and angels are able to make decisions out of their own will. This will, however, is freely capable of making a bad decision. The origin of evil is found in the bad decisions made by both humans and angels – those of the demons, who are fallen angels.[18] Augustine was able to show how an all-powerful good God can create and sustain the world and also explain the reality of evil.

The freedom of the will is absolutely crucial in understanding and appreciating the thoughts of Augustine. A new question rose up in Augustine's life. How free are humans to sin? Furthermore, how free are humans to avoid sin? These questions came from a man named Pelagius. To him Augustine turned his focus.

Pelagius

It was against the thoughts of the godly man Pelagius that Augustine wrote his most important theological works. Pelagius, a monk from Britain, had become famous by his piety. Pelagius claimed humans can attain a sinless life. He denied that human sin is inherited from Adam.[19]

---

17 Ibid. p. 213.

18 Ibid.

19 Knowles. Augustine and His World. p.120.

He believed that humans are free to act righteously. He saw no need for an outside influence. He did not believe we needed the special enabling power of the Holy Spirit. Pelagius saw the Christian life as a constant effort through which one's sins could be overcome and salvation attained.[20]

As Augustine considered the claims of Pelagius he remembered his personal experience of desiring to follow God but being unable to give up his sexual lifestyle. He both willed to obey and willed to not obey. Perhaps the will regarding sin was not as simple as Pelagius thought. Augustine's disagreement with Pelgaius centered around conversion, the question arose:

> *How can we make the decision to accept God's grace? According to Augustine, only by the power of grace itself, for before that moment we are not free to not sin, and therefore we are not free to decide to accept grace. The initiative in conversion is not human, but divine. Furthermore, grace is irresistible, and God gives it to those who have been predestined to it.*

Pelagius, for example, views salvation as a life preserver. If you find, while you are swimming, that you need help with your sin then you grab the life preserver. It's there if you need it, most people do in some way. Augustine, on the other hand, believed the Bible taught the concept of being dead in our sins. Dead people can't grab a life preserver. They're floating face-down. The only way Augustine can be saved is if God jumps in, drags him to shore and brings him back to life.

Augustine's famous statement from this debate was, "Grant what you command, and command what you will." If God desires for someone to come and follow Him, he has to grant the ability to do what He commands. The only thing we bring to our salvation, according to Augustine, is our sin.

The views of Pelagius were eventually rejected by the church.

---

20 Gonzalez. p.214.

Confessions

Augustine's book *Confessions* is without a doubt the most famous of all his writings. His autobiography, written between 397 and 401AD is unique in all ancient literature. No human being had ever written such an honest account of their own life. Augustine's perception of himself in light of His God would shape western theology for a thousand years – not only in their conclusions, but in an observant, reflective and astonishingly honest quest for truth.[21]

City of God

The other book standing out among his many volumes is his work *The City of God*. The immediate occasion compelling Augustine to write this book was the fall of the Roman Empire. At the time many of the people who had clung to the ancient pagan beliefs of the Roman Empire thought Christianity was to blame for the fall of Rome. Augustine wrote this work to respond to those people. The book is a huge sweep of history centered on two cities. Each city is built on a foundation of love. The city of God is built on love for God. The earthly city is built on love for self. In the end, all earthly cities will crumble, only the city of God will remain.

The thoughts of Augustine have had unparalleled influence in church history. It is this influence we now look at more closely.

Augustine's Influence

The influence of Augustine is broad and deep. On a personal level his finger-prints are all over: Anselm, Aquinas, Calvin, Luther, Bellarmine, Pascal and Kierkegaard. For example, it's hard to read more than two pages in Calvin's masterpiece *Institutes of the Christian Religion* without coming across a quote from Augustine.

---

21 Knowles. Augustine and His World. p.142.

During the last year of his life Jerome sent a letter from Bethlehem to Augustine to tell him that by his books he had virtually, "refounded the old faith," and that the bitter attacks on him by heretics were sufficient testimony to his achievement.[22]

It is easier, however, to mention his influence more on movements than on individuals. The theology and philosophy of medieval schoolmen and of the creators of the first universities were rooted in Augustinian ideas of the relation between faith and reason. When Peter Lombard compiled his foundational Sentences (1155) to provide a basic textbook of theology, a very high proportion was drawn from Augustine.[23]

The Reformation found much of its foundation in Augustine. Both sides in the controversy, interestingly, appealed on a large scale to the writings of Augustine.

During the 18th century enlightenment people were debating the concept of Augustine's "Original Sin." Immanuel Kant surprised the men of the Enlightenment by affirming that human nature is distorted by a pervasive radical evil.[24]

Augustine has and continues to influence those who follow Christ. Augustine, however, was not perfect. He had plenty of reasons why we should only worship Christ and view Augustine as a fellow sinner. His foibles help keep him in perspective compared to our Savior.

Augustine's Foibles

Augustine's life before coming to Christ was full of licentious living. His 15-year relationship with his live-in girlfriend seems to have not been handled properly. Right around the time Augustine is coming to Christ and should have married her is the time when he sends her on her way. This could have been a righteous decision, but it also could have been a great chance to make a wrong situation right. As he was sending her away, she vowed to never marry another man. She wanted to marry him

22 Chadwick. p.125.

23 Chadwick. Augustine: A Very Short Introduction. p.3.

24 Ibid.

but he told her to get lost. Later in his life he seems to have realized the injustice of the situation.

Many Christians would see Augustine's view of infant baptism as incorrect. Pelagius saw people free from original sin. Since there is no original sin, thought Pelagius, infants did not need baptism. Infants had not committed sin, so they did not need anything to get to heaven. Since Augustine disagreed with the premise of Pelagius, he viewed original sin to the degree that infants were unable to go to heaven unless they had been baptized. Outside of the debate with Pelagius it is possible Augustine did not hold this as strongly as some of his works suggest. He wrote in City of God some ideas which suggest some who die in infancy may be able to get to heaven without baptism. Augustine, however, wrote strongly on this topic which seems too harsh to many 21st century ears.

Additionally, some of Augustine's views on the end-times, predestination, Mary, martyrs, etc… have been criticized by certain groups of Christians throughout the centuries as not balanced or sufficiently biblical.

Augustine's Effect on Us

Dr. Bradley Green nicely summarizes Augustine's effect on us:

> *At one level all of Western theology has been – in a sense – a long series of footnotes to Augustine. He bequeathed to the church deep reflection on how to talk and think about God, how language works when speaking about God, and on the nature of the triune God. His insights as to how one must affirm one God in three divine persons – where the three are understood in terms of relationship and love – is seminal. Augustine's doctrine of man as sinner – and hence in need of radical grace – is central to understanding Scripture, and every evangelical must still come to terms with his view of original sin. Augustine is rightfully considered the Doctor of Grace, for it is in Augustine's understanding*

> *of grace that he has perhaps made his greatest mark on the church. The grace of God, set upon us from all eternity, that moves us to trust in and believe God, that transforms our hearts, that effectively moves us to obey God for salvation and moves in us that we persevere to the end – that is a grace worth believing and promulgating in the world today. For these and many other reasons, Augustine is worthy of our attention, and can help evangelicals as we strive to understand and serve the God of Scripture.* [25]

As this chapter comes to an end my hope is these mighty mentors of history will only begin to shape our lives. These ten theologians are potentially ten people God may use to mentor you to be all He has called you to be in your world. My prayer is your connection with these mentors will grow until He calls us all safely home.

I hope you have enjoyed this book as much as I have enjoyed learning from these men.

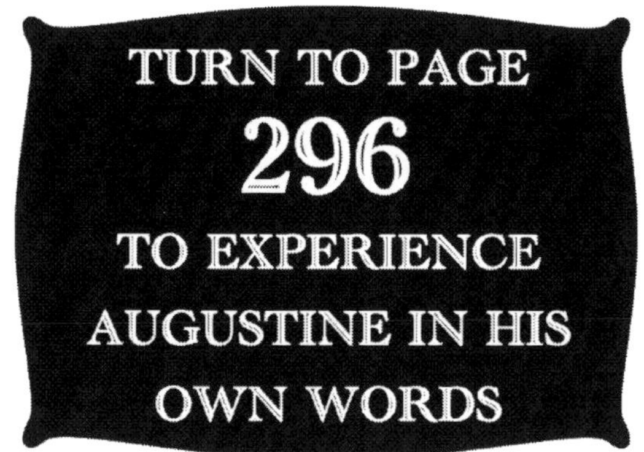

25 Green. Shapers of Christian Orthodoxy. p.288.

INTRODUCTION TO THE READER

In this section you get a taste for the original writings of the people you have hopefully came to appreciate.

It can be a daunting task to pick up and read men like Barth, Edwards, Calvin, Luther and Aquinas. Many people sit down to read their mighty works without much training. You would never try to run a marathon without first becoming comfortable running a mile.

In this section I ask you to simply run a mile with the greats; giving you the training to one day run a marathon with them.

READER

WARNING:
THE FOLLOWING PAGES
CONTAIN SOME OF THE DEEPEST
WRITING ON THE PLANET

HEART AND MIND
MAY BE BLOWN

PROCEED WITH
CAUTION

TOP TEN THEOLOGIANS

IRENAEUS:AGAINST HERESIES EXCERPT WRITTEN 180AD

BOOK I

PREFACE.

1. INASMUCH(1) as certain men have set the truth aside, and bring in lying words and vain genealogies, which, as the apostle says,(2) "minister questions rather than godly edifying which is in faith," and by means of their craftily-constructed plausibilities draw away the minds of the inexperienced and take them captive, [I have felt constrained, my dear friend, to compose the following treatise in order to expose and counteract their machinations.] These men falsify the oracles of God, and prove themselves evil interpreters of the good word of revelation. They also overthrow the faith of many, by drawing them away, under a pretence of [superior] knowledge, from Him who rounded and adorned the universe; as if, forsooth, they had something more excellent and sublime to reveal, than that God who created the heaven and the earth, and all things that are therein. By means of specious and plausible words, they cunningly allure the simple-minded to inquire into their system; but they nevertheless clumsily destroy them, while they initiate them into their blasphemous and impious opinions respecting the Demiurge;(3) and these simple ones are unable, even in such a matter, to distinguish falsehood from truth.

2. Error, indeed, is never set forth in its naked deformity, lest, being thus exposed, it should at once be detected. But it is craftily decked out in an attractive dress, so as, by its outward form, to make it appear to the inexperienced (ridiculous as the expression may seem) more true than the truth itself. One(4) far superior to me has well said, in reference to this point, "A clever imitation in glass casts contempt, as it were, on that precious jewel the emerald (which is most highly esteemed by some), unless it come under the eye of one able to test and expose the counterfeit. Or, again, what inexperienced person can with ease detect the presence of brass when it has been mixed up with silver?" Lest, therefore, through my neglect, some should be carried off, even as sheep are by wolves, while they perceive not the true character of these men,-because they outwardly are covered with sheep's clothing (against whom the Lord has enjoined(5) us to be on our guard), and because their language resembles ours, while their sentiments are very different,--I have deemed it my duty (after reading some of the Commentaries, as they call them, of the disciples of Valentinus, and after making myself acquainted with their tenets through personal intercourse with some of them) to unfold to thee, my friend, these portentous and profound mysteries, which do not fall within the range of every intellect, because all have not sufficiently purged(6) their brains. I do this, in order that thou, obtaining an acquaintance with these things, mayest in turn explain them to all those with whom thou art connected, and exhort them to avoid such an abyss of madness and of blasphemy against Christ. I intend, then, to the best of my ability, with brevity and clearness to set forth the opinions of those who are now promulgating heresy. I refer especially to the disciples of Ptolemaeus, whose school may be described as a bud from that of Valentinus. I shall also endeavour, according to my moderate ability, to furnish the means of overthrowing them, by showing how absurd and inconsistent with the truth are their statements. Not that I am practised either in composition or eloquence; but my feeling of affection prompts me to make known to thee and all thy companions those doctrines which have been kept in concealment until now, but which are at last, through the goodness of God, brought to light. "For there is nothing hidden which shall not be revealed, nor secret that shall not be made known."(1)

3. Thou wilt not expect from me, who am resident among the Keltae,(2)

and am accustomed for the most part to use a barbarous dialect, any display of rhetoric, which I have never learned, or any excellence of composition, which I have never practised, or any beauty and persuasiveness of style, to which I make no pretensions. But thou wilt accept in a kindly spirit what I in a like spirit write to thee simply, truthfully, and in my own homely way; whilst thou thyself (as being more capable than I am) wilt expand those ideas of which I send thee, as it were, only the seminal principles; and in the comprehensiveness of thy understanding, wilt develop to their full extent the points on which I briefly touch, so as to set with power before thy companions those things which I have uttered in weakness. In fine, as I (to gratify thy long-cherished desire for information regarding the tenets of these persons) have spared no pains, not only to make these doctrines known to thee, but also to furnish the means of showing their falsity; so shalt thou, according to the grace given to thee by the Lord, prove an earnest and efficient minister to others, that men may no longer be drawn away by the plausible system of these heretics, which I now proceed to describe.(3)

CHAP. I.--ABSURD IDEAS OF THE DISCIPLES OF VALENTINUS AS TO THE ORIGIN, NAME, ORDER, AND CONJUGAL PRODUCTIONS OF THEIR FANCIED AEONS, WITH THE PASSAGES OF SCRIPTURE WHICH THEY ADAPT TO THEIR OPINIONS.

1. THEY maintain, then, that in the invisible and ineffable heights above there exists a certain perfect, pre-existent AEon,(4) whom they call Proarche, Propator, and Bythus, and describe as being invisible and incomprehensible. Eternal and unbegotten, he remained throughout innumerable cycles of ages in profound serenity and quiescence. There existed along with him Ennoea, whom they also call Charis and Sige.(5) At last this Bythus determined to send forth from himself the beginning of all things, and deposited this production (which he had resolved to bring forth) in his contemporary Sige, even as seed is deposited in the womb. She then, having received this seed, and becoming pregnant, gave birth to Nous, who was both similar and equal to him who had produced him, and was alone capable of comprehending his father's greatness. This Nous they call also Monogenes, and Father, and the Beginning of all Things. Along with him was also produced Aletheia; and these four constituted the first and first-begotten Pythagorean Tetrad, which they also denominate the root of all things. For there are first Bythus and Sige, and

then Nous and Aletheia. And Monogenes, perceiving for what purpose he had been produced, also himself sent forth Logos and Zoe, being the father of all those who were to come after him, and the beginning and fashioning of the entire Pleroma. By the conjunction of Logos and Zoo were brought forth Anthropos and Ecclesia; and thus was formed the first-begotten Ogdoad, the root and substance of all things, called among them by four names, viz., Bythus, and Nous, and Logos, and Anthropos. For each of these is masculo-feminine, as follows: Propator was united by a conjunction with his Ennoea; then Monogenes, that is Nous, with Aletheia; Logos with Zoe, and Anthropos with Ecclesia.

2. These AEons having been produced for the glory of the Father, and wishing, by their own efforts, to effect this object, sent forth emanations by means of conjunction. Logos and Zoe, after producing Anthropos and Ecclesia, sent forth other ten AEons, whose names are the following: Bythius and Mixis, Ageratos and Henosis, Autophyes and Hedone, Acinetos and Syncrasis, Monogenes and Macaria.(6) These are the ten AEons whom they declare to have been produced by Logos and Zoe. They then add that Anthropos himself, along with Ecclesia, produced twelve AEons, to whom they give the following names: Paracletus and Pistis, Patricos and Elpis, Metricos and Agape, Ainos and Synesis, Ecclesiasticus and Macariotes, Theletos and Sophia.

3. Such are the thirty AEons in the erroneous system of these men; and they are described as being wrapped up, so to speak, in silence, and known to none [except these professing teachers]. Moreover, they declare that this invisible and spiritual Pleroma of theirs is tripartite, being divided into an Ogdoad, a Decad, and a Duodecad. And for this reason they affirm it was that the "Saviour"--for they do not please to call Him "Lord"--did no work in public during the space of thirty years,(1) thus setting forth the mystery of these AEons. They maintain also, that these thirty AEons are most plainly indicated in the parable(2) of the labourers sent into the vineyard. For some are sent about the first hour, others about the third hour, others about the sixth hour, others about the ninth hour, and others about the eleventh hour. Now, if we add up the numbers of the hours here mentioned, the sum total will be thirty: for one, three, six, nine, and eleven, when added together, form thirty. And by the hours, they hold that the AEons were pointed out; while they maintain that these are great, and wonderful, and hitherto unspeak-

able mysteries which it is their special function to develop; and so they proceed when they find anything in the multitude(3) of things contained in the Scriptures which they can adopt and accommodate to their baseless speculations.

CHAP. II.--THE PROPATOR WAS KNOWN TO MONO-GENES ALONE. AMBITION, DISTURBANCE, AND DANGER INTO WHICH SOPHIA FELL; HER SHAPELESS OFFSPRING: SHE IS RESTORED BY HOROS. THE PRODUCTION OF CHRIST AND OF THE HOLY SPIRIT, IN ORDER TO THE COMPLETION OF THE AEONS. MANNER OF THE PRODUCTION OF JESUS.

1. They proceed to tell us that the Propator of their scheme was known only to Monogenes, who sprang from him; in other words, only to Nous, while to all the others he was invisible and incomprehensible. And, according to them, Nous alone took pleasure in contemplating the Father, and exulting in considering his immeasurable greatness; while he also meditated how he might communicate to the rest of the AEons the greatness of the Father, revealing to them how vast and mighty he was, and how he was without beginning,--beyond comprehension, and altogether incapable of being seen. But, in accordance with the will of the Father, Sige restrained him, because it was his design to lead them all to an acquaintance with the aforesaid Propator, and to create within them a desire of investigating his nature. In like manner, the rest of the AEons also, in a kind of quiet way, had a wish to behold the Author of their being, and to contemplate that First Cause which had no beginning.

2. But there rushed forth in advance of the rest that AEon who was much the latest of them, and was the youngest of the Duodecad which sprang from Anthropos and Ecclesia, namely Sophia, and suffered passion apart from the embrace of her consort Theletos. This passion, indeed, first arose among those who were connected with Nous and Aletheia, but passed as by contagion to this degenerate AEon, who acted under a pretence of love, but was in reality influenced by temerity, because she had not, like Nous, enjoyed communion with the perfect Father. This passion, they say, consisted in a desire to search into the nature of the Father; for she wished, according to them, to comprehend his greatness. When she could not attain her end, inasmuch as she aimed at an impossibility, and thus became involved in an extreme agony of mind,

while both on account of the vast profundity as well as the unsearchable nature of the Father, and on account of the love she bore him, she was ever stretching herself forward, there was danger lest she should at last have been absorbed by his sweetness, and resolved into his absolute essence, unless she had met with that Power which supports all things, and preserves them outside of the unspeakable greatness. This power they term Horos; by whom, they say, she was restrained and supported; and that then, having with difficulty been brought back to herself, she was convinced that the Father is incomprehensible, and so laid aside her original design, along with that passion which had arisen within her from the overwhelming influence of her admiration.

3. But others of them fabulously describe the passion and restoration of Sophia as follows: They say that she, having engaged in an impossible and impracticable attempt, brought forth an amorphous substance, such as her female nature enabled her to produce.(4) When she looked upon it, her first feeling was one of grief, on account of the imperfection of its generation, and then of fear lest this should end(5) her own existence. Next she lost, as it were, all command of herself, and was in the greatest perplexity while endeavouring to discover the cause of all this, and in what way she might conceal what had happened. Being greatly harassed by these passions, she at last changed her mind, and endeavoured to return anew to the Father. When, however, she in some measure made the attempt, strength failed her, and she became a suppliant of the Father. The other AEons, Nous in particular, presented their supplications along with her. And hence they declare material substance(1) had its beginning from ignorance and grief, and fear and bewilderment.

4. The Father afterwards produces, in his own image, by means of Monogenes, the above-mentioned Horos, without conjunction,(2) masculo-feminine. For they maintain that sometimes the Father acts in conjunction with Sige, but that at other times he shows himself independent both of male and female. They term this Horos both Stauros and Lytrotes, and Carpistes, and Horothetes, and Metagoges.(3) And by this Horos they declare that Sophia was purified and established, while she was also restored to her proper conjunction. For her enthymesis (or inborn idea) having been taken away from her, along with its supervening passion, she herself certainly remained within the Pleroma; but her enthymesis, with its passion, was separated from her by Horos, fenced(4)

off, and expelled from that circle. This enthymesis was, no doubt, a spiritual substance, possessing some of the natural tendencies of an AEon, but at the same time shapeless and without form, because it had received nothing.(5) And on this account they say that it was an imbecile and feminine production.(6)

5. After this substance had been placed outside of the Pleroma of the AEons, and its mother restored to her proper conjunction, they tell us that Monogenes, acting in accordance with the prudent forethought of the Father, gave origin to another conjugal pair, namely Christ and the Holy Spirit (lest any of the AEons should fall into a calamity similar to that of Sophia), for the purpose of fortifying and strengthening the Pleroma, and who at the same time completed the number of the AEons. Christ then instructed them as to the nature of their conjunction, and taught them that those who possessed a comprehension of the Unbegotten were sufficient for themselves.(7) He also announced among them what related to the knowledge of the Father,--namely, that he cannot be understood or comprehended, nor so much as seen or heard, except in so far as he is known by Monogenes only. And the reason why the rest of the AEons possess perpetual existence is found in that part of the Father's nature which is incomprehensible; but the reason of their origin and formation was situated in that which may be comprehended regarding him, that is, in the Son.(8) Christ, then, who had just been produced, effected these things among them.

6. But the Holy Spirit(9) taught them to give thanks on being all rendered equal among themselves, and led them to a state of true repose. Thus, then, they tell us that the AEons were constituted equal to each other in form and sentiment, so that all became as Nous, and Logos, and Anthropos, and Christus. The female AEons, too, became all as Aletheia, and Zoe, and Spiritus, and Ecclesia. Everything, then, being thus established, and brought into a state of perfect rest, they next tell us that these beings sang praises with great joy to the Propator, who himself shared in the abounding exaltation. Then, out of gratitude for the great benefit which had been conferred on them, the whole Pleroma of the AEons, with one design and desire, and with the concurrence of Christ and the Holy Spirit, their Father also setting the seal of His approval on their conduct, brought together whatever each one had in himself of the greatest beauty and preciousness; and uniting all these contributions so as skilfully

to blend the whole, they produced, to the honour and glory of Bythus, a being of most perfect beauty, the very star of the Pleroma, and the perfect fruit [of it], namely Jesus. Him they also speak of under the name of Saviour, and Christ, and patronymically, Logos, and Everything, because He was formed from the contributions of all. And then we are told that, by way of honour, angels of the same nature as Himself were simultaneously produced, to act as His body-guard.

CHAP. III.--TEXTS OF HOLY SCRIPTURE USED BY THESE HERETICS TO SUPPORT THEIR OPINIONS.

1. Such, then, is the account they give of what took place within the Pleroma; such the calamities that flowed from the passion which seized upon the AEon who has been named, and who was within a little of perishing by being absorbed in the universal substance, through her inquisitive searching after the Father; such the consolidation(1) [of that AEon] from her condition of agony by Horos, and Stauros, and Lytrotes, and Carpistes, and Horothetes, and Metagoges.(2) Such also is the account of the generation of the later AEons, namely of the first Christ and of the Holy Spirit, both of whom were produced by the Father after the repentance(3) [of Sophia], and of the second(4) Christ (whom they also style Saviour), who owed his being to the joint contributions [of the AEons]. They tell us, however, that this knowledge has not been openly divulged, because all are not capable of receiving it, but has been mystically revealed by the Saviour through means of parables to those qualified for understanding it. This has been done as follows. The thirty AEons are indicated (as we have already remarked) by the thirty years during which they say the Saviour performed no public act, and by the parable of the labourers in the vineyard. Paul also, they affirm, very clearly and frequently names these AEons, and even goes so far as to preserve their order, when he says, "To all the generations of the AEons of the AEon."(5) Nay, we ourselves, when at the giving of thanks we pronounce the words, "To AEons of AEons" (for ever and ever), do set forth these AEons. And, in fine, wherever the words AEon or AEons occur, they at once refer them to these beings.

2. The production, again, of the Duodecad of the AEons, is indicated by the fact that the Lord was twelve(7) years of age when He disputed with the teachers of the law, and by the election of the apostles, for of

these there were twelve.(8) The other eighteen AEons are made manifest in this way: that the Lord, [according to them,] conversed with His disciples for eighteen months(9) after His resurrection from the dead. They also affirm that these eighteen AEons are strikingly indicated by the first two letters of His name [Ihsous], namely Iota(10) and Eta. And, in like manner, they assert that the ten AEons are pointed out by the letter Iota, which begins His name; while, for the same reason, they tell us the Saviour said, "One Iota, or one tittle, shall by no means pass away until all be fulfilled."(11)

3. They further maintain that the passion which took place in the case of the twelfth AEon is pointed at by the apostasy of Judas, who was the twelfth apostle, and also by the fact that Christ suffered in the twelfth month. For their opinion is, that He continued to preach for one year only after His baptism. The same thing is also most clearly indicated by the case of the woman who suffered from an issue of blood. For after she had been thus afflicted during twelve years, she was healed by the advent of the Saviour, when she had touched the border of His garment; and on this account the Saviour said, "Who touched me?"(12)--teaching his disciples the mystery which had occurred among the AEons, and the healing of that AEon who had been involved in suffering. For she who had been afflicted twelve years represented that power whose essence, as they narrate, was stretching itself forth, and flowing into immensity; and unless she had touched the garment of the Son,(13) that is, Aletheia of the first Tetrad, who is denoted by the hem spoken of, she would have been dissolved into the general essence(14) [of which she participated]. She stopped short, however, and ceased any longer to suffer. For the power that went forth from the Son (and this power they term Horos) healed her, and separated the passion from her.

4. They moreover affirm that the Saviour(15) is shown to be derived from all the AEons, and to be in Himself everything by the following passage: "Every male that openeth the womb."(16) For He, being everything, opened the womb(17) of the enthymesis of the suffering AEon, when it had been expelled from the Pleroma. This they also style the second Ogdoad, of which we shall speak presently. And they state that it was clearly on this account that Paul said, "And He Himself is all things;"(1) and again, "All things are to Him, and of Him are all things;"(2) and further, "In Him dwelleth all the fulness of the

Godhead;"(3) and yet again, "All things are gathered together by God in Christ."(4) Thus do they interpret these and any like passages to be found in Scripture.

5. They show, further, that that Horos of theirs, whom they call by a variety of names, has two faculties,--the one of supporting, and the other of separating; and in so far as he supports and sustains, he is Stauros, while in so far as he divides and separates, he is Horos. They then represent the Saviour as having indicated this twofold faculty: first, the sustaining power, when He said, "Whosoever doth not bear his cross (Stauros), and follow after me, cannot be my disciple;"(5) and again, "Taking up the cross follow me;"(6) but the separating power when He said, "I came not to send peace, but a word."(7) They also maintain that John indicated the same thing when he said, "The fan is in His hand, and He will thoroughly purge the floor, and will gather the wheat into His garner; but the chaff He will burn with fire unquenchable."(8) By this declaration He set forth the faculty of Horos. For that fan they explain to be the cross (Stauros), which consumes, no doubt, all material(9) objects, as fire does chaff, but it purifies all them that are saved, as a fan does wheat. Moreover, they affirm that the Apostle Paul himself made mention of this cross in the following words: "The doctrine of the cross is to them that perish foolishness, but to us who are saved it is the power of God."(10) And again: "God forbid that I should glory in anything(11) save in the cross of Christ, by whom the world is crucified to me, and I unto the world."

6. Such, then, is the account which they all give of their Pleroma, and of the formation(12) of the universe, striving, as they do, to adapt the good words of revelation to their own wicked inventions. And it is not only from the writings of the evangelists and the apostles that they endeavour to derive proofs for their opinions by means of perverse interpretations and deceitful expositions: they deal in the same way with the law and the prophets, which contain many parables and allegories that can frequently be drawn into various senses, according to the kind of exegesis to which they are subjected. And others(13) of them, with great craftiness, adapted such parts of Scripture to their own figments, lead away captive from the truth those who do not retain a stedfast faith in one God, the Father Almighty, and in one Lord Jesus Christ, the Son of God.

CHAP. IV.--ACCOUNT GIVEN BY THE HERETICS OF THE FORMATION OF ACHAMOTH; ORIGIN OF THE VISIBLE WORLD FROM HER DISTURBANCES.

1. The following are the transactions which they narrate as having occurred outside of the Pleroma: The enthymesis of that Sophia who dwells above, which they also term Achamoth,(14) being removed from the Pleroma, together with her passion, they relate to have, as a matter of course, become violently excited in those places of darkness and vacuity [to which she had been banished]. For she was excluded from light(15) and the Pleroma, and was without form or figure, like an untimely birth, because she had received nothing(16) [from a male parent]. But the Christ dwelling on high took pity upon her; and having extended himself through and beyond Stauros,(17) he imparted a figure to her, but merely as respected substance, and not so as to convey intelligence.(18) Having effected this, he withdrew his influence, and returned, leaving Achamoth to herself, in order that she, becoming sensible of her suffering as being severed from the Pleroma, might be influenced by the desire of better things, while she possessed in the meantime a kind of odour of immortality left in her by Christ and the Holy Spirit. Wherefore also she is called by two names--Sophia after her father (for Sophia is spoken of as being her father), and Holy Spirit from that Spirit who is along with Christ. Having then obtained a form, along with intelligence, and being immediately deserted by that Logos who had been invisibly present with her--that is, by Christ--she strained herself to discover that light which had forsaken her, but could not effect her purpose, inasmuch as she was prevented by Horos. And as Horos thus obstructed her further progress, he exclaimed, IAO,(1) whence, they say, this name Iao derived its origin. And when she could not pass by Horos on account of that passion in which she had been involved, and because she alone had been left without, she then resigned herself to every sort of that manifold and varied state of passion to which she was subject; and thus she suffered grief on the one hand because she had not obtained the object of her desire, and fear on the other hand, lest life itself should fail her, as light had already done, while, in addition, she was in the greatest perplexity. All these feelings were associated with ignorance. And this ignorance of hers was not like that of her mother, the first Sophia, an AEon, due to degeneracy by means of passion, but to an [innate] opposition [of nature to knowl-

edge].(2) Moreover, another kind of passion fell upon her her (Achamoth), namely, that of desiring to return to him who gave her life.

2. This collection [of passions] they declare was the substance of the matter from which this world was formed. For from [her desire of] returning [to him who gave her life], every soul belonging to this world, and that of the Demiurge(3) himself, derived its origin. All other things owed their beginning to her terror and sorrow. For from her tears all that is of a liquid nature was formed; from her smile all that is lucent; and from her grief and perplexity all the corporeal elements of the world. For at one time, as they affirm, she would weep and lament on account of being left alone in the midst of darkness and vacuity; while, at another time, reflecting on the light which had forsaken her, she would be filled with joy, and laugh; then, again, she would be struck with terror; or, at other times, would sink into consternation and bewilderment.

3. Now what follows from all this? No light tragedy comes out of it, as the fancy of every man among them pompously explains, one in one way, and another in another, from what kind of passion and from what element being derived its origin. They have good reason, as seems to me, why they should not feel inclined to teach these things to all in public, but only to such as are able to pay a high price for an acquaintance with such profound mysteries. For these doctrines are not at all similar to those of which our Lord said, "Freely ye have received, freely give."(4) They are, on the contrary, abstruse, and portentous, and profound mysteries, to be got at only with great labour by such as are in love with falsehood. For who would not expend lull that he possessed, if only he might learn in return, that from the tears of the enthymesis of the AEon involved in passion, seas, and fountains, and rivers, and every liquid substance derived its origin; that light burst forth from her smile; and that from her perplexity and consternation the corporeal elements of the world had their formation?

4. I feel somewhat inclined myself to contribute a few hints towards the development of their system. For when I perceive that waters are in part fresh, such as fountains, rivers, showers, and so on, and in part salt; such as those in the sea, I reflect with myself that all such waters cannot be derived from her tears, inasmuch as these are of a saline quality only. It

is clear, therefore, that the waters which are salt are alone those which are derived from her tears. But it is probable that she, in her intense agony and perplexity, was covered with perspiration. And hence, following out their notion, we may conceive that fountains and rivers, and all the fresh water in the world, are due to this source. For it is difficult, since we know that all tears are of the same quality, to believe that waters both salt and fresh proceeded from them. The more plausible supposition is, that some are from her tears, and some from her perspiration. And since there are also in the world certain waters which are hot and acrid in their nature, thou must be left to guess their origin, how and whence. Such are some of the results of their hypothesis.

5. They go on to state that, when the mother Achamoth had passed through all sorts of passion, and had with difficulty escaped from them, she turned herself to supplicate the light which had forsaken her, that is, Christ. He, however, having returned to the Pleroma, and being probably unwilling again to descend from it, sent forth to her the Paraclete, that is, the Saviour.(5) This being was endowed with all power by the Father, who placed everything under his authority, the AEons(6) doing so likewise, so that "by him were all things, visible and invisible, created, thrones, divinities, dominions."(7) He then was sent to her along with his contemporary angels. And they related that Achamoth, filled with reverence, at first veiled herself through modesty, but that by and by, when she had looked upon him with all his endowments, and had acquired strength from his appearance, she ran forward to meet him. He then imparted to her form as respected intelligence, and brought healing to her passions, separating them from her, but not so as to drive them out of thought altogether. For it was not possible that they should be annihilated as in the former case,(1) because they had already taken root and acquired strength [so as to possess an indestructible existence]. All that he could do was to separate them and set them apart, and then commingle and condense them, so as to transmute them from incorporeal passion into unorganized matter.(2) He then by this process conferred upon them a fitness and a nature to become concretions and corporeal structures, in order that two substances should be formed,--the one evil, resulting from the passions, and the other subject indeed to suffering, but originating from her conversion. And on this account (i.e., on account of this hypostatizing of ideal matter) they say that the Saviour virtually(3) created the world. But when Achamoth was freed from her

passion, she gazed with rapture on the dazzling vision of the angels that were with him; and in her ecstasy, conceiving by them, they tell us that she brought forth new beings, partly after her oven image, and partly a spiritual progeny after the image of the Saviour's attendants.

CHAP. V.--FORMATION OF THE DEMIURGE; DESCRIPTION OF HIM. HE IS THE CREATOR OF EVERYTHING OUTSIDE OF THE PLEROMA.

1. These three kinds of existence, then, having, according to them, been now formed,--one from the passion, which was matter; a second from the conversion, which was animal; and the third, that which she (Achamoth) herself brought forth, which was spiritual,--she next addressed herself to the task of giving these form. But she could not succeed in doing this as respected the spiritual existence, because it was of the same nature with herself. She therefore applied herself to give form to the animal substance which had proceeded from her own conversion, and to bring forth to light the instructions of the Saviour.(4) And they say she first formed out of animal substance him who is Father and King of all things, both of these which are of the same nature with himself, that is, animal substances, which they also call right-handed, and those which sprang from the passion, and from matter, which they call left-handed. For they affirm that he formed all the things which came into existence after him, being secretly impelled thereto by his mother. From this circumstance they style him Metropator,(5) Apator, Demiurge, and Father, saying that he is Father of the substances on the right hand, that is, of the animal, but Demiurge of those on the left, that is, of the material, while he is at the same time the king of all. For they say that this Enthymesis, desirous of making all things to the honour of the AEons, formed images of them, or rather that the Saviour(6) did so through her instrumentality. And she, in the image(7) of the invisible Father, kept herself concealed from the Demiurge. But he was in the image of the only-begotten Son, and the angels and archangels created by him were in the image of the rest of the AEons.

2. They affirm, therefore, that he was constituted the Father and God of everything outside of the Pleroma, being the creator of all animal and material substances. For he it was that discriminated these two kinds of existence hitherto confused, and made corporeal from incor-

poreal substances, fashioned things heavenly and earthly, and became the Framer (Demiurge) of things material and animal, of those on the right and those on the left, of the light and of the heavy, and of those tending upwards as well as of those tending downwards. He created also seven heavens, above which they say that he, the Demiurge, exists. And on this account they term him Hebdomas, and his mother Achamoth Ogdoads, preserving the number of the first-begotten and primary Ogdoad as the Pleroma. They affirm, moreover, that these seven heavens are intelligent, and speak of them as being angels, while they refer to the Demiurge himself as being an angel bearing a likeness to God; and in the same strain, they declare that Paradise, situated above the third heaven, is a fourth angel possessed of power, from whom Adam derived certain qualities while he conversed with him.

3. They go on to say that the Demiurge imagined that he created all these things of himself, while he in reality made them in conjunction with the productive power of Achamoth. He formed the heavens, yet was ignorant of the heavens; he fashioned man, yet knew not man; he brought to light the earth, yet had no acquaintance with the earth; and, in like manner. they declare that he was ignorant of the forms of all that he made, and knew not even of the existence of his own mother, but imagined that he himself was all things. They further affirm that his mother originated this opinion in his mind, because she desired to bring him forth possessed of such a character that he should be the head and source of his own essence, and the absolute ruler over every kind of operation [that was afterwards attempted]. This mother they also call Ogdoad, Sophia; Terra, Jerusalem, Holy Spirit, and, with a masculine reference, Lord. (1) Her place of habitation is an intermediate one, above the Demiurge indeed, but below and outside of the Pleroma, even to the end.(2)

4. As, then, they represent all material substance to be formed from three passions, viz., fear, grief, and perplexity, the account they give is as follows: Animal substances originated from fear and from conversion; the Demiurge they also describe as owing his origin to conversion; but the existence of all the other animal substances they ascribe to fear, such as the souls of irrational animals, and of wild beasts, and men. And on this account, he (the Demiurge), being incapable of recognising any spiritual essences, imagined himself to be God alone, and declared through the prophets, "I am God, and besides me there is none else."(3) They further

teach that the spirits of wickedness derived their origin from grief. Hence the devil, whom they also call Cosmocrator (the ruler of the world), and the demons, and the angels, and every wicked spiritual being that exists, found the source Of their existence. They represent the Demiurge as being the son of that mother of theirs (Achamoth), and Cosmocrator as the creature of the Demiurge. Cosmocrator has knowledge of what is above himself, because he is a spirit of wickedness; but the Demiurge is ignorant of such things, inasmuch as he is merely animal. Their mother dwells in that place which is above the heavens, that is, in the intermediate abode; the Demiurge in the heavenly place, that is, in the hebdomad; but the Cosmocrator in this our world. The corporeal elements of the world, again, sprang, as we before remarked, from bewilderment and perplexity, as from a more ignoble source. Thus the earth arose from her state of stupor; water from the agitation caused by her fear; air from the consolidation of her grief; while fire, producing death and corruption, was inherent in all these elements, even as they teach that ignorance also lay concealed in these three passions.

5. Having thus formed the world, he (the Demiurge) also created the earthy [part of] man, not taking him from this dry earth, but from an invisible substance consisting of fusible and fluid matter, and then afterwards, as they define the process, breathed into him the animal part of his nature. It was this latter which was created after his image and likeness. The material part, indeed, was very near to. God, so far as the image went, but not of the same substance with him. The animal, on the Other hand, was so in respect to likeness; and hence his substance was called the spirit of life, because it took its rise from a spiritual outflowing. After all this, he was, they say, enveloped all round with a covering of skin; and by this they mean the outward sensitive flesh.

6. But they further affirm that the Demiurge himself was ignorant of that offspring of his mother Achamoth, which she brought forth as a consequence of her contemplation of those angels who waited on the Saviour, and which was, like herself, of a spiritual nature. She took advantage of this ignorance to deposit it (her production) in him without his knowledge, in order that, being by his instrumentality infused into that animal soul proceeding from himself, and being thus carried as in a womb in this material body, while it gradually increased in strength, might in course of time become fitted for the reception of perfect

rationality.(4) Thus it came to pass, then, according to them, that, without any knowledge on the part of the Demiurge, the man formed by his inspiration was at the same time, through an unspeakable providence, rendered a spiritual man by the simultaneous inspiration received from Sophia. For, as he was ignorant of his mother, so neither did he recognise her offspring. This [offspring] they also declare to be the Ecclesia, an emblem of the Ecclesia which is above. This, then, is the kind of man whom they conceive of: he has his animal soul from the Demiurge, his body from the earth, his fleshy part from matter, and his spiritual man from the mother Achamoth.

READER

KARL BARTH: BARMEN DECLARATION

TOP TEN THEOLOGIANS

Theological Declaration of Barmen

Written by Karl Barth and the confessing church in Nazi Germany in response to Hitler's national church. Its central doctrines concern the sin of idolatry and the lordship of Christ

I. An Appeal to the Evangelical Congregations and Christians in Germany

8.01 The Confessional Synod of the German Evangelical Church met in Barmen, May 29-31, 1934. Here representatives from all the German Confessional Churches met with one accord in a confession of the one Lord of the one, holy, apostolic Church. In fidelity to their Confession of Faith, members of Lutheran, Reformed, and United Churches sought a common message for the need and temptation of the Church in our day. With gratitude to God they are convinced that they have been given a common word to utter. It was not their intention to found a new Church or to form a union. For nothing was farther from their minds than the abolition of the confessional status of our Churches. Their intention was, rather, to withstand in faith and unanimity the destruction of the Confession of Faith, and thus of the Evangelical Church in Germany. In opposition to attempts to establish the unity of the German Evangelical Church by means of false doctrine, by the use of force and insincere practices, the Confessional Synod insists that the unity of the Evangelical Churches in Germany can come only from the Word of God in faith through the Holy Spirit. Thus alone is the Church renewed.

8.02 Therefore the Confessional Synod calls upon the congregations to range themselves behind it in prayer, and steadfastly to gather around those pastors and teachers who are loyal to the Confessions.

8.03 Be not deceived by loose talk, as if we meant to oppose the unity of the German nation! Do not listen to the seducers who pervert our intentions, as if we wanted to break up the unity of the German Evangelical Church or to forsake the Confessions of the Fathers!

8.04 Try the spirits whether they are of God! Prove also the words of the Confessional Synod of the German Evangelical Church to see whether they agree with Holy Scripture and with the Confessions of the Fathers. If you find that we are speaking contrary to Scripture, then do not listen to us! But if you find that we are taking our stand upon Scripture, then let no fear or temptation keep you from treading with us the path of faith and obedience to the Word of God, in order that God's people be of one mind upon earth and that we in faith experience what he himself has said: "I will never leave you, nor forsake you." Therefore, "Fear not, little flock, for it is your Father's good pleasure to give you the kingdom."

II. Theological Declaration Concerning the Present Situation of the German Evangelical Church

8.05 According to the opening words of its constitution of July 11, 1933, the German Evangelical Church is a federation of Confessional Churches that grew our of the Reformation and that enjoy equal rights. The theological basis for the unification of these Churches is laid down in Article 1 and Article 2(1) of the constitution of the German Evangelical Church that was recognized by the Reich Government on July 14, 1933:

> Article 1. The inviolable foundation of the German Evangelical Church is the gospel of Jesus Christ as it is attested for us in Holy Scripture and brought to light again in the Confessions of the Reformation. The full powers that the Church needs for its mission are hereby determined and limited.
>
> Article 2 (1). The German Evangelical Church is divided into member Churches Landeskirchen).

8.06 We, the representatives of Lutheran, Reformed, and United Churches, of free synods, Church assemblies, and parish organizations united in the Confessional Synod of the German Evangelical Church, declare that we stand together on the ground of the German Evangelical Church as a federation of German Confessional Churches. We are bound together by the confession of the one Lord of the one, holy, catholic, and apostolic Church.

8.07 We publicly declare before all evangelical Churches in Germany that what they hold in common in this Confession is grievously imperiled, and with it the unity of the German Evangelical Church. It is threatened by the teaching methods and actions of the ruling Church party of the "German Christians" and of the Church administration carried on by them. These have become more and more apparent during the first year of the existence of the German Evangelical Church. This threat consists in the fact that the theological basis, in which the German Evangelical Church is united, has been continually and systematically thwarted and rendered ineffective by alien principles, on the part of the leaders and spokesmen of the "German Christians" as well as on the part of the Church administration. When these principles are held to be valid, then, according to all the Confessions in force among us, the Church ceases to be the Church and the German Evangelical Church, as a federation of Confessional Churches, becomes intrinsically impossible.

8.08 As members of Lutheran, Reformed, and United Churches we may and must speak with one voice in this matter today. Precisely because we want to be and to remain faithful to our various Confessions, we may not keep silent, since we believe that we have been given a common message to utter in a time of common need and temptation. We commend to God what this may mean for the interrelations of the Confessional Churches.

8.09 In view of the errors of the "German Christians" of the present Reich Church government which are devastating the Church and also therefore breaking up the unity of the German Evangelical Church, we confess the following evangelical truths:

8.10 - 1. "I am the way, and the truth, and the life; no one comes to the Father, but by me." (John 14.6). "Truly, truly, I say to you, he who does not enter the sheepfold by the door, but climbs in by another way, that man is a thief and a robber. . . . I am the door; if anyone enters by me, he will be saved." (John 10:1, 9.)

8.11 Jesus Christ, as he is attested for us in Holy Scripture, is the one Word of God which we have to hear and which we have to trust and obey in life and in death.

8.12 We reiect the false doctrine, as though the church could and would have to acknowledge as a source of its proclamation, apart from and besides this one Word of God, still other events and powers, figures and truths, as God's revelation.

8.13 - 2. "Christ Jesus, whom God has made our wisdom, our righteousness and sanctification and redemption." (1 Cor. 1:30.)

8.14 As Jesus Christ is God's assurance of the forgiveness of all our sins, so, in the same way and with the same seriousness he is also God's mighty claim upon our whole life. Through him befalls us a joyful deliverance from the godless fetters of this world for a free, grateful service to his creatures.

8.15 We reiect the false doctrine, as though there were areas of our life in which we would not belong to Jesus Christ, but to other lords--areas in which we would not need justification and sanctification through him.

8.16 - 3. "Rather, speaking the truth in love, we are to grow up in every way into him who is the head, into Christ, from whom the whole body [is] joined and knit together." (Eph. 4:15,16.)

8.17 The Christian Church is the congregation of the brethren in which Jesus Christ acts presently as the Lord in Word and sacrament through the Holy Spirit. As the Church of pardoned sinners, it has to testify in the midst of a sinful world, with its faith as with its obedience, with its message as with its order, that it is solely his property, and that it lives and wants to live solely from his comfort and from his direction in the expectation of his
appearance.

8.18 We reject the false doctrine, as though the Church were permitted to abandon the form of its message and order to its own pleasure or to changes in prevailing ideological and political convictions.

8.19 - 4. "You know that the rulers of the Gentiles lord it over them, and their great men excercise authority over them. It shall not be so among you; but whoever would be great among you must be your srvant." (Matt. 20:25,26.)

8.20 The various offices in the Church do not establish a dominion of some over the others; on the contrary, they are for the excercise of the ministry entrusted to and enjoined upon the whole congregation.

8.21 We reject the false doctrine, as though the Church, apart from this ministry, could and were permitted to give itself, or allow to be given to it, special leaders vested with ruling powers.

8.22 - 5. "Fear God. Honor the emperor." (1 Peter 2:17.)
Scripture tells us that, in the as yet unredeemed world in which the Church also exists, the State has by divine appointment the task of providing for justice and peace. [It fulfills this task] by means of the threat and exercise of force, according to the measure of human judgment and human ability. The Church acknowledges the benefit of this divine appointment in gratitude and reverence before him. It calls to mind the Kingdom of God, God's commandment and righteousness, and thereby the responsibility both of rulers and of the ruled. It trusts and obeys the power of the Word by which God upholds all things.

8.23 We reject the false doctrine, as though the State, over and beyond its special commision, should and could become the single and totalitarian order of human life, thus fulfilling the Church's vocation as well.

8.24 We reject the false doctrine, as though the Church, over and beyond its special commission, should and could appropriate the characteristics, the tasks, and the dignity of the State, thus itself becoming an organ of the State.

8.25 - 6. "Lo, I am with you always, to the close of the age." (Matt. 28:20.) "The word of God is not fettered." (2 Tim. 2:9.)

8.26 The Church's commission, upon which its freedom is founded, consists in delivering the message of the free grace of God to all people in Christ's stead, and therefore in the ministry of his own Word and work through sermon and sacrament.

8.27 We reject the false doctrine, as though the Church in human arrogance could place the Word and work of the Lord in the service of any arbitrarily chosen desires, purposes, and plans.

8.28 The Confessional Synod of the German Evangelical Church declares that it sees in the acknowledgment of these truths and in the rejection of these errors the indispensable theological basis of the German Evangelical Church as a federation of Confessional Churches. It invites all who are able to accept its declaration to be mindful of these theological principles in their decisions in Church politics. It entreats all whom it concerns to return to the unity of faith, love, and hope.

READER

ANSELM: A MEDITATION ON HUMAN REDEMPTION WRITTEN 1099AD

TOP TEN THEOLOGIANS

0 Christian soul, soul raised up from grievous death, soul re- deemed and freed by the blood of God from wretched bondage: arouse your mind, remember your resurrection, contemplate your redemption and liberation. Consider anew where and what the strength of your salvation is, spend time in meditating upon this strength, delight in reflecting upon it. Shake off your disinclination, constrain yourself, strive with your mind toward this end. Taste the goodness of your Redeemer, be af lame with love for your Savior, chew His words as a honey-comb, suck out their flavor, which is sweeter than honey, swallow their health-giving sweet- ness. Chew by thinking, suck by understanding, swallow by loving and rejoicing. Rejoice in chewing, be glad in sucking, delight in swallowing.

Where, then, and what is the strength and might of your sal- vation? Assuredly, Christ has resurrected you. That Good Samar- itan has healed you, that Good Friend has redeemed and freed you by [sacrificing] His own soul [life]. Yes, it was Christ. Therefore, the strength of Christ is the strength of your salvation. Where is the strength of Christ? Surely horns are in His hands; there His strength is hidden. Horns are indeed in His hands because His hands were nailed to the arms of the cross. But what strength can there be in such great weakness, what sublimity in such great humiliation, what worthy of reverence in such great contempt? But surely because it is [disguised] in weakness it is something hidden, because [veiled] in humiliation it is something concealed, because [covered with] contempt it is something unseen. 0 hidden might! A man appended to a cross suspends the eternal death impend- ing over the human race; a man fastened to a cross unfastens a world affixed to endless death! 0 concealed power! A man con- demned with thieves saves men condemned with demons; a man stretched out on a cross draws all things unto Himself! 0 unseen strength! One soul yielded up in the torment [of crucifixion] draws countless souls [from the torments of] Hell; a man undergoes bodily death and abolishes spiritual death!

Why did you, 0 good Lord, gracious Redeemer, mighty Savior, why did You veil such great strength with such great lowliness? Was it in order to deceive the Devil, who by deceiving man thrust him forth from Paradise? Surely, Truth deceives no one; someone deceives himself if he does not know the truth, if he does not be- lieve it. He deceives himself if, seeing the truth, he hates it or de- spises it; thus, Truth deceives no one. Well, then, [did You con- ceal Your power] in order that the Devil might deceive himself? Surely, just as Truth deceives no one, so it does not intend that anyone deceive himself, (even though we do say that Truth intends this when Truth permits it to occur). For You did not assume a human nature in order to conceal what was known about You but in order to reveal what was unknown about You. You said that You were truly divine and truly human, and You demonstrated this fact through Your works. The hiddenness was unavoidable, not delib- erate. The reason that the event occurred as it did was not in order to be hidden, but in order to be performed in the right way. [It happened in that way] not in order to deceive anyone, but in order to be done as was fitting. If this event is called concealed, then it is called so only because it is not revealed to everyone. Al- though Truth does not manifest itself to everyone, it does not withhold itself from anyone. Therefore, 0 Lord, in becoming incarnate it was not Your purpose to deceive anyone or to cause anyone to deceive himself. You remained in the truth in every respect so that You might do what had to be done in the way it had to be done. Hence, let anyone who has deceived himself regarding Your truth complain not about You but about the falsehood in himself.

Did the Devil justly have against God or against man some claim which obliged God to act against him on man's behalf in this manner [i.e., by incarnation] before acting by open force, so that when the Devil unjustly killed a just man [Jesus] he would justly lose the power he was holding over unjust men? But surely God did not owe the Devil anything except punishment. Nor did man [owe the Devil anything] except requital, so that just as man by sin- ning permitted himself easily to be defeated by the Devil, so by keeping justice intact even on pain of death, he would defeat the Devil. But even this [conquering of the Devil] man owed only to God; for he sinned against God, not against the Devil. Nor did he belong to the Devil; rather both man and the Devil belonged to God. But even in vexing man the Devil acted not out of zeal for justice but out of zeal for iniquity. God did not command [this vexation]; He [only] permitted it. God's justice, not the Devil's, required [man's punishment]. Therefore, the Devil had no claim which obliged God to conceal His power from him or to postpone its use against him in order to secure man's salvation.

Did some necessity compel the Most High thus to humble Himself as He did; was the Almighty compelled to toil in order to accomplish so great a thing? But all necessity and impossibility are subject to His will. Indeed, what He wills must occur; and what He does not will cannot occur. Therefore, He acted of His own will; and because His will is always good, He acted out of goodness alone. God did not need to secure man's salvation in the way He did; but human nature needed in that way to make satisfaction to God. God did not need to suffer such troubles; but man needed to be reconciled in this way. God did not need thus to humble Himself; but man needed in this way to be rescued from the depth of Hell. The Divine Nature did not need, and was not able, to be abased or to toil. It was necessary for human nature to do all these things in order to be restored to that end for which it was created. But neither human nature nor anyone other than God Himself was able to accomplish these things. Man is not restored to that end for which he was made unless he attains to the likeness of those angels in whom there is no sin. This attainment cannot possibly occur unless the remission of all sins is obtained. And remission occurs only by means of an antecedent complete satisfaction.

This satisfaction ought to be such that the sinner or someone on his behalf gives to God something of his own which is not owed—something which exceeds everything that is not God. For to sin is to dishonor God; and man ought not to dishonor God even if [as a consequence] it were necessary for everything that is other than God to be destroyed. Therefore, without doubt, un- changing truth and clear reason demand that the sinner give to God, in place of the honor stolen, something greater than that for which he ought not to have dishonored God. But human nature by itself did not have this payment. And without the required satisfaction human nature could not be reconciled, lest Divine Justice leave a sin unreckoned-with in His kingdom. Therefore, Divine Goodness gave assistance. The Son of God assumed a human nature into His own person, so that in this person He was the God- man, who possessed what exceeded not only every being which is not God but also every debt which sinners ought to pay. And since He owed nothing for Himself, He paid this sum for others who did not have what they were indebted to pay.

For the life of that man [Jesus] is more precious than everything that is not God, and it surpasses every debt owed by sinners as satisfaction. For if putting Him to death [is a sin which] surpass- es the multitude and magnitude of all conceivable sins which are not against the person of God, clearly His life is a good greater than the evil of all those sins which are not against the person of God. To honor the Father, that man [Jesus]—although not oblig- ed to die, because not a sinner—freely gave something of His own when He permitted His life to be taken from Him for the sake of justice. [He permitted this] in order to show to all others by example that they ought not to forsake the justice of God even because of death, which inevitably they are obliged to undergo at some time or other; for He who was not obliged [to undergo] death and who, having kept justice, could have avoided death, freely and for the sake of justice endured death, which was in- flicted upon Him. Thus, in that man human nature freely and out of no obligation gave to God something its own, so that it might redeem itself in others in whom it did not have what it, as a result of indebtedness, was required to pay.

In all these occurrences the divine nature [in the God-man] was not abased but the human nature was exalted. The divine nature was not weakened but the human nature was mercifully assisted. Moreover, in that man the human nature did not suffer anything out of necessity but suffered only voluntarily. That man did not succumb to any compelling force; but out of voluntary goodness, and for the honor of God and the benefit of other men, He bore mercifully and laudably what was inflicted upon Him out of malev- olence. The requirement of obedience did not constrain Him, but His mighty wisdom disposed Him. For the Father by His command did not compel that man to die, but that man freely performed what He knew would please the Father and would be helpful to [other] men. The Father could not compel Him with respect to that which He ought not to have required of Him. The very great honor which the Son with such a good will freely offered to the Father could not fail to please the Father. Therefore, when the Son freely willed to do what he knew would please the Father, in this way He displayed free obedience to the Father. Furthermore, since the Father gave the Son this good will—a will nonetheless free [i.e., even though bestowed by another]—the Son is rightly said to have received this will as the Father's command. Therefore, in this way, the Son was obedient to the Father even unto death; and He did as the Father gave Him command- ment; and He drank of the chalice which the Father gave Him.

For this is human nature's perfect and completely free obedience when [in Jesus] it freely sub- mitted its own free will to the will of God and when it freely and without any constraint exercised the good will which it had re- ceived.

Thus, that man redeemed all other men when what He freely gave to God God reckoned for the debt they owed. Through this payment a man is redeemed from his faults not once only; rather, he is received as often as he returns again in worthy penitence. Nevertheless, this peni- tence is not promised to the sinner. But since [payment] was made on the cross, our Christ has redeemed us through the cross. Therefore, those who will to come to this grace with worthy affection are saved; but those who despise this grace are justly condemned because they do not pay the debt they owe.

Behold, 0 Christian soul, this is the strength of your salvation, this is the basis of your freedom, this is the cost of your redemption. You were in bondage, but in this way you have been redeemed. You were a servant, but in this way you have been set free. You are an exile who in this manner has been led back home, someone lost who has been found, someone dead who has been revived. 0 man, let your heart feed upon these thoughts, let it chew continually upon them, let it suck upon them and swallow them whenever your mouth receives the flesh and blood of your Redeemer. In this life make these thoughts your daily bread, your nourishment, your provision. For through these thoughts and only through them will you remain in Christ and Christ in you; and only through them will your joy be full in the life to come.

But You, 0 Lord, You who underwent death so that I might live, how can I rejoice over my freedom, which results only from Your bonds ? How can I be glad about my salvation when it comes only because of Your sorrows ? How can I delight in my life, which is secured only by Your death? Shall I rejoice over what You have suffered and over the cruelty of those who have inflicted these sufferings upon You? For had they not done so, You would not have suffered; and had You not suffered, I would not have possessed these goods. On the other hand, if I grieve over Your sufferings, how can I delight in these goods for the sake of which Your sufferings occurred and which would not have existed had Your suf- ferings not occurred? But surely those wicked men were not able to do anything except because You freely permitted it; nor did You suffer except because You graciously willed to. And so, I ought to detest the cruelty of those wicked men, to imitate Your sufferings and death by grieving over them, to love Your gracious will by giving thanks, and in these ways to exult, free of distress, over the goods conferred upon me.

Therefore, 0 insignificant man, leave the cruelty of these men to the judgment of God, and meditate upon what you owe your Savior. Consider what your condition was and what has been done for you; reflect upon how worthy of love is He who has done this for you. Behold your need and His goodness; see what thanks you may give and how much you owe to His love. You were in dark- ness, on slippery footing, on the downward road to the chaos of Hell, from which there is no return. An enormous lead-like weight hanging from your neck was causing you to stoop. A burden too heavy for your back was pressing upon you. Invisible foes were urging you onward with all their fury. Such was your helplessness and you did not know it, because you were conceived and born in that condition. 0 how desperate was that condition! To what a destination these forces were impelling you! Let the memory of it terrify you; tremble at the very thought!

0 good Lord Jesus Christ, in this state I was neither seeking nor deliberating; but like the sun You shined forth upon me and showed me my plight. You cast off the leaden weight which was drawing me down; You removed the burden which was pushing me down; You repelled the foes who were impelling me onward, ward- ing them off for my sake. You called me by a new name which You derived from Your name. Stooped over as I was, You stood me upright to face You, saying: "Be confident, I have redeemed You and given my soul [life] for you. If you will cling to me, you will escape the evils of your former condition and will not fall into the abyss toward which you were hastening; instead, I will lead you to my kingdom and will make you an heir of God and a joint-heir with me." Thereafter, You brought me under Your protection so that nothing might harm my soul against its will. And, lo, although I did not yet cling to You as You had exhorted, You still did not permit me to fall into Hell. But You awaited the time when I would cling to You and You would do what You had promised.

Yes, 0 Lord, such was my condition, and these things You have done for me. I was in darkness because I knew nothing—not even my very self. I was on slippery footing because I was weak and prone to sin. I was on the downward road to the chaos of Hell because in our first parents I had descended from justice to injustice (and injustice leads down to Hell), from happiness to the misery of this life (from which one falls into eternal misery). The weight of original sin was dragging me down; the unbearable burden of God's judgment was pushing me down; demons hostile to me were urging me on, as strenuously as they could, so that they might make me deserving of even greater condemnation because of added sins.
Being thus destitute of all help, I was illumined by You and shown my condition. For while I was not yet able to know my condition You taught all these things to others on my behalf; and later You taught these same things to me even before I inquired. You cast aside the leaden weight, the heavy burden, and the impelling foes, for You removed the sin in which I had been conceived and born, You removed also the condemnation of this sin, and You forbade evil spirits to constrain my

soul. You gave me the name Christian, which derives from Your own name; through Your name I confess, and You acknowledge, that I am among the redeemed. You stood me upright and lifted me to the knowledge and love of You. You made me confident of my soul's salvation, for which You gave Your soul [life]. You promised me Your glory if I would follow You. And, behold, while I was not yet following You, as You had exhorted, but was even continuing to commit manifold sins, which You had proscribed, You awaited the time when I would follow You and You would give what You had promised.

Consider, 0 my soul, peer into, 0 my inmost being, how much my entire substance owes to Him. Yes, 0 Lord, because You cre- ated me I owe my entire self to Your love; because You redeemed me I owe my entire self; because Your promises are so great I owe my entire self. Indeed, I owe to Your love much more than myself—as much more as You are greater than I, for whom You gave Yourself and to whom You promise Yourself. I pray You, 0 Lord, make me to taste by loving, what I taste by knowing. Let me sense by affection what I sense by understanding. I owe more than my entire self, but I have no more to give; of myself I am not even able to give my entire self. 0 Lord, draw my whole self into Your love. The whole of what I am is Yours through Your creating; make it Yours through its loving commitment.

Behold, 0 Lord, my heart is before You. It strains, but can do nothing of itself; do, 0 Lord, what it cannot do. Receive me into the inner chamber of Your love. I ask, I seek, I knock. You who cause me to ask, cause me also to receive. You grant that I seek; grant that I also may find. You teach me to knock; open to me when I knock. If You deny to him who asks, to whom do You then give ? If he who seeks seeks in vain, who then finds? If You keep [the chamber door] closed for one who knocks, for whom do You open ? If You withhold Your love from one who implores, what do You give to one who does not implore? You cause me to desire; cause me also to obtain. 0 my soul, cling to Him, cling tenaciously. Good Lord, 0 good Lord, do not scorn my soul, which faints out of hunger for Your love. Revive my soul; let Your tender kindness satisfy it, let Your affection make it fat, let Your love fill it. Let Your love seize my whole being; let it possess me com- pletely, because together with the Father and the Holy Spirit You are the only God, blessed forever. Amen.

READER

THOMAS AQUINAS: SUMMA THEOLOGICA EXCERPT

TOP TEN THEOLOGIANS

Whether, besides philosophy, any further doctrine is required?

Objection 1: It seems that, besides philosophical science, we have no need of any further knowledge. For man should not seek to know what is above reason: "Seek not the things that are too high for thee" (Ecclus. 3:22). But whatever is not above reason is fully treated of in philosophical science. Therefore any other knowledge besides philosophical science is superfluous.

Objection 2: Further, knowledge can be concerned only with being, for nothing can be known, save what is true; and all that is, is true. But everything that is, is treated of in philosophical science---even God Himself; so that there is a part of philosophy called theology, or the divine science, as Aristotle has proved (Metaph. vi). Therefore, besides philosophical science, there is no need of any further knowledge.

On the contrary, It is written (2 Tim. 3:16): "All Scripture, inspired of God is profitable to teach, to reprove, to correct, to instruct in justice." Now Scripture, inspired of God, is no part of philosophical science, which has been built up by human reason. Therefore it is useful that besides philosophical science, there should be other knowledge, i.e. inspired of God.

I answer that, It was necessary for man's salvation that there should be a knowledge revealed by God besides philosophical science built up by human reason. Firstly, indeed, because man is directed to God, as to an end that surpasses the grasp of his reason: "The eye hath not seen, O God, besides Thee, what things Thou hast prepared for them that wait for Thee" (Is. 66:4). But the end must first be known by men who are to direct their thoughts and actions to the end. Hence it was necessary for the salvation of man that certain truths which exceed human reason should be made known to him by divine revelation. Even as regards those truths about God which human reason could have discovered, it was necessary that man should be taught by a divine revelation; because the truth about God such as reason could discover, would only be known by a few, and that after a long time, and with the admixture of many errors. Whereas man's whole salvation, which is in God, depends upon the knowledge of this truth. Therefore, in order that the salvation of men might be brought about more fitly and more surely, it was necessary that they should be taught divine truths by divine revelation. It was therefore necessary that besides philosophical science built up by reason, there should be a sacred science learned through revelation.

Reply to Objection 1: Although those things which are beyond man's knowledge may not be sought for by man through his reason, nevertheless, once they are revealed by God, they must be accepted by faith. Hence the sacred text continues, "For many things are shown to thee above the understanding of man" (Ecclus. 3:25). And in this, the sacred science consists.

Reply to Objection 2: Sciences are differentiated according to the various means through which knowledge is obtained. For the astronomer and the physicist both may prove the same conclusion: that the earth, for instance, is round: the astronomer by means of mathematics (i.e. abstracting from matter), but the physicist by means of matter itself. Hence there is no reason why those things which may be learned from philosophical science, so far as they can be known by natural reason, may not also be taught us by another science so far as they fall within revelation. Hence theology included in sacred doctrine differs in kind from that theology which is part of philosophy.

Whether God is truth?

Objection 1: It seems that God is not truth. For truth consists in the intellect composing and dividing. But in God there is not composition and division. Therefore in Him there is not truth.

Objection 2: Further, truth, according to Augustine (De Vera Relig. xxxvi) is a "likeness to the principle." But in God there is no likeness to a principle. Therefore in God there is not truth.

Objection 3: Further, whatever is said of God, is said of Him as of the first cause of all things; thus the being of God is the cause of all being; and His goodness the cause of all good. If therefore there is truth in God, all truth will be from Him. But it is true that someone sins. Therefore this will be from God; which is evidently false.

On the contrary, Our Lord says, "I am the Way, the Truth, and the Life" (Jn. 14:6).

I answer that, As said above (A[1]), truth is found in the intellect according as it apprehends a thing as it is; and in things according as they have being conformable to an intellect. This is to the greatest degree found in God. For His being is not only conformed to His intellect, but it is the very act of His intellect; and His act of understanding is the measure and cause of every other being and of every other intellect, and He Himself is His own existence and act of understanding. Whence it follows not only that truth is in Him, but that He is truth itself, and the sovereign and first truth.

Reply to Objection 1: Although in the divine intellect there is neither composition nor division, yet in His simple act of intelligence He judges of all things and knows all things complex; and thus there is truth in His intellect.

Reply to Objection 2: The truth of our intellect is according to its conformity with its principle, that is to say, to the things from which it receives knowledge. The truth also of things is according to their conformity with their principle, namely, the divine intellect. Now this cannot be said, properly speaking, of divine truth; unless perhaps in so far as truth is appropriated to the Son, Who has a principle. But if we speak of divine truth in its essence, we cannot understand this unless the affirmative must be resolved into the negative, as when one says: "the Father is of Himself, because He is not from another." Similarly, the divine truth can be called a "likeness to the principle," inasmuch as His existence is not dissimilar to His intellect.

Reply to Objection 3: Not-being and privation have no truth of themselves, but only in the apprehension of the intellect. Now all apprehension of the intellect is from God. Hence all the truth that exists in the statement---"that a person commits fornication is true"---is entirely from God. But to argue, "Therefore that this person fornicates is from God", is a fallacy of Accident.

READER

RESOLUTIONS OF JONTHAN EDWARDS 1723AD

TOP TEN THEOLOGIANS

Being sensible that I am unable to do anything without God's help, I do humbly entreat him by his grace to enable me to keep these Resolutions, so far as they are agreeable to his will, for Christ's sake.

Remember to read over these Resolutions once a week.

Overall Life Mission

1. Resolved, that I will do whatsoever I think to be most to God's glory, and my own good, profit and pleasure, in the whole of my duration, without any consideration of the time, whether now, or never so many myriad's of ages hence. Resolved to do whatever I think to be my duty and most for the good and advantage of mankind in general. Resolved to do this, whatever difficulties I meet with, how many and how great soever.

2. Resolved, to be continually endeavoring to find out some new invention and contrivance to promote the aforementioned things.

3. Resolved, if ever I shall fall and grow dull, so as to neglect to keep

any part of these Resolutions, to repent of all I can remember, when I come to myself again.

4. Resolved, never to do any manner of thing, whether in soul or body, less or more, but what tends to the glory of God; nor be, nor suffer it, if I can avoid it.

6. Resolved, to live with all my might, while I do live.

22. Resolved, to endeavor to obtain for myself as much happiness, in the other world, as I possibly can, with all the power; might, vigor, and vehemence, yea violence, I am capable of, or can bring myself to exert, in any way that can be thought of.

62. Resolved, never to do anything but duty; and then according to Eph. 6:6-8, do it willingly and cheerfully as unto the Lord, and not to man; "knowing that whatever good thing any man doth, the same shall he receive of the Lord." June 25 and July 13, 1723.

Good Works

11. Resolved, when I think of any theorem in divinity to be solved, immediately to do what I can towards solving it, if circumstances don't hinder.

13. Resolved, to be endeavoring to find out fit objects of charity and liberality.

69. Resolved, always to do that, which I shall wish I had done when I see others do it. Aug. 11, 1723.

Time Management

5. Resolved, never to lose one moment of time; but improve it the most profitable way I possibly can.

7. Resolved, never to do anything, which I should be afraid to do, if it were the last hour of my life.

17. Resolved, that I will live so as I shall wish I had done when I come to die.

18. Resolved, to live so at all times, as I think is best in my devout frames, and when I have clearest notions of things of the gospel, and another world.

19. Resolved, never to do anything, which I should be afraid to do, if I expected it would not be above an hour, before I should hear the last trump.

37. Resolved, to inquire every night, as I am going to bed, wherein I have been negligent, what sin I have committed, and wherein I have denied myself: also at the end of every week, month and year. Dec. 22 and 26, 1722.

40. Resolved, to inquire every night, before I go to bed, whether I have acted in the best way I possibly could, with respect to eating and drinking. Jan. 7, 1723.

41. Resolved, to ask myself at the end of every day, week, month and year, wherein I could possibly in any respect have done better. Jan. 11, 1723.

50.Resolved, I will act so as I think I shall judge would have been best, and most prudent, when I come into the future world. July 5, 1723.

51.Resolved, that I will act so, in every respect, as I think I shall wish I had done, if I should at last be damned. July 8, 1723.

52. I frequently hear persons in old age say how they would live, if they were to live their lives over again: Resolved, that I will live just so as I can think I shall wish I had done, supposing I live to old age. July 8, 1723.

55. Resolved, to endeavor to my utmost to act as I can think I should do, if I had already seen the happiness of heaven, and hell torments. July 8, 1723.

61. Resolved, that I will not give way to that listlessness which I find unbends and relaxes my mind from being fully and fixedly set on religion, whatever excuse I may have for it-that what my listlessness inclines me to do, is best to be done, etc. May 21, and July 13, 1723.

Relationships

14. Resolved, never to do anything out of revenge.

15. Resolved, never to suffer the least motions of anger to irrational beings.

16. Resolved, never to speak evil of anyone, so that it shall tend to his dishonor, more or less, upon no account except for some real good.

31. Resolved, never to say anything at all against anybody, but when it is perfectly agreeable to the highest degree of Christian honor, and of love to mankind, agreeable to the lowest humility, and sense of my own faults and failings, and agreeable to the golden rule; often, when I have said anything against anyone, to bring it to, and try it strictly by the test of this Resolution.

33. Resolved, always to do what I can towards making, maintaining, establishing and preserving peace, when it can be without over-balancing detriment in other respects. Dec. 26, 1722.

34. Resolved, in narration's never to speak anything but the pure and simple verity.

36. Resolved, never to speak evil of any, except I have some particular good call for it. Dec. 19, 1722.

46. Resolved, never to allow the least measure of any fretting uneasiness at my father or mother. Resolved to suffer no effects of it, so much as in the least alteration of speech, or motion of my eve: and to be especially careful of it, with respect to any of our family.

58. Resolved, not only to refrain from an air of dislike, fretfulness, and anger in conversation, but to exhibit an air of love, cheerfulness and benignity. May 27, and July 13, 1723.

59. Resolved, when I am most conscious of provocations to ill nature and anger, that I will strive most to feel and act good-naturedly; yea, at such times, to manifest good nature, though I think that in other respects it would be disadvantageous, and so as would be imprudent at other times. May 12, July 2, and July 13.

66. Resolved, that I will endeavor always to keep a benign aspect, and air of acting and speaking in all places, and in all companies, except it should so happen that duty requires otherwise.

70. Let there be something of benevolence, in all that I speak.

Suffering

9. Resolved, to think much on all occasions of my own dying, and of the common circumstances which attend death.

10. Resolved, when I feel pain, to think of the pains of martyrdom, and of hell.

67. Resolved, after afflictions, to inquire, what I am the better for them, what good I have got by them, and what I might have got by them.

57. Resolved, when I fear misfortunes and adversities, to examine whether ~ have done my duty, and resolve to do it; and let it be just as providence orders it, I will as far as I can, be concerned about nothing but my duty and my sin. June 9, and July 13, 1723.

Character

8. Resolved, to act, in all respects, both speaking and doing, as if nobody had been so vile as I, and as if I had committed the same sins, or had the same infirmities or failings as others; and that I will let the knowledge of their failings promote nothing but shame in myself, and

prove only an occasion of my confessing my own sins and misery to God.

12. Resolved, if I take delight in it as a gratification of pride, or vanity, or on any such account, immediately to throw it by.

21. Resolved, never to do anything, which if I should see in another, I should count a just occasion to despise him for, or to think any way the more meanly of him.

32. Resolved, to be strictly and firmly faithful to my trust, that that in Prov. 20:6, "A faithful man who can find?" may not be partly fulfilled in me.

47. Resolved, to endeavor to my utmost to deny whatever is not most agreeable to a good, and universally sweet and benevolent, quiet, peaceable, contented, easy, compassionate, generous, humble, meek, modest, submissive, obliging, diligent and industrious, charitable, even, patient, moderate, forgiving, sincere temper; and to do at all times what such a temper would lead me to. Examine strictly every week, whether I have done so. Sabbath morning. May 5, 1723.

54. Whenever I hear anything spoken in conversation of any person, if I think it would be praiseworthy in me, Resolved to endeavor to imitate it. July 8, 1723.

63. On the supposition, that there never was to be but one individual in the world, at any one time, who was properly a complete Christian, in all respects of a right stamp, having Christianity always shining in its true luster, and appearing excellent and lovely, from whatever part and under whatever character viewed: Resolved, to act just as I would do, if I strove with all my might to be that one, who should live in my time. Jan. 14 and July 3, 1723.

27. Resolved, never willfully to omit anything, except the omission be for the glory of God; and frequently to examine my omissions.

39. Resolved, never to do anything that I so much question the lawfulness of, as that I intend, at the same time, to consider and examine

afterwards, whether it be lawful or no; except I as much question the lawfulness of the omission.

20. Resolved, to maintain the strictest temperance in eating and drinking.

Spiritual Life

Assurance

25. Resolved, to examine carefully, and constantly, what that one thing in me is, which causes me in the least to doubt of the love of God; and to direct all my forces against it.

26. Resolved, to cast away such things, as I find do abate my assurance.

48. Resolved, constantly, with the utmost niceness and diligence, and the strictest scrutiny, to be looking into the state of my soul, that I may know whether I have truly an interest in Christ or no; that when I come to die, I may not have any negligence respecting this to repent of. May 26, 1723.

49. Resolved, that this never shall be, if I can help it.

The Scriptures

28. Resolved, to study the Scriptures so steadily, constantly and frequently, as that I may find, and plainly perceive myself to grow in the knowledge of the same.

Prayer

29. Resolved, never to count that a prayer, nor to let that pass as a prayer, nor that as a petition of a prayer, which is so made, that I cannot hope that God will answer it; nor that as a confession, which I cannot hope God will accept.

64. Resolved, when I find those "groanings which cannot be uttered"

(Rom. 8:26), of which the Apostle speaks, and those "breakings of soul for the longing it hath," of which the Psalmist speaks, Psalm 119:20, that I will promote them to the utmost of my power, and that I will not be wear', of earnestly endeavoring to vent my desires, nor of the repetitions of such earnestness. July 23, and August 10, 1723.

The Lord's Day

38. Resolved, never to speak anything that is ridiculous, sportive, or matter of laughter on the Lord's day. Sabbath evening, Dec. 23, 1722.

Vivification of Righteousness

30. Resolved, to strive to my utmost every week to be brought higher in religion, and to a higher exercise of grace, than I was the week before.

42. Resolved, frequently to renew the dedication of myself to God, which was made at my baptism; which I solemnly renewed, when I was received into the communion of the church; and which I have solemnly re-made this twelfth day of January, 1722-23.

43. Resolved, never henceforward, till I die, to act as if I were any way my own, but entirely and altogether God's, agreeable to what is to be found in Saturday, January 12, 1723.

44- Resolved, that no other end but religion, shall have any influence at all on any of my actions; and that no action shall be, in the least circumstance, any otherwise than the religious end will carry it. Jan.12, 1723.

45. Resolved, never to allow any pleasure or grief, joy or sorrow, nor any affection at all, nor any degree of affection, nor any circumstance relating to it, but what helps religion. Jan. 12-13, 1723.

Mortification of Sin and Self Examination

23. Resolved, frequently to take some deliberate action, which seems most unlikely to be done, for the glory of God, and trace it back to the original intention, designs and ends of it; and if I find it not to be for God's glory, to repute it as a breach of the 4th Resolution.

24. Resolved, whenever I do any conspicuously evil action, to trace it back, till I come to the original cause; and then both carefully endeavor to do so no more, and to fight and pray with all my might against the original of it.

35. Resolved, whenever I so much question whether I have done my duty, as that my quiet and calm is thereby disturbed, to set it down, and also how the question was resolved. Dec. 18, 1722.

60. Resolved, whenever my feelings begin to appear in the least out of order, when I am conscious of the least uneasiness within, or the least irregularity without, I will then subject myself to the strictest examination. July 4 and 13, 1723.

68. Resolved, to confess frankly to myself all that which I find in myself, either infirmity or sin; and, if it be what concerns religion, also to confess the whole case to God, and implore needed help. July 23 and August 10, 1723.

56. Resolved, never to give over, nor in the least to slacken my fight with my corruptions, however unsuccessful I may be.

Communion with God

53. Resolved, to improve every opportunity, when I am in the best and happiest frame of mind, to cast and venture my soul on the Lord Jesus Christ, to trust and confide in him, and consecrate myself wholly to him; that from this I may have assurance of my safety, knowing that I confide in my Redeemer. July 8, 1723.

65. Resolved, very much to exercise myself in this all my life long,

viz. with the greatest openness I am capable of, to declare my ways to God, and lay open my soul to him: all my sins, temptations, difficulties, sorrows, fears, hopes, desires, and every thing, and every circumstance; according to Dr. Manton's 27th Sermon on Psalm 119. July 26 and Aug. 10, 1723.

Aug. 17, 1723

READER

ATHANASIUS ON THE INCARNATION EXCERPT - 318AD

TOP TEN THEOLOGIANS

The Divine Dilemma and Its Solution in the Incarnation

We saw in the last chapter that, because death and corruption were gaining ever firmer hold on them, the human race was in process of destruction. Man, who was created in God's image and in his possession of reason reflected the very Word Himself, was disappearing, and the work of God was being undone. The law of death, which followed from the Transgression, prevailed upon us, and from it there was no escape. The thing that was happening was in truth both monstrous and unfitting. It would, of course, have been unthinkable that God should go back upon His word and that man, having transgressed, should not die; but it was equally monstrous that beings which once had shared the nature of the Word should perish and turn back again into non-existence through corruption. It was unworthy of the goodness of God that creatures made by Him should be brought to nothing through the deceit wrought upon man by the devil; and it was supremely unfitting that the work of God in mankind should disappear, either through their own negligence or through the deceit of evil spirits. As, then, the creatures whom He had created reasonable, like the Word, were in fact perishing, and such noble works were on the road to ruin, what then was God, being Good, to do? Was He to let corruption and death have their way with them? In that case, what was the use of having made them in the beginning? Surely it would have been better never to have been created at all than, having been created, to be neglected and perish; and, besides that, such indifference to the ruin of His own work before His very eyes would argue not goodness in God but limitation, and that far more than if He had never created men at all. It was impossible, therefore, that God should leave man to be carried off by corruption, because it would be unfitting and unworthy of Himself.

(7) Yet, true though this is, it is not the whole matter. As we have already noted, it was unthinkable that God, the Father of Truth, should go back upon His word regarding death in order to ensure our continued existence. He could not falsify Himself; what, then, was God to do? Was He to demand repentance from men for their transgression? You might say that that was worthy of God, and argue further that, as through the Transgression they became subject to corruption, so through repentance they might return to incorruption again. But repentance would not guard the Divine consistency, for, if death did not hold dominion over men, God would still remain untrue. Nor does repentance recall men from what is according to their nature; all that it does is to make them cease from sinning. Had it been a case of a trespass only, and not of a subsequent corruption, repentance would have been well enough; but when once transgression had begun men came under the power of the corruption proper to their nature and were bereft of the grace which belonged to them as creatures in the Image of God. No, repentance could not meet the case. What—or rather Who was it that was needed for such grace and such recall as we required? Who, save the Word of God Himself, Who also in the beginning had made all things out of nothing? His part it was, and His alone, both to bring again the corruptible to incorruption and to maintain for the Father His consistency of character with all. For He alone, being Word of the Father and above all, was in consequence both able to recreate all, and worthy to suffer on behalf of all and to be an ambassador for all with the Father.

(8) For this purpose, then, the incorporeal and incorruptible and immaterial Word of God entered our world. In one sense, indeed, He was not far from it before, for no part of creation had ever been without Him

Who, while ever abiding in union with the Father, yet fills all things that are. But now He entered the world in a new way, stooping to our level in His love and Self-revealing to us. He saw the reasonable race, the race of men that, like Himself, expressed the Father's Mind, wasting out of existence, and death reigning over all in corruption. He saw that corruption held us all the closer, because it was the penalty for the Transgression; He saw, too, how unthinkable it would be for the law to be repealed before it was fulfilled. He saw how unseemly it was that the very things of which He Himself was the Artificer should be disappearing. He saw how the surpassing wickedness of men was mounting up against them; He saw also their universal liability to death. All this He saw and, pitying our race, moved with compassion for our limitation, unable to endure that death should have the mastery, rather than that His creatures should perish and the work of His Father for us men come to nought, He took to Himself a body, a human body even as our own. Nor did He will merely to become embodied or merely to appear; had that been so, He could have revealed His divine majesty in some other and better way. No, He took our body, and not only so, but He took it directly from a spotless, stainless virgin, without the agency of human father—a pure body, untainted by intercourse with man. He, the Mighty One, the Artificer of all, Himself prepared this body in the virgin as a temple for Himself, and took it for His very own, as the instrument through which He was known and in which He dwelt. Thus, taking a body like our own, because all our bodies were liable to the corruption of death, He surrendered His body to death instead of all, and offered it to the Father. This He did out of sheer love for us, so that in His death all might die, and the law of death thereby be abolished because, having fulfilled in His body that for which it was appointed, it was thereafter voided of its power for men. This He did that He might turn again to incorruption men who had turned back to corruption, and make them alive through death by the appropriation of His body and by the grace of His resurrection. Thus He would make death to disappear from them as utterly as straw from fire.

(9) The Word perceived that corruption could not be got rid of otherwise than through death; yet He Himself, as the Word, being immortal and the Father's Son, was such as could not die. For this reason, therefore, He assumed a body capable of death, in order that it, through belonging to the Word Who is above all, might become in dying a

sufficient exchange for all, and, itself remaining incorruptible through His indwelling, might thereafter put an end to corruption for all others as well, by the grace of the resurrection. It was by surrendering to death the body which He had taken, as an offering and sacrifice free from every stain, that He forthwith abolished death for His human brethren by the offering of the equivalent. For naturally, since the Word of God was above all, when He offered His own temple and bodily instrument as a substitute for the life of all, He fulfilled in death all that was required. Naturally also, through this union of the immortal Son of God with our human nature, all men were clothed with incorruption in the promise of the resurrection. For the solidarity of mankind is such that, by virtue of the Word's indwelling in a single human body, the corruption which goes with death has lost its power over all. You know how it is when some great king enters a large city and dwells in one of its houses; because of his dwelling in that single house, the whole city is honored, and enemies and robbers cease to molest it. Even so is it with the King of all; He has come into our country and dwelt in one body amidst the many, and in consequence the designs of the enemy against mankind have been foiled and the corruption of death, which formerly held them in its power, has simply ceased to be. For the human race would have perished utterly had not the Lord and Savior of all, the Son of God, come among us to put an end to death.

(10) This great work was, indeed, supremely worthy of the goodness of God. A king who has founded a city, so far from neglecting it when through the carelessness of the inhabitants it is attacked by robbers, avenges it and saves it from destruction, having regard rather to his own honor than to the people's neglect. Much more, then, the Word of the All-good Father was not unmindful of the human race that He had called to be; but rather, by the offering of His own body He abolished the death which they had incurred, and corrected their neglect by His own teaching. Thus by His own power He restored the whole nature of man. The Savior's own inspired disciples assure us of this. We read in one place: " For the love of Christ constraineth us, because we thus judge that, if One died on behalf of all, then all died, and He died for all that we should no longer live unto ourselves, but unto Him who died and rose again from the dead, even our Lord Jesus Christ."[1] And again another says: "But we behold Him Who hath been made a little lower than the angels, even Jesus, because of the suffering of death crowned

with glory and honor, that by the grace of God He should taste of death on behalf of every man." The same writer goes on to point out why it was necessary for God the Word and none other to become Man: "For it became Him, for Whom are all things and through Whom are all things, in bringing many sons unto glory, to make the Author of their salvation perfect through suffering.[2] He means that the rescue of mankind from corruption was the proper part only of Him Who made them in the beginning. He points out also that the Word assumed a human body, expressly in order that He might offer it in sacrifice for other like bodies: "Since then the children are sharers in flesh and blood, He also Himself assumed the same, in order that through death He might bring to nought Him that hath the power of death, that is to say, the Devil, and might rescue those who all their lives were enslaved by the fear of death."[3] For by the sacrifice of His own body He did two things: He put an end to the law of death which barred our way; and He made a new beginning of life for us, by giving us the hope of resurrection. By man death has gained its power over men; by the Word made Man death has been destroyed and life raised up anew. That is what Paul says, that true servant of Christ: For since by man came death, by man came also the resurrection of the dead. Just as in Adam all die, even so in Christ shall all be made alive,"[4] and so forth. Now, therefore, when we die we no longer do so as men condemned to death, but as those who are even now in process of rising we await the general resurrection of all, "which in its own times He shall show,"[5] even God Who wrought it and bestowed it on us.

This, then, is the first cause of the Savior's becoming Man. There are, however, other things which show how wholly fitting is His blessed presence in our midst; and these we must now go on to consider.

The Divine Dilemma and Its Solution in the Incarnation—continued

When God the Almighty was making mankind through His own Word, He perceived that they, owing to the limitation of their nature, could not of themselves have any knowledge of their Artificer, the Incorporeal and Uncreated. He took pity on them, therefore, and did not leave them destitute of the knowledge of Himself, lest their very existence should prove purposeless. For of what use is existence to the creature if it cannot know its Maker? How could men be reasonable beings if they had no knowledge of the Word and Reason of the Father, through Whom they had received their being? They would be no better than the beasts, had they no knowledge save of earthly things; and why should God have made them at all, if He had not intended them to know Him? But, in fact, the good God has given them a share in His own Image, that is, in our Lord Jesus Christ, and has made even themselves after the same Image and Likeness. Why? Simply in order that through this gift of Godlikeness in themselves they may be able to perceive the Image Absolute, that is the Word Himself, and through Him to apprehend the Father; which knowledge of their Maker is for men the only really happy and blessed life.

But, as we have already seen, men, foolish as they are, thought little of the grace they had received, and turned away from God. They defiled their own soul so completely that they not only lost their apprehension of God, but invented for themselves other gods of various kinds. They fashioned idols for themselves in place of the truth and reverenced things that are not, rather than God Who is, as St. Paul says, "worshipping the creature rather than the Creator."[1] Moreover, and much worse, they transferred the honor which is due to God to material objects such as wood and stone, and also to man; and further even than that they went, as we said in our former book. Indeed, so impious were they that they worshipped evil spirits as gods in satisfaction of their lusts. They sacrificed brute beasts and immolated men, as the just due of these deities, thereby bringing themselves more and more under their insane control. Magic arts also were taught among them, oracles in sundry places led men astray, and the cause of everything in human life was traced to the stars as though nothing existed but that which could be seen. In a word, impiety and lawlessness were everywhere, and neither God nor His Word was known. Yet He had not hidden Himself from the sight of men nor given the knowledge of Himself in one way only; but rather He had unfolded it in many forms and by many ways.

(12) God knew the limitation of mankind, you see; and though the grace of being made in His Image was sufficient to give them knowledge of the Word and through Him of the Father, as a safeguard against their neglect of this grace, He provided the works of creation also as means by

which the Maker might be known. Nor was this all. Man's neglect of the indwelling grace tends ever to increase; and against this further frailty also God made provision by giving them a law, and by sending prophets, men whom they knew. Thus, if they were tardy in looking up to heaven, they might still gain knowledge of their Maker from those close at hand; for men can learn directly about higher things from other men. Three ways thus lay open to them, by which they might obtain the knowledge of God. They could look up into the immensity of heaven, and by pondering the harmony of creation come to know its Ruler, the Word of the Father, Whose all-ruling providence makes known the Father to all. Or, if this was beyond them, they could converse with holy men, and through them learn to know God, the Artificer of all things, the Father of Christ, and to recognize the worship of idols as the negation of the truth and full of all impiety. Or else, in the third place, they could cease from lukewarmness and lead a good life merely by knowing the law. For the law was not given only for the Jews, nor was it solely for their sake that God sent the prophets, though it was to the Jews that they were sent and by the Jews that they were persecuted. The law and the prophets were a sacred school of the knowledge of God and the conduct of the spiritual life for the whole world.

So great, indeed, were the goodness and the love of God. Yet men, bowed down by the pleasures of the moment and by the frauds and illusions of the evil spirits, did not lift up their heads towards the truth. So burdened were they with their wickednesses that they seemed rather to be brute beasts than reasonable men, reflecting the very Likeness of the Word.

(13) What was God to do in face of this dehumanising of mankind, this universal hiding of the knowledge of Himself by the wiles of evil spirits? Was He to keep silence before so great a wrong and let men go on being thus deceived and kept in ignorance of Himself? If so, what was the use of having made them in His own Image originally? It would surely have been better for them always to have been brutes, rather than to revert to that condition when once they had shared the nature of the Word. Again, things being as they were, what was the use of their ever having had the knowledge of God? Surely it would have been better for God never to have bestowed it, than that men should subsequently be found unworthy to receive it. Similarly, what possible profit could it be

to God Himself, Who made men, if when made they did not worship Him, but regarded others as their makers? This would be tantamount to His having made them for others and not for Himself. Even an earthly king, though he is only a man, does not allow lands that he has colonized to pass into other hands or to desert to other rulers, but sends letters and friends and even visits them himself to recall them to their allegiance, rather than allow His work to be undone. How much more, then, will God be patient and painstaking with His creatures, that they be not led astray from Him to the service of those that are not, and that all the more because such error means for them sheer ruin, and because it is not right that those who had once shared His Image should be destroyed.

What, then, was God to do? What else could He possibly do, being God, but renew His Image in mankind, so that through it men might once more come to know Him? And how could this be done save by the coming of the very Image Himself, our Savior Jesus Christ? Men could not have done it, for they are only made after the Image; nor could angels have done it, for they are not the images of God. The Word of God came in His own Person, because it was He alone, the Image of the Father Who could recreate man made after the Image.

In order to effect this re-creation, however, He had first to do away with death and corruption. Therefore He assumed a human body, in order that in it death might once for all be destroyed, and that men might be renewed according to the Image. The Image of the Father only was sufficient for this need. Here is an illustration to prove it.

(14) You know what happens when a portrait that has been painted on a panel becomes obliterated through external stains. The artist does not throw away the panel, but the subject of the portrait has to come and sit for it again, and then the likeness is re-drawn on the same material. Even so was it with the All-holy Son of God. He, the Image of the Father, came and dwelt in our midst, in order that He might renew mankind made after Himself, and seek out His lost sheep, even as He says in the Gospel: "I came to seek and to save that which was lost.[2] This also explains His saying to the Jews: "Except a man be born anew . . ."[3] a He was not referring to a man's natural birth from his mother, as they thought, but to the re-birth and re-creation of the soul in the Image of God.

Nor was this the only thing which only the Word could do. When the madness of idolatry and irreligion filled the world and the knowledge of God was hidden, whose part was it to teach the world about the Father? Man's, would you say? But men cannot run everywhere over the world, nor would their words carry sufficient weight if they did, nor would they be, unaided, a match for the evil spirits. Moreover, since even the best of men were confused and blinded by evil, how could they convert the souls and minds of others? You cannot put straight in others what is warped in yourself. Perhaps you will say, then, that creation was enough to teach men about the Father. But if that had been so, such great evils would never have occurred. Creation was there all the time, but it did not prevent men from wallowing in error. Once more, then, it was the Word of God, Who sees all that is in man and moves all things in creation, Who alone could meet the needs of the situation. It was His part and His alone, Whose ordering of the universe reveals the Father, to renew the same teaching. But how was He to do it? By the same means as before, perhaps you will say, that is, through the works of creation. But this was proven insufficient. Men had neglected to consider the heavens before, and now they were looking in the opposite direction. Wherefore, in all naturalness and fitness. desiring to do good to men, as Man He dwells, taking to Himself a body like the rest; and through His actions done in that body, as it were on their own level, He teaches those who would not learn by other means to know Himself, the Word of God, and through Him the Father.

(15) He deals with them as a good teacher with his pupils, coming down to their level and using simple means. St. Paul says as much: "Because in the wisdom of God the world in its wisdom knew not God, God thought fit through the simplicity of the News proclaimed to save those who believe."[4] Men had turned from the contemplation of God above, and were looking for Him in the opposite direction, down among created things and things of sense. The Savior of us all, the Word of God, in His great love took to Himself a body and moved as Man among men, meeting their senses, so to speak, half way. He became Himself an object for the senses, so that those who were seeking God in sensible things might apprehend the Father through the works which He, the Word of God, did in the body. Human and human minded as men were, therefore, to whichever side they looked in the sensible world

they found themselves taught the truth. Were they awe-stricken by creation? They beheld it confessing Christ as Lord. Did their minds tend to regard men as Gods? The uniqueness of the Savior's works marked Him, alone of men, as Son of God. Were they drawn to evil spirits? They saw them driven out by the Lord and learned that the Word of God alone was God and that the evil spirits were not gods at all. Were they inclined to hero-worship and the cult of the dead? Then the fact that the Savior had risen from the dead showed them how false these other deities were, and that the Word of the Father is the one true Lord, the Lord even of death. For this reason was He both born and manifested as Man, for this He died and rose, in order that, eclipsing by His works all other human deeds, He might recall men from all the paths of error to know the Father. As He says Himself, "I came to seek and to save that which was lost."[5]
(16) When, then, the minds of men had fallen finally to the level of sensible things, the Word submitted to appear in a body, in order that He, as Man, might center their senses on Himself, and convince them through His human acts that He Himself is not man only but also God, the Word and Wisdom of the true God. This is what Paul wants to tell us when he says: "That ye, being rooted and grounded in love, may be strong to apprehend with all the saints what is the length and breadth and height and depth, and to know the love of God that surpasses knowledge, so that ye may be filled unto all the fullness of God."[6] The Self- revealing of the Word is in every dimension—above, in creation; below, in the Incarnation; in the depth, in Hades; in the breadth, throughout the world. All things have been filled with the knowledge of God.

For this reason He did not offer the sacrifice on behalf of all immediately He came, for if He had surrendered His body to death and then raised it again at once He would have ceased to be an object of our senses. Instead of that, He stayed in His body and let Himself be seen in it, doing acts and giving signs which showed Him to be not only man, but also God the Word. There were thus two things which the Savior did for us by becoming Man. He banished death from us and made us anew; and, invisible and imperceptible as in Himself He is, He became visible through His works and revealed Himself as the Word of the Father, the Ruler and King of the whole creation.

(17) There is a paradox in this last statement which we must now exam-

ine. The Word was not hedged in by His body, nor did His presence in the body prevent His being present elsewhere as well. When He moved His body He did not cease also to direct the universe by His Mind and might. No. The marvelous truth is, that being the Word, so far from being Himself contained by anything, He actually contained all things Himself. In creation He is present everywhere, yet is distinct in being from it; ordering, directing, giving life to all, containing all, yet is He Himself the Uncontained, existing solely in His Father. As with the whole, so also is it with the part. Existing in a human body, to which He Himself gives life, He is still Source of life to all the universe, present in every part of it, yet outside the whole; and He is revealed both through the works of His body and through His activity in the world. It is, indeed, the function of soul to behold things that are outside the body, but it cannot energize or move them. A man cannot transport things from one place to another, for instance, merely by thinking about them; nor can you or I move the sun and the stars just by sitting at home and looking at them. With the Word of God in His human nature, however, it was otherwise. His body was for Him not a limitation, but an instrument, so that He was both in it and in all things, and outside all things, resting in the Father alone. At one and the same time—this is the wonder— as Man He was living a human life, and as Word He was sustaining the life of the universe, and as Son He was in constant union with the Father. Not even His birth from a virgin, therefore, changed Him in any way, nor was He defiled by being in the body. Rather, He sanctified the body by being in it. For His being in everything does not mean that He shares the nature of everything, only that He gives all things their being and sustains them in it. Just as the sun is not defiled by the contact of its rays with earthly objects, but rather enlightens and purifies them, so He Who made the sun is not defiled by being made known in a body, but rather the body is cleansed and quickened by His indwelling, "Who did no sin, neither was guile found in His mouth."[7]

(18) You must understand, therefore, that when writers on this sacred theme speak of Him as eating and drinking and being born, they mean that the body, as a body, was born and sustained with the food proper to its nature; while God the Word, Who was united with it, was at the same time ordering the universe and revealing Himself through His bodily acts as not man only but God. Those acts are rightly said to be His acts, because the body which did them did indeed belong to Him and none

other; moreover, it was right that they should be thus attributed to Him as Man, in order to show that His body was a real one and not merely an appearance. From such ordinary acts as being born and taking food, He was recognized as being actually present in the body; but by the extraordinary acts which He did through the body He proved Himself to be the Son of God. That is the meaning of His words to the unbelieving Jews: "If I do not the works of My Father, believe Me not; but if I do, even if ye believe not Me, believe My works, that ye may know that the Father is in Me and I in the Father."

Invisible in Himself, He is known from the works of creation; so also, when His Godhead is veiled in human nature, His bodily acts still declare Him to be not man only, but the Power and Word of God. To speak authoritatively to evil spirits, for instance, and to drive them out, is not human but divine; and who could see-Him curing all the diseases to which mankind is prone, and still deem Him mere man and not also God? He cleansed lepers, He made the lame to walk, He opened the ears of the deaf and the eyes of the blind, there was no sickness or weakness that-He did not drive away. Even the most casual observer can see that these were acts of God. The healing of the man born blind, for instance, who but the Father and Artificer of man, the Controller of his whole being, could thus have restored the faculty denied at birth? He Who did thus must surely be Himself the Lord of birth. This is proved also at the outset of His becoming Man. He formed His own body from the virgin; and that is no small proof of His Godhead, since He Who made that was the Maker of all else. And would not anyone infer from the fact of that body being begotten of a virgin only, without human father, that He Who appeared in it was also the Maker and Lord of all beside?

Again, consider the miracle at Cana. Would not anyone who saw the substance of water transmuted into wine understand that He Who did it was the Lord and Maker of the water that He changed? It was for the same reason that He walked on the sea as on dry land—to prove to the onlookers that He had mastery over all. And the feeding of the multitude, when He made little into much, so that from five loaves five thousand mouths were filled—did not that prove Him none other than the very Lord Whose Mind is over all?

READER

CALVIN'S INSTITUTES BOOK III EXCERPTS WRITTEN MID-1500'S

TOP TEN THEOLOGIANS

CHAPTER 8: OF BEARING THE CROSS—ONE BRANCH OF SELF-DENIAL.

1. The pious mind must ascend still higher, namely, whither Christ calls his disciples when he says, that every one of them must "take up his cross," (Mt. 16:24). Those whom the Lord has chosen and honoured with his intercourse must prepare for a hard, laborious, troubled life, a life full of many and various kinds of evils; it being the will of our heavenly Father to exercise his people in this way while putting them to the proof. Having begun this course with Christ the first-born, he continues it towards all his children. For though that Son was dear to him above others, the Son in whom he was "well pleased," yet we see, that far from being treated gently and indulgently, we may say, that not only was he subjected to a perpetual cross while he dwelt on earth, but his whole life was nothing else than a kind of perpetual cross. The Apostle assigns the reason, "Though he was a Son, yet learned he obedience by the things which he suffered," (Heb. 5:8). Why then should we exempt ourselves 2017from that condition to which Christ our Head behoved to submit;

especially since he submitted on our account, that he might in his own person exhibit a model of patience? Wherefore, the Apostle declares, that all the children of God are destined to be conformed to him. Hence it affords us great consolation in hard and difficult circumstances, which men deem evil and adverse, to think that we are holding fellowship with the sufferings of Christ; that as he passed to celestial glory through a labyrinth of many woes, so we too are conducted thither through various tribulations. For, in another passage, Paul himself thus speaks, "we must through much tribulation enter the kingdom of God," (Acts 14:22); and again, "that I may know him, and the power of his resurrection, and the fellowship of his sufferings, being made conformable unto his death," (Rom 8:29). How powerfully should it soften the bitterness of the cross, to think that the more we are afflicted with adversity, the surer we are made of our fellowship with Christ; by communion with whom our sufferings are not only blessed to us, but tend greatly to the furtherance of our salvation.

2. We may add, that the only thing which made it necessary for our Lord to undertake to bear the cross, was to testify and prove his obedience to the Father; whereas there are many reasons which make it necessary for us to live constantly under the cross. Feeble as we are by nature, and prone to ascribe all perfection to our flesh, unless we receive as it were ocular demonstration of our weakness, we readily estimate our virtue above its proper worth, and doubt not that, whatever happens, it will stand unimpaired and invincible against all difficulties. Hence we indulge a stupid and empty confidence in the flesh, and then trusting to it wax proud against the Lord himself; as if our own faculties were sufficient without his grace. This arrogance cannot be better repressed than when He proves to us by experience, not only how great our weakness, but also our frailty is. Therefore, he visits us with disgrace, or poverty, or bereavement, or disease, or other afflictions. Feeling altogether unable to support them, we forthwith, in so far as regards ourselves, give way, and thus humbled learn to invoke his strength, which alone can enable us to bear up under a weight of affliction. Nay, even the holiest of men, however well aware that they stand not in their own strength, but by the grace of God, would feel too secure in their own fortitude and constancy, were they not brought to a more thorough knowledge of themselves by the trial of the cross. This feeling gained even upon David, "In my prosperity I Said, I shall never be moved. Lord, by thy favour thou hast made my

mountain to stand strong: thou didst hide thy face, and I was troubled," (Ps. 30:6, 7). He confesses that in prosperity his feelings were dulled and blunted, so that, neglecting the grace of God, on which alone he ought to have depended, he leant to himself, and promised himself perpetuity. If it so happened to this great prophet, who of us should not fear and study caution? 2018Though in tranquillity they flatter themselves with the idea of greater constancy and patience, yet, humbled by adversity, they learn the deception. Believers, I say, warned by such proofs of their diseases, make progress in humility, and, divesting themselves of a depraved confidence in the flesh, betake themselves to the grace of God, and, when they have so betaken themselves, experience the presence of the divine power, in which is ample protection.

3. This Paul teaches when he says that tribulation worketh patience, and patience experience. God having promised that he will be with believers in tribulation, they feel the truth of the promise; while supported by his hand, they endure patiently. This they could never do by their own strength. Patience, therefore, gives the saints an experimental proof that God in reality furnishes the aid which he has promised whenever there is need. Hence also their faith is confirmed, for it were very ungrateful not to expect that in future the truth of God will be, as they have already found it, firm and constant. We now see how many advantages are at once produced by the cross. Overturning the overweening opinion we form of our own virtue, and detecting the hypocrisy in which we delight, it removes our pernicious carnal confidence, teaching us, when thus humbled, to recline on God alone, so that we neither are oppressed nor despond. Then victory is followed by hope, inasmuch as the Lord, by performing what he has promised, establishes his truth in regard to the future. Were these the only reasons, it is surely plain how necessary it is for usto bear the cross. It is of no little importance to be rid of your self-love, and made fully conscious of your weakness; so impressed with a sense of your weakness as to learn to distrust yourself—to distrust yourself so as to transfer your confidence to God, reclining on him with such heartfelt confidence as to trust in his aid, and continue invincible to the end, standing by his grace so as to perceive that he is true to his promises, and so assured of the certainty of his promises as to be strong in hope.

4. Another end which the Lord has in afflicting his people is to try their

patience, and train them to obedience—not that they can yield obedience to him except in so far as he enables them; but he is pleased thus to attest and display striking proofs of the graces which he has conferred upon his saints, lest they should remain within unseen and unemployed. Accordingly, by bringing forward openly the strength and constancy of endurance with which he has provided his servants, he is said to try their patience. Hence the expressions that God tempted Abraham (Gen. 21:1, 12), and made proof of his piety by not declining to sacrifice his only son. Hence, too, Peter tells us that our faith is proved by tribulation, just as gold is tried in a furnace of fire. But who will say it is not expedient that the most excellent gift of patience which the believer has received from his God should be applied to uses by being made sure and manifest? Otherwise men would never value it according to its worth. But if God himself, to prevent the virtues which he has conferred upon believers from 2019lurking in obscurity, nay, lying useless and perishing, does aright in supplying materials for calling them forth, there is the best reason for the afflictions of the saints, since without them their patience could not exist. I say, that by the cross they are also trained to obedience, because they are thus taught to live not according to their own wish, but at the disposal of God. Indeed, did all things proceed as they wish, they would not know what it is to follow God. Seneca mentions (De Vit. Beata, cap. 15) that there was an old proverb when any one was exhorted to endure adversity, "Follow God;" thereby intimating, that men truly submitted to the yoke of God only when they gave their back and hand to his rod. But if it is most right that we should in all things prove our obedience to our heavenly Father, certainly we ought not to decline any method by which he trains us to obedience.

5. Still, however, we see not how necessary that obedience is, unless we at the same time consider how prone our carnal nature is to shake off the yoke of God whenever it has been treated with some degree of gentleness and indulgence. It just happens to it as with refractory horses, which, if kept idle for a few days at hack and manger, become ungovernable, and no longer recognize the rider, whose command before they implicitly obeyed. And we invariably become what God complains of in the people of Israel—waxing gross and fat, we kick against him who reared and nursed us (Deut. 32:15). The kindness of God should allure us to ponder and love his goodness; but since such is our malignity, that we are invariably corrupted by his indulgence, it is more than necessary for us

to be restrained by discipline from breaking forth into such petulance. Thus, lest we become emboldened by an over-abundance of wealth; lest elated with honour, we grow proud; lest inflated with other advantages of body, or mind, or fortune, we grow insolent, the Lord himself interferes as he sees to be expedient by means of the cross, subduing and curbing the arrogance of our flesh, and that in various ways, as the advantage of each requires. For as we do not all equally labour under the same disease, so we do not all need the same difficult cure. Hence we see that all are not exercised with the same kind of cross. While the heavenly Physician treats some more gently, in the case of others he employs harsher remedies, his purpose being to provide a cure for all. Still none is left free and untouched, because he knows that all, without a single exception, are diseased.

6. We may add, that our most merciful Father requires not only to prevent our weakness, but often to correct our past faults, that he may keep us in due obedience. Therefore, whenever we are afflicted we ought immediately to call to mind our past life. In this way we will find that the faults which we have committed are deserving of such castigation. And yet the exhortation to patience is not to be founded chiefly on the acknowledgment of sin. For Scripture supplies a far better consideration when it says, that in adversity "we are chastened of the Lord, that we should not be condemned with the 2020world," (1 Cor. 11:32). Therefore, in the very bitterness of tribulation we ought to recognise the kindness and mercy of our Father, since even then he ceases not to further our salvation. For he afflicts, not that he may ruin or destroy but rather that he may deliver us from the condemnation of the world. Let this thought lead us to what Scripture elsewhere teaches: "My son, despise not the chastening of the Lord; neither be weary of his correction: For whom the Lord loveth he correcteth; even as a father the son in whom he delighteth," (Prov. 3:11, 12). When we perceive our Father's rod, is it not our part to behave as obedient docile sons rather than rebelliously imitate desperate men, who are hardened in wickedness? God dooms us to destruction, if he does not, by correction, call us back when we have fallen off from him, so that it is truly said, "If ye be without chastisement," "then are ye bastards, and not sons," (Heb. 12:8). We are most perverse then if we cannot bear him while he is manifesting his good-will to us, and the care which he takes of our salvation. Scripture states the difference between believers and unbelievers to be, that the latter, as

the slaves of inveterate and deep-seated iniquity, only become worse and more obstinate under the lash; whereas the former, like free-born sons turn to repentance. Now, therefore, choose your class. But as I have already spoken of this subject, it is sufficient to have here briefly adverted to it.

7. There is singular consolation, moreover, when we are persecuted for righteousness' sake. For our thought should then be, How high the honour which God bestows upon us in distinguishing us by the special badge of his soldiers. By suffering persecution for righteousness' sake, I mean not only striving for the defence of the Gospel, but for the defence of righteousness in any way. Whether, therefore, in maintaining the truth of God against the lies of Satan, or defending the good and innocent against the injuries of the bad, we are obliged to incur the offence and hatred of the world, so as to endanger life, fortune, or honour, let us not grieve or decline so far to spend ourselves for God; let us not think ourselves wretched in those things in which he with his own lips has pronounced us blessed (Mt. 5:10). Poverty, indeed considered in itself, is misery; so are exile, contempt, imprisonment, ignominy: in fine, death itself is the last of all calamities. But when the favour of God breathes upon is, there is none of these things which may not turn out to our happiness. Let us then be contented with the testimony of Christ rather than with the false estimate of the flesh, and then, after the example of the Apostles, we will rejoice in being "counted worthy to suffer shame for his name," (Acts 5:41). For why? If, while conscious of our innocence, we are deprived of our substance by the wickedness of man, we are, no doubt, humanly speaking, reduced to poverty; but in truth our riches in heaven are increased: if driven from our homes we have a more welcome reception into the family of God; if vexed and despised, we are more firmly rooted in Christ; if stigmatised by disgrace and ignominy, we have a higher place in the kingdom of God; and if we are slain, entrance is thereby given us to eternal life. The Lord having set such a price upon us, let us be ashamed to estimate ourselves at less than the shadowy and evanescent allurements of the present life.

8. Since by these, and similar considerations, Scripture abundantly solaces us for the ignominy or calamities which we endure in defence of righteousness, we are very ungrateful if we do not willingly and cheerfully receive them at the hand of the Lord, especially since this form of

the cross is the most appropriate to believers, being that by which Christ desires to be glorified in us, as Peter also declares (1 Pet. 4:11, 14). But as to ingenuous natures, it is more bitter to suffer disgrace than a hundred deaths, Paul expressly reminds us that not only persecution, but also disgrace awaits us, "because we trust in the living God," (1 Tim. 4:10). So in another passage he bids us, after his example, walk "by evil report and good report," (2 Cor. 6:8). The cheerfulness required, however, does not imply a total insensibility to pain. The saints could show no patience under the cross if they were not both tortured with pain and grievously molested. Were there no hardship in poverty, no pain in disease, no sting in ignominy, no fear in death, where would be the fortitude and moderation in enduring them? But while every one of these, by its inherent bitterness, naturally vexes the mind, the believer in this displays his fortitude, that though fully sensible of the bitterness and labouring grievously, he still withstands and struggles boldly; in this displays his patience, that though sharply stung, he is however curbed by the fear of God from breaking forth into any excess; in this displays his alacrity, that though pressed with sorrow and sadness, he rests satisfied with spiritual consolation from God.

9. This conflict which believers maintain against the natural feeling of pain, while they study moderation and patience, Paul elegantly describes in these words: "We are troubled on every side, yet not distressed; we are perplexed, but not in despair; persecuted, but not forsaken; cast down, but not destroyed," (2 Cor. 4:8, 9). You see that to bear the cross patiently is not to have your feelings altogether blunted, and to be absolutely insensible to pain, according to the absurd description which the Stoics of old gave of their hero as one who, divested of humanity, was affected in the same way by adversity and prosperity, grief and joy; or rather, like a stone, was not affected by anything. And what did they gain by that sublime wisdom? they exhibited a shadow of patience, which never did, and never can, exist among men. Nay, rather by aiming at a too exact and rigid patience, they banished it altogether from human life. Now also we have among Christians a new kind of Stoics, who hold it vicious not only to groan and weep, but even to be sad and anxious. These paradoxes are usually started by indolent men who, employing themselves more in speculation than in action, can do nothing else for us than beget such paradoxes. But we have nothing to do with 2022that iron philosophy which our Lord and Master condemned—not only in word, but also

by his own example. For he both grieved and shed tears for his own and others' woes. Nor did he teach his disciples differently: "Ye shall weep and lament, but the world shall rejoice," (John 16:20). And lest any one should regard this as vicious, he expressly declares, "Blessed are they that mourn," (Mt. 5:4). And no wonder. If all tears are condemned, what shall we think of our Lord himself, whose "sweat was as it were great drops of blood falling down to the ground?" (Luke 22:44; Mt. 26:38). If every kind of fear is a mark of unbelief, what place shall we assign to the dread which, it is said, in no slight degree amazed him; if all sadness is condemned, how shall we justify him when he confesses, "My soul is exceeding sorrowful, even unto death?"

10. I wished to make these observations to keep pious minds from despair, lest, from feeling it impossible to divest themselves of the natural feeling of grief, they might altogether abandon the study of patience. This must necessarily be the result with those who convert patience into stupor, and a brave and firm man into a block. Scripture gives saints the praise of endurance when, though afflicted by the hardships they endure, they are not crushed; though they feel bitterly, they are at the same time filled with spiritual joy; though pressed with anxiety, breathe exhilarated by the consolation of God. Still there is a certain degree of repugnance in their hearts, because natural sense shuns and dreads what is adverse to it, while pious affection, even through these difficulties, tries to obey the divine will. This repugnance the Lord expressed when he thus addressed Peter: "Verily, verily, I say unto thee, When thou wast young, thou girdedst thyself and walkedst whither thou wouldst; but when thou shalt be old, thou shalt stretch forth thy hands, and another shall gird thee; and carry thee whither thou wouldest not," (John 21:18). It is not probable, indeed, that when it became necessary to glorify God by death he was driven to it unwilling and resisting; had it been so, little praise would have been due to his martyrdom. But though he obeyed the divine ordination with the greatest alacrity of heart, yet, as he had not divested himself of humanity, he was distracted by a double will. When he thought of the bloody death which he was to die, struck with horror, he would willingly have avoided it: on the other hand, when he considered that it was God who called him to it, his fear was vanquished and suppressed, and he met death chcerfully. It must therefore be our study, if we would be disciples of Christ, to imbue our minds with such reverence and obedience to God as may tame and subjugate all affections contrary to his appoint-

ment. In this way, whatever be the kind of cross to which we are subjected, we shall in the greatest straits firmly maintain our patience. Adversity will have its bitterness, and sting us. When afflicted with disease, we shall groan and be disquieted, and long for health; pressed with 2023poverty, we shall feel the stings of anxiety and sadness, feel the pain of ignominy, contempt, and injury, and pay the tears due to nature at the death of our friends: but our conclusion will always be, The Lord so willed it, therefore let us follow his will. Nay, amid the pungency of grief, among groans and tears this thought will necessarily suggest itself and incline us cheerfully to endure the things for which we are so afflicted.

11. But since the chief reason for enduring the cross has been derived from a consideration of the divine will, we must in few words explain wherein lies the difference between philosophical and Christian patience. Indeed, very few of the philosophers advanced so far as to perceive that the hand of God tries us by means of affliction, and that we ought in this matter to obey God. The only reason which they adduce is, that so it must be. But is not this just to say, that we must yield to God, because it is in vain to contend against him? For if we obey God only because it is necessary, provided we can escape, we shall cease to obey him. But what Scripture calls us to consider in the will of God is very different, namely, first justice and equity, and then a regard to our own salvation. Hence Christian exhortations to patience are of this nature, Whether poverty, or exile, or imprisonment, or contumely, or disease, or bereavement, or any such evil affects us, we must think that none of them happens except by the will and providence of God; moreover, that every thing he does is in the most perfect order. What! do not our numberless daily faults deserve to be chastised, more severely, and with a heavier rod than his mercy lays upon us? Is it not most right that our flesh should be subdued, and be, as it were, accustomed to the yoke, so as not to rage and wanton as it lists? Are not the justice and the truth of God worthy of our suffering on their account? But if the equity of God is undoubtedly displayed in affliction, we cannot murmur or struggle against them without iniquity. We no longer hear the frigid cant, Yield, because it is necessary; but a living and energetic precept, Obey, because it is unlawful to resist; bear patiently, because impatience is rebellion against the justice of God. Then as that only seems to us attractive which we perceive to be for our own safety and advantage, here also our heavenly Father consoles us, by the assurance, that in the very cross with which he afflicts us he provides for our

salvation. But if it is clear that tribulations are salutary to us, why should we not receive them with calm and grateful minds? In bearing them patiently we are not submitting to necessity but resting satisfied with our own good. The effect of these thoughts is, that to whatever extent our minds are contracted by the bitterness which we naturally feel under the cross, to the same extent will they be expanded with spiritual joy. Hence arises thanksgiving, which cannot exist unless joy be felt. But if the praise of the Lord and thanksgiving can emanate only from a cheerful and gladdened breasts and there is nothing which ought to interrupt these feelings in us, it is clear how necessary it is to temper the bitterness of the cross with spiritual joy.

CHAPTER 9: OF MEDITATING ON THE FUTURE LIFE

1. Whatever be the kind of tribulation with which we are afflicted, we should always consider the end of it to be, that we may be trained to despise the present, and thereby stimulated to aspire to the future life. For since God well knows how strongly we are inclined by nature to a slavish love of this world, in order to prevent us from clinging too strongly to it, he employs the fittest reason for calling us back, and shaking off our lethargy. Every one of us, indeed, would be thought to aspire and aim at heavenly immortality during the whole course of his life. For we would be ashamed in no respect to excel the lower animals; whose condition would not be at all inferior to ours, had we not a hope of immortality beyond the grave. But when you attend to the plans, wishes, and actions of each, you see nothing in them but the earth. Hence our stupidity; our minds being dazzled with the glare of wealth, power, and honours, that they can see no farther. The heart also, engrossed with avarice, ambition, and lust, is weighed down and cannot rise above them. In short, the whole soul, ensnared by the allurements of the flesh, seeks its happiness on the earth. To meet this disease, the Lord makes his people sensible of the vanity of the present life, by a constant proof of its miseries. Thus, that they may not promise themselves deep and lasting peace in it, he often allows them to be assailed by war, tumult, or rapine, or to be disturbed by other injuries. That they may not long with too much eager-

ness after fleeting and fading riches, or rest in those which they already possess, he reduces them to want, or, at least, restricts them to a moderate allowance, at one time by exile, at another by sterility, at another by fire, or by other means. That they may not indulge too complacently in the advantages of married life, he either vexes them by the misconduct of their partners, or humbles them by the wickedness of their children, or afflicts them by bereavement. But if in all these he is indulgent to them, lest they should either swell with vain-glory, or be elated with confidence, by diseases and dangers he sets palpably before them how unstable and evanescent are all the advantages competent to mortals. We duly profit by the discipline of the cross, when we learn that this life, estimated in itself, is restless, troubled, in numberless ways wretched, and plainly in no respect happy; that what are estimated its blessings are uncertain, fleeting, vain, and vitiated by a great admixture of evil. From this we conclude, that all we have to seek or hope for here is contest; that when we think of the crown we must raise our eyes to heaven. For we must hold, that our mind never rises seriously to desire and aspire after the future, until it has learned to despise the present life.

2. For there is no medium between the two things: the earth must either be worthless in our estimation, or keep us enslaved by an intemperate love of it. Therefore, if we have any regard to eternity, we must carefully strive to disencumber ourselves of these fetters. Moreover, since the present life has many enticements to allure us, and great semblance of delight, grace, and sweetness to soothe us, it is of great consequence to us to be now and then called off from its fascinations. For what, pray, would happen, if we here enjoyed an uninterrupted course of honour and felicity, when even the constant stimulus of affliction cannot arouse us to a due sense of our misery? That human life is like smoke or a shadow, is not only known to the learned; there is not a more trite proverb among the vulgar. Considering it a fact most useful to be known, they have recommended it in many well-known expressions. Still there is no fact which we ponder less carefully, or less frequently remember. For we form all our plans just as if we had fixed our immortality on the earth. If we see a funeral, or walk among graves, as the image of death is then present to the eye, I admit we philosophise admirably on the vanity of life. We do not indeed always do so, for those things often have no effect upon us at all. But, at the best, our philosophy is momentary. It vanishes as soon as we turn our back, and leaves not the vestige of remembrance

behind; in short, it passes away, just like the applause of a theatre at some pleasant spectacle. Forgetful not only of death, but also of mortality itself, as if no rumour of it had ever reached us, we indulge in supine security as expecting a terrestrial immortality. Meanwhile, if any one breaks in with the proverb, that man is the creature of a day, we indeed acknowledge its truth, but, so far from giving heed to it, the thought of perpetuity still keeps hold of our minds. Who then can deny that it is of the highest importance to us all, I say not, to be admonished by words, but convinced by all possible experience of the miserable condition of our earthly life; since even when convinced we scarcely cease to gaze upon it with vicious, stupid admiration, as if it contained within itself the sum of all that is good? But if God finds it necessary so to train us, it must be our duty to listen to him when he calls, and shakes us from our torpor, that we may hasten to despise the world, and aspire with our whole heart to the future life.

3. Still the contempt which believers should train themselves to feel for the present life, must not be of a kind to beget hatred of it or ingratitude to God. This life, though abounding in all kinds of wretchedness, is justly classed among divine blessings which are not to be despised. Wherefore, if we do not recognize the kindness of God in it, we are chargeable with no little ingratitude towards him. To believers, especially, it ought to be a proof of divine benevolence, since it is wholly destined to promote their salvation. Before openly exhibiting the inheritance of eternal glory, God is pleased to manifest himself to us as a Father by minor proofs—viz. the blessings which he daily bestows upon us. Therefore, while this life serves to acquaint us with the goodness of God, shall we disdain it as if it did not contain one particle of good? We ought, therefore, to feel and be affected towards it in such a manner as to place it among those gifts of the divine benignity which are by no means to be despised. Were there no proofs in Scripture (they are most numerous and clear), yet nature herself exhorts us to return thanks to God for having brought us forth into light, granted us the use of it, and bestowed upon us all the means necessary for its preservation. And there is a much higher reason when we reflect that here we are in a manner prepared for the glory of the heavenly kingdom. For the Lord hath ordained, that those who are ultimately to be crowned in heaven must maintain a previous warfare on the earth, that they may not triumph before they have overcome the difficulties of war, and obtained the vic-

tory. Another reason is, that we here begin to experience in various ways a foretaste of the divine benignity, in 2028order that our hope and desire may be whetted for its full manifestation. When once we have concluded that our earthly life is a gift of the divine mercy, of which, agreeably to our obligation, it behoves us to have a grateful remembrance, we shall then properly descend to consider its most wretched condition, and thus escape from that excessive fondness for it, to which, as I have said, we are naturally prone.

4. In proportion as this improper love diminishes, our desire of a better life should increase. I confess, indeed, that a most accurate opinion was formed by those who thought, that the best thing was not to be born, the next best to die early. For, being destitute of the light of God and of true religion, what could they see in it that was not of dire and evil omen? Nor was it unreasonable for those who felt sorrow and shed tears at the birth of their kindred, to keep holiday at their deaths. But this they did without profit; because, devoid of the true doctrine of faith, they saw not how that which in itself is neither happy nor desirable turns to the advantage of the righteous: and hence their opinion issued in despair. Let believers, then, in forming an estimate of this mortal life, and perceiving that in itself it is nothing but misery, make it their aim to exert themselves with greater alacrity, and less hinderance, in aspiring to the future and eternal life. When we contrast the two, the former may not only be securely neglected, but, in comparison of the latter, be disdained and contemned. If heaven is our country, what can the earth be but a place of exile? If departure from the world is entrance into life, what is the world but a sepulchre, and what is residence in it but immersion in death? If to be freed from the body is to gain full possession of freedom, what is the body but a prison? If it is the very summit of happiness to enjoy the presence of God, is it not miserable to want it? But "whilst we are at home in the body, we are absent from the Lord," (2 Cor. 5:6). Thus when the earthly is compared with the heavenly life, it may undoubtedly be despised and trampled under foot. We ought never, indeed, to regard it with hatred, except in so far as it keeps us subject to sin; and even this hatred ought not to be directed against life itself. At all events, we must stand so affected towards it in regard to weariness or hatred as, while longing for its termination, to be ready at the Lord's will to continue in it, keeping far from everything like murmuring and impatience. For it is as if the Lord had assigned us

a post, which we must maintain till he recalls us. Paul, indeed, laments his condition, in being still bound with the fetters of the body, and sighs earnestly for redemption (Rom. 7:24); nevertheless, he declared that, in obedience to the command of Gods he was prepared for both courses, because he acknowledges it as his duty to God to glorify his name whether by life or by death, while it belongs to God to determine what is most conducive to His glory (Phil. 1:20-24). Wherefore, if it becomes us to live and die to the Lord, let us leave the period of our life and death at his disposal. Still let us ardently long for death, and constantly meditate upon it, and in comparison with future immortality, let us despise life, and, on account of the bondage of sin, long to renounce it whenever it shall so please the Lord.

5. But, most strange to say, many who boast of being Christians, instead of thus longing for death, are so afraid of it that they tremble at the very mention of it as a thing ominous and dreadful. We cannot wonder, indeed, that our natural feelings should be somewhat shocked at the mention of our dissolution. But it is altogether intolerable that the light of piety should not be so powerful in a Christian breast as with greater consolation to overcome and suppress that fear. For if we reflect that this our tabernacle, unstable, defective, corruptible, fading, pining, and putrid, is dissolved, in order that it may forthwith be renewed in sure, perfect, incorruptible, in fine, in heavenly glory, will not faith compel us eagerly to desire what nature dreads? If we reflect that by death we are recalled from exile to inhabit our native country, a heavenly country, shall this give us no comfort? But everything longs for permanent existence. I admit this, and therefore contend that we ought to look to future immortality, where we may obtain that fixed condition which nowhere appears on the earth. For Paul admirably enjoins believers to hasten cheerfully to death, not because they "would be unclothed, but clothed upon," (2 Cor. 5:2). Shall the lower animals, and inanimate creatures themselves even wood and stone, as conscious of their present vanity, long for the final resurrection, that they may with the sons of God be delivered from vanity (Rom. 8:19); and shall we, endued with the light of intellect, and more than intellect, enlightened by the Spirit of God, when our essence is in question, rise no higher than the corruption of this earth? But it is not my purpose, nor is this the place, to plead against this great perverseness. At the outset, I declared that I had no wish to engage in a diffuse discussion of common-places. My advice to those whose minds are thus

timid is to read the short treatise of Cyprian De Mortalitate, unless it be more accordant with their deserts to send them to the philosophers, that by inspecting what they say on the contempt of death, they may begin to blush. This, however let us hold as fixed, that no man has made much progress in the school of Christ who does not look forward with joy to the day of death and final resurrection (2 Tim. 4:18; Tit. 2:13) for Paul distinguishes all believers by this mark; and the usual course of Scripture is to direct us thither whenever it would furnish us with an argument for substantial joy. "Look up," says our Lord, "and lift up your heads: for your redemption draweth nigh," (Luke 21:28). Is it reasonable, I ask, that what he intended to have a powerful effect in stirring us up to alacrity and exultation should produce nothing but sadness and consternation? If it is so, why do we still glory in him as our Master? Therefore, let us come to a sounder mind, and how repugnant so ever the blind and stupid longing of the flesh may be, let us doubt not to desire the advent of the Lord not in wish only, but with earnest sighs, as the most propitious of all events. He will come as a Redeemer to deliver us from an immense abyss of evil and misery, and lead us to the blessed inheritance of his life and glory.

6. Thus, indeed, it is; the whole body of the faithful, so long as they live on the earth, must be like sheep for the slaughter, in order that they may be conformed to Christ their head (Rom. 8:36). Most deplorable, therefore, would their situation be did they not, by raising their mind to heaven, become superior to all that is in the world, and rise above the present aspect of affairs (1 Cor. 15:19). On the other hand, when once they have raised their head above all earthly objects, though they see the wicked flourishing in wealth and honour, and enjoying profound peace, indulging in luxury and splendour, and revelling in all kinds of delights, though they should moreover be wickedly assailed by them, suffer insult from their pride, be robbed by their avarice, or assailed by any other passion, they will have no difficulty in bearing up under these evils. They will turn their eye to that day (Isaiah 25:8; Rev. 7:17), on which the Lord will receive his faithful servants, wipe away all tears from their eyes, clothe them in a robe of glory and joy, feed them with the ineffable sweetness of his pleasures, exalt them to share with him in his greatness; in fine, admit them to a participation in his happiness. But the wicked who may have flourished on the earth, he will cast forth in extreme ignominy, will change their delights into torments, their laughter and joy into wailing

and gnashing of teeth, their peace into the gnawing of conscience, and punish their luxury with unquenchable fire. He will also place their necks under the feet of the godly, whose patience they abused. For, as Paul declares, "it is a righteous thing with God to recompense tribulation to them that trouble you; and to you who are troubled rest with us, when the Lord Jesus shall be revealed from heaven," (2 Thess. 1:6, 7). This, indeed, is our only consolation; deprived of it, we must either give way to despondency, or resort to our destruction to the vain solace of the world. The Psalmist confesses, "My feet were almost gone: my steps had well nigh slipt: for I was envious at the foolish when I saw the prosperity of the wicked," (Psalm 73:3, 4); and he found no resting-place until he entered the sanctuary, and considered the latter end of the righteous and the wicked. To conclude in one word, the cross of Christ then only triumphs in the breasts of believers over the devil and the flesh, sin and sinners, when their eyes are directed to the power of his resurrection.

APPENDIX

MARTIN LUTHER'S COMMENTARY ON GALATIANS 3

TOP TEN THEOLOGIANS

CHAPTER III

Verse 3. Are ye so foolish? having begun in the Spirit, are ye now made perfect by the flesh?

Paul now begins to warn the Galatians against a twofold danger. The first danger is: "Are ye so foolish, that after ye have begun in the Spirit, ye would now end in the flesh?"

"Flesh" stands for the righteousness of reason which seeks justification by the accomplishment of the Law. I am told that I began in the spirit under the papacy, but am ending up in the flesh because I got married. As though single life were a spiritual life, and married life a carnal life. They are silly. All the duties of a Christian husband, e.g., to love his wife, to bring up his children, to govern his family, etc., are the very fruits of the Spirit.

The righteousness of the Law which Paul also terms the righteousness of the flesh is so far from justifying a person that those who once had the Holy Spirit and lost Him, end up in the Law to their complete destruction.

Verse 4. Have ye suffered so many things in vain?

The other danger against which the Apostle warns the Galatians is this: "Have ye suffered so many things in vain?" Paul wants to say: "Consider not only the good start you had and lost, but consider also the many things you have suffered for the sake of the Gospel and for the name of Christ. You have suffered the loss of your possessions, you have borne reproaches, you have passed through many dangers of body and life. You endured much for the name of Christ and you endured it faithfully. But now you have lost everything, the Gospel, faith, and the spiritual benefit of your sufferings for Christ's sake. What a miserable thing to endure so many afflictions for nothing."

Verse 4. If it be yet in vain.

The Apostle adds the afterthought: "If it be yet in vain. I do not despair of all hope for you. But if you continue to look to the Law for righteousness, I think you should be told that all your past true worship of God and 95all the afflictions that you have endured for Christ's sake are going to help you not at all. I do not mean to discourage you altogether. I do hope you will repent and amend."

Verse 5. He therefore that ministereth to you the Spirit, and worketh miracles among you, doeth he it by the works of the law, or by the hearing of faith?

This argument based on the experience of the Galatians, pleased the Apostle so well that he returns to it after he had warned them against their twofold danger. "You have not only received the Spirit by the preaching of the Gospel, but by the same Gospel you were enabled to do things." "What things?" we ask. Miracles. At least the Galatians had manifested the striking fruits of faith which true disciples of the Gospel manifested in those days. On one occasion the Apostle wrote: "The kingdom of God is not in word, but in power." This "power" revealed itself not only in readiness of speech, but in demonstrations of the supernatural ability of the Holy Spirit.

When the Gospel is preached unto faith, hope, love, and patience, God gives His wonder-working Spirit. Paul reminds the Galatians of this. "God had not only brought you to faith by my preaching. He had also sanctified you to bring forth the fruits of faith. And one of the fruits of your faith was that you loved me so devotedly that you were willing to pluck out your eyes for me." To love a fellow-man so devotedly as to be ready to bestow upon him money, goods, eyes in order to secure his salvation, such love is the fruit of the Holy Spirit.

"These products of the Spirit you enjoyed before the false apostles misled you," the Apostle reminds the Galatians. "But you haven't manifested any of these fruits under the regime of the Law. How does it come that you do not grow the same fruits now? You no longer teach truly; you do not believe boldly; you do not live well; you do not work hard; you do not bear things patiently. Who has spoiled you that you no longer love me; that you are not now ready to pluck out your eyes for me? What has happened to cool your personal interest in me?"

The same thing happened to me. When I began to proclaim the Gospel, there were many, very many who were delighted with our doctrine and had a good opinion of us. And now? Now they have succeeded in making us so odious to those who formerly loved us that they now hate us like poison.

Paul argues: "Your experience ought to teach you that the fruits of love do not grow on the stump of the Law. You had not virtue prior to the preaching of the Gospel and you have no virtues now under the regime of the false apostles."

We, too, may say to those who misname themselves "evangelical" and flout their new-found liberty: Have you put down the tyranny of the Pope and obtained liberty in Christ through the Anabaptists and other fanatics? Or have you obtained your freedom from us who preach faith in Christ Jesus? If there is any honesty left in them they will have to confess that their freedom dates from the preaching of the Gospel.

Verse 6. Even as Abraham believed God, and it was accounted to him for righteousness.

The Apostle next adduces the example of Abraham and reviews the testimony of the Scriptures concerning faith. The first passage is taken from Genesis 15:6: "And he believed in the Lord; and he counted it to him for righteousness." The Apostle makes the most of this passage. Abraham may have enjoyed a good standing with men for his upright life, but not with God. In the sight of God, Abraham was a condemned sinner. That he was justified before God was not due to his own exertions, but due to his faith. The Scriptures expressly state: "Abraham believed in the Lord; and he counted it to him for righteousness."

Paul places the emphasis upon the two words: Abraham believed. Faith in God constitutes the highest worship, the prime duty, the first obedience, and the foremost sacrifice. Without faith God forfeits His glory, wisdom, truth, and mercy in us. The first duty of man is to believe in God and to honor Him with his faith. Faith is truly the height of wisdom, the right kind of righteousness, the only real religion. This will give us an idea of the excellence of faith.

To believe in God as Abraham did is to be right with God because faith honors God. Faith says to God: "I believe what you say."

When we pay attention to reason, God seems to propose impossible matters in the Christian Creed. To reason it seems absurd that Christ should offer His body and blood in the Lord's Supper; that Baptism should be the washing of regeneration; that the dead shall rise; that Christ the Son of God was conceived in the womb of the Virgin Mary, etc. Reason shouts that all this is preposterous. Are you surprised that reason thinks little of faith? Reason thinks it ludicrous that faith should be the foremost service any person can render unto God.

Let your faith supplant reason. Abraham mastered reason by faith in the Word of God. Not as though reason ever yields meekly. It put up a fight against the faith of Abraham. Reason protested that it was absurd to think that Sarah who was ninety years old and barren by nature, should give birth to a son. But faith won the victory and routed reason, that ugly beast and enemy of God. Everyone who by faith slays reason, the world's biggest monster, renders God a real service, a better service than the religions of all races and all the drudgery of meritorious monks can render.

Men fast, pray, watch, suffer. They intend to appease the wrath of God and to deserve God's grace by their exertions. But there is no glory in it for God, because by their exertions these workers pronounce God an unmerciful slave driver, an unfaithful and angry Judge. They despise God, make a liar out of Him, snub Christ and all His benefits; in short they pull God from His throne and perch themselves on it.

Faith truly honors God. And because faith honors God, God counts faith for righteousness.

Christian righteousness is the confidence of the heart in God through Christ Jesus. Such confidence is accounted righteousness for Christ's sake. Two things make for Christian righteousness: Faith in Christ, which is a gift of God; and God's acceptance of this imperfect faith of ours for perfect righteousness. Because of my faith in Christ, God overlooks my distrust, the unwillingness of my spirit, my many other sins. Because the shadow of Christ's wing covers me I have no fear that God will cover all my sins and take my imperfections for perfect righteousness.

God "winks" at my sins and covers them up. God says: "Because you believe in My Son I will forgive your sins until death shall deliver you from the body of sin."

Learn to understand the constitution of your Christian righteousness. Faith is weak, but it means enough to God that He will not lay sin to our charge. He will not punish nor condemn us for it. He will forgive our sins as though they amount to nothing at all. He will do it not because we are worthy of such mercy. He will do it for Jesus' sake in whom we believe.

Paradoxically, a Christian is both right and wrong, holy and profane, an enemy of God and a child of God. These contradictions no person can harmonize who does not understand the true way of salvation. Under the papacy we were told to toil until the feeling of guilt had left us. But the authors of this deranged idea were frequently driven to despair in the hour of death. It would have happened to me, if Christ had not mercifully delivered me from this error.

We comfort the afflicted sinner in this manner: Brother, you can never be perfect in this life, but you can be holy. He will say: "How can I be holy when I feel my sins?" I answer: You feel sin? That is a good sign. To realize that one is ill is a step, and a very necessary step, toward recovery. "But how will I get rid of my sin?" he will ask. I answer: See the heavenly Physician, Christ, who heals the broken-hearted. Do not consult that Quackdoctor, Reason. Believe in Christ and your sins will be pardoned. His righteousness will become your righteousness, and your sins will become His sins.

On one occasion Jesus said to His disciples: "The Father loveth you." Why? Not because the disciples were Pharisees, or circumcised, or particularly attentive to the Law. Jesus said: "The Father loveth you, because ye have loved me, and have believed that I came out from God. It pleased you to know that the Father sent me into the world. And because you believed it the Father loves you." On another occasion Jesus called His disciples evil and commanded them to ask for forgiveness.

A Christian is beloved of God and a sinner. How can these two contradictions be harmonized: I am a sinner and deserve God's wrath and punishment, and yet the Father loves me? Christ alone can harmonize these contradictions. He is the Mediator.

Do you now see how faith justifies without works? Sin lingers in us, and God hates sin. A transfusion of righteousness therefore becomes vitally necessary. This transfusion of righteousness we obtain from Christ because we believe in Him.

Verse 7. Know ye therefore that they which are of faith, the same are the children of Abraham.

This is the main point of Paul's argument against the Jews: The children of Abraham are those who believe and not those who are born of Abraham's flesh and blood. This point Paul drives home with all his might because the Jews attached saving value to the genealogical fact: "We are the seed and children of Abraham."

Let us begin with Abraham and learn how this friend of God was justified and saved. Not because he left his country, his relatives, his father's house; not because he was circumcised; not because he stood ready to sacrifice his own son Isaac in whom he had the promise of posterity. Abraham was justified because he believed. Paul's argumentation runs like this: "Since this is the unmistakable testimony of Holy Writ, why do you take your stand upon circumcision and the Law? Was not Abraham, your father, of whom you make so much, justified and saved without circumcision and the Law by faith alone?" Paul therefore concludes: "They which are of faith, the same are the children of Abraham."

Abraham was the father of the faithful. In order to be a child of the believing Abraham you must believe as he did. Otherwise you are merely the physical offspring of the procreating Abraham, i.e., you were conceived and born in sin unto wrath and condemnation.

Ishmael and Isaac were both the natural children of Abraham. By rights Ishmael should have enjoyed the prerogatives of the firstborn, if physical generation had any special value. Nevertheless he was left out in the cold while Isaac was called. This goes to prove that the children of faith are the real children of Abraham.

Some find fault with Paul for applying the term "faith" in Genesis 15:6 to Christ. They think Paul's use of the term too wide and general. They think its meaning should be restricted to the context. They claim Abraham's faith had no more in it than a belief in the promise of God that he should have seed.

We reply: Faith presupposes the assurance of God's mercy. This assurance takes in the confidence that our sins are forgiven for Christ's sake. Never will the conscience trust in God unless it can be sure of God's mercy and promises in Christ. Now all the promises of God lead back to the first promise concerning Christ: "And I will put enmity between thee and the woman, and between thy seed and her seed; it shall bruise thy head, and thou shalt bruise his heel." The faith of the fathers in the Old Testament era, and our faith in the New Testament are one and the same faith in Christ Jesus, although times and conditions may differ. Peter acknowledged this in the words: "Which neither our fathers nor we were able to bear? But we believe that through the grace of the Lord Jesus Christ we shall be saved, even as they" (Acts 15: 10, 11). And Paul writes: "And did all drink the spiritual drink; for they drank of that spiritual Rock that followed them: and that Rock was Christ" (I Cor. 10:4). And Christ Himself declared: "Your father Abraham rejoiced to see my day: and he saw it and was glad" (John 8:56). The faith of the fathers was directed at the Christ who was to come, while ours rests in the Christ who has come. Time does not change the object of true faith, or the Holy Spirit. There has always been and always will be one mind, one impression, one faith concerning Christ among true believers whether they live in times past, now, or in times to come. We too believe in the Christ to come as the fathers did in the Old Testament, for we look for Christ to come again on the last day to judge the quick and the dead.

Verse 7. Know ye therefore that they which are of faith, the same are the children of Abraham.

Paul is saying: "You know from the example of Abraham and from the plain testimony of the Scriptures that they are the children of Abraham, who have faith in Christ, regardless of their nationality, regardless of the Law, regardless of works, regardless of their parentage. The promise was made unto Abraham, 'Thou shalt be a father of many nations'; again, 'And in thee shall all families of the earth be blessed.'" To prevent the Jews from misinterpreting the word "nations," the Scriptures are careful to say "many nations." The true children of Abraham are the believers in Christ from all nations.

Verse 8. And the Scripture, foreseeing that God would justify the heathen through faith.

"Your boasting does not get you anywhere," says Paul to the Galatians, "because the Sacred Scriptures foresaw and foretold long before the Law was ever given, that the heathen should be justified by the blessed 'seed' of Abraham and not by the Law. This promise was made four hundred and thirty years before the Law was given. Because the Law was given so many years after Abraham, it could not abolish the promised blessing." This argument is strong because it is based on the exact factor of time. "Why should you boast of the Law, my Galatians, when the Law came four hundred and thirty years after the promise?"

The false apostles glorified the Law and despised the promise made unto Abraham, although it antedated the Law by many years. It was after Abraham was accounted righteous because of his faith that the Scriptures first make mention of circumcision. "The Scriptures," says Paul, "meant to forestall your infatuation for the righteousness of the Law by installing the righteousness of faith before circumcision and the Law ever were ordained."

Verse 8. Preached before the gospel unto Abraham, saying, In thee shall all nations be blessed.

The Jews misconstrue this passage. They want the term "to bless" to mean "to praise." They want the passage to read: In thee shall all the nations of the earth be praised. But this is a perversion of the words of Holy Writ. With the words "Abraham believed" Paul describes a spiritual Abraham, renewed by faith and regenerated by the Holy Ghost, that he should be the spiritual father of many nations. In that way all the Gentiles could be given to him for an inheritance.

The Scriptures ascribe no righteousness to Abraham except through faith. The Scriptures speak of Abraham as he stands before God, a man justified by faith. Because of his faith God extends to him the promise: "In thee shall all nations be blessed."

Verse 9. So then they which be of faith are blessed with faithful Abraham.

The emphasis lies on the words "with faithful Abraham." Paul distinguishes between Abraham and Abraham. There is a working and there is a believing Abraham. With the working Abraham we have nothing to do. Let the Jews glory in the generating Abraham; we glory in the believing Abraham of whom the Scriptures say that he received the blessing of righteousness by faith, not only for himself but for all who believe as he did. The world was promised to Abraham because he believed. The whole world is blessed if it believes as Abraham believed.

The blessing is the promise of the Gospel. That all nations are to be blessed means that all nations are to hear the Gospel. All nations are to be declared righteous before God through faith in Christ Jesus. To bless simply means to spread abroad the knowledge of Christ's salvation. This is the office of the New Testament Church which distributes the promised blessing by preaching the Gospel, by administering the sacraments, by comforting the broken-hearted, in short, by dispensing the benefits of Christ.

The Jews exhibited a working Abraham. The Pope exhibits a working Christ, or an exemplary Christ. The Pope quotes Christ's saying recorded in John 13:15, "I have given you an example, that ye should do as I have done to you." We do not deny that Christians ought to imitate the example of Christ; but mere imitation will not satisfy God. And bear in mind that Paul is not now discussing the example of Christ, but the salvation of Christ.

That Abraham submitted to circumcision at the command of God, that he was endowed with excellent virtues, that he obeyed God in all things, was certainly admirable of him. To follow the example of Christ, to love one's neighbor, to do good to them that persecute you, to pray for one's enemies, patiently to bear the ingratitude of those who return evil for good, is certainly praiseworthy. But praiseworthy or not, such virtues do not acquit us before God. It takes more than that to make us righteous before God. We need Christ Himself, not His example, to save us. We need a redeeming, not an exemplary Christ, to save us. Paul is here speaking of the redeeming Christ and the believing Abraham, not of the model Christ or the sweating Abraham.

The believing Abraham is not to lie buried in the grave. He is to be dusted off and brought out before the world. He is to be praised to the sky for his faith. Heaven and earth ought to know about him and about his faith in Christ. The working Abraham ought to look pretty small next to the believing Abraham.

Paul's words contain the implication of contrast. When he quotes Scripture to the effect that all nations that share the faith of faithful Abraham are to be blessed, Paul means to imply the contrast that all nations are accursed without faith in Christ.

Verse 10. For as many as are of the works of the law are under the curse.

The curse of God is like a flood that swallows everything that is not of faith. To avoid the curse we must hold on to the promise of the blessing in Christ.

The reader is reminded that all this has no bearing upon civil laws, customs, or political matters. Civil laws and ordinances have their place and purpose. Let every government enact the best possible laws. But civil righteousness will never deliver a person from the condemnation of God's Law.

I have good reason for calling your attention to this. People easily mistake civil righteousness for spiritual righteousness. In civil life we must, of course, pay attention to laws and deeds, but in the spiritual life we must not think to be justified by laws and works, but always keep in mind the promise and blessing of Christ, our only Savior.

According to Paul everything that is not of faith is sin. When our opponents hear us repeat this statement of Paul, they make it appear as if we taught that governments should not be honored, as if we favored rebellion against the constituted authorities, as if we condemned all laws. Our opponents do us a great wrong, for we make a clear-cut distinction between civil and spiritual affairs.

Governmental laws and ordinances are blessings of God for this life only. As for everlasting life, temporal blessings are not good enough. Unbelievers enjoy more temporal blessings than the Christians. Civil or legal righteousness may be good enough for this life but not for the life hereafter. Otherwise the infidels would be nearer heaven than the Christians, for infidels often excel in civil righteousness.

Verse 10. For it is written, Cursed is every one that continueth not in all things which are written in the book of the law to do them.

Paul goes on to prove from this quotation out of the Book of Deuteronomy that all men who are under the Law are under the sentence of sin, of the wrath of God, and of everlasting death. Paul produces his proof in a roundabout way. He turns the negative statement, "Cursed is every one that continueth not in all things which are written in the book of the law to do them," into a positive statement, "As many as are of the works of the law are under the curse." These two statements, one by Paul and the other by Moses, appear to conflict. Paul declares, "Whosoever shall do the works of the Law, is accursed." Moses declares, "Whosoever shall not do the works of the Law, is accursed." How can these two contradictory statements be reconciled? How can the one statement prove the other? No person can hope to understand Paul unless he understands the article of justification. These two statements are not at all inconsistent.

We must bear in mind that to do the works of the Law does not mean only to live up to the superficial requirements of the Law, but to obey the spirit of the Law to perfection. But where will you find the person who can do that? Let him step forward and we will praise him.

Our opponents have their answer ready-made. They quote Paul's own statement in Romans 2:13, "The doers of the law shall be justified." Very well. But let us first find out who the doers of the law are. They call a "doer" of the Law one who performs the Law in its literal sense. This is not to "do" the Law. This is to sin. When our opponents go about to perform the Law, they sin against the first, the second, and the third commandments; in fact they sin against the whole Law. For God requires above all that we worship Him in spirit and in faith. In observing the Law for the purpose of obtaining righteousness without faith in Christ these law-workers go smack against the Law and against God. They deny the righteousness of God, His mercy, and His promises. They deny Christ and all His benefits.

In their ignorance of the true purpose of the Law the exponents of the Law abuse the Law, as Paul says, Romans 10:3, "For they, being ignorant of God's righteousness, and going about to establish their own righteousness, have not submitted themselves unto the righteousness of God."

In their folly our opponents rush into the Scriptures, pick out a sentence here and a sentence there about the Law and imagine they know all about it. Their work-righteousness is plain idolatry and blasphemy against God. No wonder they abide under the curse of God.

Because God saw that we could not fulfill the Law, He provided a way of salvation long before the Law was ever given, a salvation that He promised to Abraham, saying, "In thee shall all nations be blessed."

The very first thing for us to do is to believe in Christ. First, we must receive the Holy Spirit, who enlightens and sanctifies us so that we can begin to do the Law, i.e., to love God and our neighbor. Now, the Holy Ghost is not obtained by the Law, but by faith in Christ. In the last analysis, to do the Law means to believe in Jesus Christ. The tree comes first, and then come the fruits.

The scholastics admit that a mere external and superficial performance of the Law without sincerity and good will is plain hypocrisy. Judas acted like the other disciples. What was wrong with Judas? Mark what Rome answers, "Judas was a reprobate. His motives were perverse, therefore his works were hypocritical and no good." Well, well. Rome does admit, after all, that works in themselves do not justify unless they issue from a sincere heart. Why do our opponents not profess the same truth in spiritual matters? There, above all, faith must precede everything. The heart must be purified by faith before a person can lift a finger to please God.

There are two classes of doers of the Law, true doers and hypocritical doers. The true doers of the Law are those who are moved by faith in Christ to do the Law. The hypocritical doers of the Law are those who seek to obtain righteousness by a mechanical performance of good works while their hearts are far removed from God. They act like the foolish carpenter who starts with the roof when he builds a house. Instead of doing the Law, these law-conscious hypocrites break the Law. They break the very first commandment of God by denying His promise in Christ. They do not worship God in faith. They worship themselves.

No wonder Paul was able to foretell the abominations that Antichrist would bring into the Church. That Antichrists would come, Christ Himself prophesied, Matthew 24:5, "For many shall come in my name, saying, I am Christ; and shall deceive many." Whoever seeks righteousness by works denies God and makes himself God. He is an Antichrist because he ascribes to his own works the omnipotent capability of conquering sin, death, devil, hell, and the wrath of God. An Antichrist lays claim to the honor of Christ. He is an idolater of himself. The law-righteous person is the worst kind of infidel.

Those who intend to obtain righteousness by their own efforts do not say in so many words: "I am God; I am Christ." But it amounts to that. They usurp the divinity and office of Christ. The effect is the same as if they said, "I am Christ; I am a Savior. I save myself and others." This is the impression the monks give out.

The Pope is the Antichrist, because he is against Christ, because he takes liberties with the things of God, because he lords it over the temple of God.

I cannot tell you in words how criminal it is to seek righteousness before God without faith in Christ, by the works of the Law. It is the abomination standing in the holy place. It deposes the Creator and deifies the creature.

The real doers of the Law are the true believers. The Holy Spirit enables them to love God and their neighbor. But because we have only the first-fruits of the Spirit and not the tenth-fruits, we do not observe the Law perfectly. This imperfection of ours, however, is not imputed to us, for Christ's sake.

Hence, the statement of Moses, "Cursed is every one that continueth not in all things which are written in the book of the law to do them," is not contrary to Paul. Moses requires perfect doers of the Law. But where will you find them? Nowhere. Moses himself confessed that he was not a perfect doer of the Law. He said to the Lord: "Pardon our iniquity and our sin." Christ alone can make us innocent of any transgression. How so? First, by the forgiveness of our sins and the imputation of His righteousness. Secondly, by the gift of the Holy Ghost, who engenders new life and activity in us.

Objections to the Doctrine of Faith Disproved

Here we shall take the time to enter upon the objections which our opponents raise against the doctrine of faith. There are many passages in the Bible that deal with works and the reward of works which our opponents cite against us in the belief that these will disprove the doctrine of faith which we teach.

The scholastics grant that according to the reasonable order of nature being precedes doing. They grant that any act is faulty unless it proceeds from a right motive. They grant that a person must be right before he can do right. Why don't they grant that the right inclination of the heart toward God through faith in Christ must precede works?

In the eleventh chapter of the Epistle to the Hebrews we find a catalogue of various works and deeds of the saints of the Bible. David, who killed a lion and a bear, and defeated Goliath, is mentioned. In the heroic deeds of David the scholastic can discover nothing more than outward achievement. But the deeds of David must be evaluated according to the personality of David. When we understand that David was a man of faith, whose heart trusted in the Lord, we shall understand why he could do such heroic deeds. David said: "The Lord that delivered me out of the paw of the lion, and out of the paw of the bear, he will deliver me out of the hand of this Philistine." Again: "Thou comest to me with a sword, and with a spear, and with a shield: but I come to thee in the name of the Lord of hosts, the God of the armies of Israel, whom thou hast defied. This day will the Lord deliver thee into mine hand; and I will smite thee, and take thine head from thee" (I Samuel 17:37, 45, 46). Before David could achieve a single heroic deed he was already a man beloved of God, strong and constant in faith.

Of Abel it is said in the same Epistle: "By faith Abel offered unto God a more excellent sacrifice than Cain." When the scholastics come upon the parallel passage in Genesis 4:4, they get no further than the words: "And the Lord had respect unto Abel and to his offering." "Aha!" they cry. "See, God has respect to offerings. Works do justify." With mud in their eyes they cannot see that the text says in Genesis that the Lord had respect to the person of Abel first. Abel pleased the Lord because of his faith. Because the person of Abel pleased the Lord, the offering of Abel pleased the Lord also. The Epistle to the Hebrews expressly states: "By faith Abel offered unto God a more excellent sacrifice."

In our dealings with God the work is worth nothing without faith, for "without faith it is impossible to please him" (Hebrews 11:6). The sacrifice of Abel was better than the sacrifice of Cain, because Abel had faith. As to Cain he had no faith or trust in God's grace, but strutted about in his own fancied worth. When God refused to recognize Cain's worth, Cain got angry at God and at Abel.

The Holy Spirit speaks of faith in different ways in the Sacred Scriptures. Sometimes He speaks of faith independently of other matters. When the Scriptures speak of faith in the absolute or abstract, faith refers to justification directly. But when the Scripture speaks of rewards and works it speaks of compound or relative faith. We will furnish some examples. Galatians 5:6, "Faith which worketh by love." Leviticus 18:5, "Which if a man do, he shall live in them." Matthew 19:17, "If thou wilt enter into life, keep the commandments." Psalm 37:27, "Depart from evil, and do good." In these and other passages where mention is made of doing, the Scriptures always speak of a faith-ful doing, a doing inspired by faith. "Do this and thou shalt live,," means: First have faith in Christ, and Christ will enable you to do and to live.

In the Word of God all things that are attributed to works are attributable to faith. Faith is the divinity of works. Faith permeates all the deeds of the believer, as Christ's divinity permeated His humanity. Abraham was accounted righteous because faith pervaded his whole personality and his every action.

When you read how the fathers, prophets, and kings accomplished great deeds, remember to explain them as the Epistle to the Hebrews accounts for them: "Who through faith subdued kingdoms, wrought righteousness, obtained promises, stopped the mouths of lions" (Hebrews 11:33). In this way will we correctly interpret all those passages that seem to support the righteousness of works. The Law is truly observed only through faith. Hence, every "holy," "moral" law-worker is accursed.

Supposing that this explanation will not satisfy the scholastics, supposing that they should completely wrap me up in their arguments (they cannot do it), I would rather be wrong and give all credit to Christ alone. Here is Christ. Paul, Christ's apostle, declares that "Christ hath redeemed us from the curse of the law, being made a curse for us" (Gal. 3:13). I hear with my own ears that I cannot be saved except by the blood and death of Christ. I conclude, therefore, that it is up to Christ to overcome my sins, and not up to the Law, or my own efforts. If He is the price of my redemption, if He was made sin for my justification, I don't give a care if you quote me a thousand Scripture passages for the righteousness of works against the righteousness of faith. I have the Author and Lord of the Scriptures on my side. I would rather believe Him than all that riffraff of "pious" law-workers.

Verse 11. But that no man is justified by the law in the sight of God, it is evident: for, The just shall live by faith.

The Apostle draws into his argument the testimony of the Prophet Habakkuk: "The just shall live by his faith." This passage carries much weight because it eliminates the Law and the deeds of the Law as factors in the process of our justification.

The scholastics misconstrue this passage by saying: "The just shall live by faith, if it is a working faith, or a faith formed and performed by charitable works." Their annotation is a forgery. To speak of formed or unformed faith, a sort of double faith, is contrary to the Scriptures. If charitable works can form and perfect faith I am forced to say eventually that charitable deeds constitute the essential factor in the Christian religion. Christ and His benefits would be lost to us.

Verse 12. And the law is not of faith.

In direct opposition to the scholastics Paul declares: "The law is not of faith." What is this charity the scholastics talk so much about? Does not the Law command charity? The fact is the Law commands nothing but charity, as we may gather from the following Scripture passages: "Thou shalt love the Lord thy God with all thine heart, and with all thy soul, and with all thy might" (Deut. 6:5). "Shewing mercy unto thousands of them that love me, and keep my commandments" (Exodus 20:6). "On these two commandments hang all the law and the prophets" (Matt. 22:40). If the law requires charity, charity is part of the Law and not of faith. Since Christ has displaced the Law which commands charity, it follows that charity has been abrogated with the Law as a factor in our justification, and only faith is left.

Verse 12. But, The man that doeth them shall live in them.

Paul undertakes to explain the difference between the righteousness of the Law and the righteousness of faith. The righteousness of the Law is the fulfillment of the Law according to the passage: "The man that doeth them shall live in them." The righteousness of faith is to believe the Gospel according to the passage: "The just shall live by faith." The Law is a statement of debit, the Gospel a statement of credit. By this distinction Paul explains why charity which is the commandment of the Law cannot justify, because the Law contributes nothing to our justification.

Indeed, works do follow after faith, but faith is not therefore a meritorious work. Faith is a gift. The character and limitations of the Law must be rigidly maintained.

When we believe in Christ we live by faith. When we believe in the Law we may be active enough but we have no life. The function of the Law is not to give life; the function of the Law is to kill. True, the Law says: "The man that doeth them shall live in them." But where is the person who can do "them," i.e., love God with all his heart, soul, and mind, and his neighbor as himself?

Paul has nothing against those who are justified by faith and therefore are true doers of the Law. He opposes those who think they can fulfill the Law when in reality they can only sin against the Law by trying to obtain righteousness by the Law. The Law demands that we fear, love, and worship God with a true faith. The law-workers fail to do this. Instead, they invent new modes of worship and new kinds of works which God never commanded. They provoke His anger according to the passage: "But in vain they do worship me, teaching for doctrines the commandments of men" (Matthew 15:9). Hence, the law-righteous workers are downright rebels against God, and idolaters who constantly sin against the first commandment. In short, they are no good at all though outwardly they seem to be extremely solicitous of the honor of God.

We who are justified by faith as the saints of old, may be under the Law, but we are not under the curse of the Law because sin is not imputed to us for Christ's sake. If the Law cannot be fulfilled by the believers, if sin continues to cling to them despite their love for God, what can you expect of people who are not yet justified by faith, who are still enemies of God and His Word, like the unbelieving law-workers? It goes to show how impossible it is for those who have not been justified by faith to fulfill the Law.

Verse 13. Christ hath redeemed us from the curse of the law, being made a curse for us: for it is written, Cursed is every one that hangeth on a tree.

Jerome and his present-day followers rack their miserable brains over this comforting passage in an effort to save Christ from the fancied insult of being called a curse. They say: "This quotation from Moses does not apply to Christ. Paul is taking liberties with Moses by generalizing the statements in Deuteronomy 21:23. Moses has 'he that is hanged.' Paul puts it 'every one that hangeth.' On the other hand, Paul omits the words 'of God' in his quotation from Moses: 'For he that is hanged is accursed of God.' Moses speaks of a criminal who is worthy of death." "How," our opponents ask, "can this passage be applied to the holy Christ as if He were accursed of God and worthy to be hanged?" This piece of exegesis may impress the naive as a zealous attempt to defend the honor and glory of Christ. Let us see what Paul has in mind.

Paul does not say that Christ was made a curse for Himself. The accent is on the two words "for us." Christ is personally innocent. Personally, He did not deserve to be hanged for any crime of His own doing. But because Christ took the place of others who were sinners, He was hanged like any other transgressor. The Law of Moses leaves no loopholes. It says that a transgressor should be hanged. Who are the other sinners? We are. The sentence of death and everlasting damnation had long been pronounced over us. But Christ took all our sins and died for them on the Cross. "He was numbered with the transgressors; and he bare the sin of many, and made intercession for the transgressors" (Isaiah 53:12).

All the prophets of old said that Christ should be the greatest transgressor, murderer, adulterer, thief, blasphemer that ever was or ever could be on earth. When He took the sins of the whole world upon Himself, Christ was no longer an innocent person. He was a sinner burdened with the sins of a Paul who was a blasphemer; burdened with the sins of a Peter who denied Christ; burdened with the sins of a David who committed adultery and murder, and gave the heathen occasion to laugh at the Lord. In short, Christ was charged with the sins of all men, that He should pay for them with His own blood. The curse struck Him. The Law found Him among sinners. He was not only in the company of sinners. He had gone so far as to invest Himself with the flesh and blood of sinners. So the Law judged and hanged Him for a sinner.

In separating Christ from us sinners and holding Him up as a holy exemplar, errorists rob us of our best comfort. They misrepresent Him as a threatening tyrant who is ready to slaughter us at the slightest provocation.

I am told that it is preposterous and wicked to call the Son of God a cursed sinner. I answer: If you deny that He is a condemned sinner, you are forced to deny that Christ died. It is not less preposterous to say, the Son of God died, than to say, the Son of God was a sinner.

John the Baptist called Him "the lamb of God, which taketh away the sin of the world." Being the unspotted Lamb of God, Christ was personally innocent. But because He took the sins of the world, His sinlessness was defiled with the sinfulness of the world. Whatever sins I, you, all of us have committed or shall commit, they are Christ's sins as if He had committed them Himself. Our sins have to be Christ's sins or we shall perish forever.

Isaiah declares of Christ: "The Lord hath laid on him the iniquity of us all." We have no right to minimize the force of this declaration. God does not amuse Himself with words. What a relief for a Christian to know that Christ is covered all over with my sins, your sins, and the sins of the whole world.

The papists invented their own doctrine of faith. They say charity creates and adorns their faith. By stripping Christ of our sins, by making Him sinless, they cast our sins back at us, and make Christ absolutely worthless to us. What sort of charity is this? If that is a sample of their vaunted charity, we want none of it.

Our merciful Father in heaven saw how the Law oppressed us and how impossible it was for us to get out from under the curse of the Law. He therefore sent His only Son into the world and said to Him: "You are now Peter, the liar; Paul, the persecutor; David, the adulterer; Adam, the disobedient; the thief on the cross. You, My Son, must pay the world's iniquity." The Law growls: "All right. If Your Son is taking the sin of the world, I see no sins anywhere else but in Him. He shall die on the Cross." And the Law kills Christ. But we go free.

The argument of the Apostle against the righteousness of the Law is impregnable. If Christ bears our sins, we do not bear them. But if Christ is innocent of our sins and does not bear them, we must bear them, and we shall die in our sins. "But thanks be to God, which giveth us the victory through our Lord Jesus Christ."

Let us see how Christ was able to gain the victory over our enemies. The sins of the whole world, past, present, and future, fastened themselves upon Christ and condemned Him. But because Christ is God, He had an everlasting and unconquerable righteousness. These two, the sin of the world and the righteousness of God, met in a death struggle. Furiously the sin of the world assailed the righteousness of God. Righteousness is immortal and invincible. On the other hand, sin is a mighty tyrant who subdues all men. This tyrant pounces on Christ. But Christ's righteousness is unconquerable. The result is inevitable. Sin is defeated and righteousness triumphs and reigns forever.

In the same manner was death defeated. Death is emperor of the world. He strikes down kings, princes, all men. He has an idea to destroy all life. But Christ has immortal life, and life immortal gained the victory over death. Through Christ death has lost her sting. Christ is the Death of death.

The curse of God waged a similar battle with the eternal mercy of God in Christ. The curse meant to condemn God's mercy. But it could not do it because the mercy of God is everlasting. The curse had to give way. If the mercy of God in Christ had lost out, God Himself would have lost out, which, of course, is impossible.

"Christ," says Paul, "spoiled principalities and powers, He made a show of them openly, triumphing over them in it" (Col. 2:15). They cannot harm those who hide in Christ. Sin, death, the wrath of God, hell, and the devil are mortified in Christ. Where Christ is near the powers of evil must keep their distance. St. John says: "And this is the victory that overcometh the world, even our faith" (I John 5:4).

You may now perceive why it is imperative to believe and confess the divinity of Christ. To overcome the sin of a whole world, and death, and the wrath of God was no work for any creature. The power of sin and death could be broken only by a greater power. God alone could abolish sin, destroy death, and take away the curse of the Law. God alone could bring righteousness, life, and mercy to light. In attributing these achievements to Christ the Scriptures pronounce Christ to be God forever. The article of justification is indeed fundamental. If we remain sound in this one article, we remain sound in all the other articles of the Christian faith. When we teach justification by faith in Christ we confess at the same time that Christ is God.

I cannot get over the blindness of the Pope's theologians. To imagine that the mighty forces of sin, death, and the curse can be vanquished by the righteousness of man's paltry works, by fasting, pilgrimages, masses, vows, and such gewgaws. These blind leaders of the blind turn the poor people over to the mercy of sin, death, and the devil. What chance has a defenseless human creature against these powers of darkness? They train sinners who are ten times worse than any thief, whore, murderer. The divine power of God alone can destroy sin and death, and create righteousness and life.

When we hear that Christ was made a curse for us, let us believe it with joy and assurance. By faith Christ changes places with us. He gets our sins, we get His holiness.

By faith alone can we become righteous, for faith invests us with the sinlessness of Christ. The more fully we believe this, the fuller will be our joy. If you believe that sin, death, and the curse are void, why, they are null, zero. Whenever sin and death make you nervous, write it down as an illusion of the devil. There is no sin now, no curse, no death, no devil because Christ has done away with them. This fact is sure. There is nothing wrong with the fact. The defect lies in our lack of faith.

In the Apostolic Creed we confess: "I believe in the holy Christian

Church." That means, I believe that there is no sin, no curse, no evil in the Church of God. Faith says: "I believe that." But if you want to believe your eyes, you will find many shortcomings and offenses in the members of the holy Church. You see them succumb to temptation, you see them weak in faith, you see them giving way to anger, envy, and other evil dispositions. "How can the Church be holy?" you ask. It is with the Christian Church as it is with the individual Christian. If I examine myself, I find enough unholiness to shock me. But when I look at Christ in me, I find that I am altogether holy. And so it is with the Church.

Holy Writ does not say that Christ was under the curse. It says directly that Christ was made a curse. In II Corinthians 5:21 Paul writes: "For he (God) hath made him (Christ) to be sin for us, who knew no sin; that we might be made the righteousness of God in him." Although this and similar passages may be properly explained by saying that Christ was made a sacrifice for the curse and for sin, yet in my judgment it is better to leave these passages stand as they read: Christ was made sin itself; Christ was made the curse itself. When a sinner gets wise to himself, he does not only feel miserable, he feels like misery personified; he does not only feel like a sinner, he feels like sin itself.

To finish with this verse: All evils would have overwhelmed us, as they shall overwhelm the unbelievers forever, if Christ had not become the great transgressor and guilty bearer of all our sins. The sins of the world got Him down for a moment. They came around Him like water. Of Christ, the Old Testament Prophet complained: "Thy fierce wrath goeth over me; thy terrors have cut me off" (Psalm 88:16). By Christ's salvation we have been delivered from the terrors of God to a life of eternal felicity.

Verse 14. That the blessing of Abraham might come on the Gentiles through Jesus Christ.

Paul always keeps this text before him: "In thy seed shall all the nations of the earth be blessed." The blessing promised unto Abraham could come upon the Gentiles only by Christ, the seed of Abraham. To become a blessing unto all nations Christ had to be made a curse to take away the curse from the nations of the earth. The merit that we plead, and the work that we proffer is Christ who was made a curse for us.

Let us become expert in the art of transferring our sins, our death, and every evil from ourselves to Christ; and Christ's righteousness and blessing from Christ to ourselves.

Verse 14. That we might receive the promise of the Spirit through faith.

"The promise of the Spirit" is Hebrew for "the promised Spirit." The Spirit spells freedom from the Law, sin, death, the curse, hell, and the judgment of God. No merits are mentioned in connection with this promise of the Spirit and all the blessings that go with Him. This Spirit of many blessings is received by faith alone. Faith alone builds on the promises of God, as Paul says in this verse.

Long ago the prophets visualized the happy changes Christ would effect in all things. Despite the fact that the Jews had the Law of God they never ceased to look longingly for Christ. After Moses no prophet or king added a single law to the Book. Any changes or additions were deferred to the time of Christ's coming. Moses told the people: "The Lord thy God will raise up unto thee a Prophet from the midst of thee, of thy brethren, like unto me; unto him ye shall hearken" (Deut. 18:15).

God's people of old felt that the Law of Moses could not be improved upon until the Messiah would bring better things than the Law, i.e., grace and remission of sins.

Verse 15. Brethren, I speak after the manner of men; Though it be but a man's covenant, yet if it be confirmed, no man disannulleth, or addeth thereto.

After the preceding, well-taken argument, Paul offers another based on the similarity between a man's testament and God's testament. A man's testament seems too weak a premise for the Apostle to argue from in confirmation of so important a matter as justification. We ought to prove earthly things by heavenly things, and not heavenly things by earthly things. But where the earthly thing is an ordinance of God, we may use it to prove divine matters. In Matthew 7:11 Christ Himself argued from earthly to heavenly things when He said: "If ye then, being evil, know how to give good gifts to your children, how much more shall your Father which is in heaven give good things to them that ask him?"

To come to Paul's argument. Civil law, which is God's ordinance, prohibits tampering with any testament of man. Any person's last will and testament must be respected. Paul asks: "Why is it that man's last will is scrupulously respected and not God's testament? You would not think of breaking faith with a man's testament. Why do you not keep faith with God's testament?"

The Apostle says that he is speaking after the manner of men. He means to say: "I will give you an illustration from the customs of men. If a man's last will is respected, and it is, how much more ought the testament of God be honored: 'In thy seed shall all the nations of the earth be blessed.' When Christ died, this testament was sealed by His blood. After His death the testament was opened, it was published to the nations. No man ought to alter God's testament as the false apostles do who substitute the Law and traditions of men for the testament of God."

As the false prophets tampered with God's testament in the days of Paul, so many do in our day. They will observe human laws punctiliously, but the laws of God they transgress without the flicker of an eyelid. But the time will come when they will find out that it is no joke to pervert the testament of God.

Verse 16. Now to Abraham and his seed were the promises made. He saith not, And to seeds, as of many; but as of one, And to thy seed, which is Christ.

The word testament is another name for the promise that God made unto Abraham concerning Christ. A testament is not a law, but an inheritance. Heirs do not look for laws and assessments when they open a last will; they look for grants and favors. The testament which God made out to Abraham did not contain laws. It contained promises of great spiritual blessings.

The promises were made in view of Christ, in one seed, not in many seeds. The Jews will not accept this interpretation. They insist that the singular "seed" is put for the plural "seeds." We prefer the interpretation of Paul, who makes a fine case for Christ and for us out of the singular "seed," and is after all inspired to do so by the Holy Ghost.

Verse 17. And this I say, that the covenant, that was confirmed before of God in Christ, the law which was four hundred and thirty years after, cannot disannul, that it should make the promise of none effect.

The Jews assert that God was not satisfied with His promises, but after four hundred and thirty years He gave the Law. "God," they say, "must have mistrusted His own promises, and considered them inadequate for salvation. Therefore He added to His promises something better, the Law. The Law," they say, "canceled the promises."

Paul answers: "The Law was given four hundred and thirty years after the promise was made to Abraham. The Law could not cancel the promise because the promise was the testament of God, confirmed by God in Christ many years before the Law. What God has once promised He does not take back. Every promise of God is a ratified promise."

Why was the Law added to the promise? Not to serve as a medium by which the promise might be obtained. The Law was added for these reasons: That there might be in the world a special people, rigidly controlled by the Law, a people out of which Christ should be born in due time; and that men burdened by many laws might sigh and long for Him, their Redeemer, the seed of Abraham. Even the ceremonies prescribed by the Law foreshadowed Christ. Therefore the Law was never meant to cancel the promise of God. The Law was meant to confirm the promise until the time should come when God would open His testament in the Gospel of Jesus Christ.

God did well in giving the promise so many years before the Law, that it may never be said that righteousness is granted through the Law and not through the promise. If God had meant for us to be justified by the Law, He would have given the Law four hundred and thirty years before the promise, at least He would have given the Law at the same time He gave the promise. But He never breathed a word about the Law until four hundred years after. The promise is therefore better than the Law. The Law does not cancel the promise, but faith in the promised Christ cancels the Law.

The Apostle is careful to mention the exact number of four hundred and thirty years. The wide divergence in the time between the promise and the Law helps to clinch Paul's argument that righteousness is not obtained by the Law.

Let me illustrate. A man of great wealth adopts a strange lad for his son. Remember, he does not owe the lad anything. In due time he appoints the lad heir to his entire fortune. Several years later the old man asks the lad to do something for him. And the young lad does it. Can the lad then go around and say that he deserved the inheritance by his obedience to the old man's request? How can anybody say that righteousness is obtained by obedience to the Law when the Law was given four hundred and thirty years after God's promise of the blessing?

One thing is certain, Abraham was never justified by the Law, for the simple reason that the Law was not in his day. If the Law was non-existent how could Abraham obtain righteousness by the Law? Abraham had nothing else to go by but the promise. This promise he believed and that was counted unto him for righteousness. If the father obtained righteousness through faith, the children get it the same way.

We use the argument of time also. We say our sins were taken away by the death of Christ fifteen hundred years ago, long before there were any religious orders, canons, or rules of penance, merits, etc. What did people do about their sins before these new inventions were hatched up?

Paul finds his arguments for the righteousness of faith everywhere. Even the element of time serves to build his case against the false apostles. Let us fortify our conscience with similar arguments. They help us in the trials of our faith. They turn our attention from the Law to the promises, from sin to righteousness; from death to life.

It is not for nothing that Paul bears down on this argument. He foresaw this confusion of the promise and the Law creeping into the Church. Accustom yourself to separate Law and Gospel even in regard to time. When 123the Law comes to pay your conscience a visit, say: "Mister Law, you come too soon. The four hundred and thirty years aren't up yet. When they are up, you come again. Won't you?"

Verse 18. For if the inheritance be of the law, it is no more of promise.

In Romans 4:14, the Apostle writes: "For if they which are made of the law be heirs, faith is made void, and the promise made of none effect." It cannot be otherwise. That the Law is something entirely different from the promise is plain. The Law thunders: "Thou shalt, thou shalt not." The promise of the "seed" pleads: "Take this gift of God." If the inheritance of the gifts of God were obtained by the Law, God would be a liar. We would have the right to ask Him: "Why did you make this promise in the first place: 'In thy seed shall all the nations of the earth be blessed'? Why did you not say: 'In thy works thou shalt be blessed'?"

Verse 18. But God gave it to Abraham by promise.

So much is certain, before the Law ever existed, God gave Abraham the inheritance or blessing by the promise. In other words, God granted unto Abraham remission of sins, righteousness, salvation, and everlasting life. And not only to Abraham but to all believers, because God said: "In thy seed shall all the nations of the earth be blessed." The blessing was given unconditionally. The Law had no chance to butt in because Moses was not yet born. "How then can you say that righteousness is obtained by the Law?"

The Apostle now goes to work to explain the province and purpose of the Law.

Verse 19. Wherefore then serveth the law?

The question naturally arises: If the Law was not given for righteousness or salvation, why was it given? Why did God give the Law in the first place if it cannot justify a person?

The Jews believed if they kept the Law they would be saved. When they heard that the Gospel proclaimed a Christ who had come into the world to save sinners and not the righteous; when they heard that sinners were to enter the kingdom of heaven before the righteous, the Jews were very much put out. They murmured: "These last have wrought but one hour, and thou hast made them equal unto us, which have borne the burden and heat of the day" (Matthew 20:12). They complained that the heathen who at one time had been worshipers of idols obtained grace without the drudgery of the Law that was theirs.

Today we hear the same complaints. "What was the use of our having lived in a cloister, twenty, thirty, forty years; what was the sense of having vowed chastity, poverty, obedience; what good are all the masses and canonical hours that we read; what profit is there in fasting, praying, etc., if any man or woman, any beggar or scour woman is to be made equal to us, or even be considered more acceptable unto God than we?"

Reason takes offense at the statement of Paul: "The law was added because of transgressions." People say that Paul abrogated the Law, that he is a radical, that he blasphemed God when he said that. People say: "We might as well live like wild people if the Law does not count. Let us abound in sin that grace may abound. Let us do evil that good may come of it."

What are we to do? Such scoffing distresses us, but we cannot stop it. Christ Himself was accused of being a blasphemer and rebel. Paul and all the other apostles were told the same things. Let the scoffers slander us, let them spare us not. But we must not on their own account keep silent. We must speak frankly in order that afflicted consciences may find surcease. Neither are we to pay any attention to the foolish and ungodly people for abusing our doctrine. They are the kind that would scoff, Law or no Law. Our first consideration must be the comfort of troubled consciences, that they may not perish with the multitudes.

When he saw that some were offended at his doctrine, while others found in it encouragement to live after the flesh, Paul comforted himself with the thought that it was his duty to preach the Gospel to the elect of God, and that for their sake he must endure all things. Like Paul we also do all these things for the sake of God's elect. As for the scoffers and skeptics, I am so disgusted with them that in all my life I would not open my mouth for them once. I wish that they were back there where they belong under the iron heel of the Pope.

People foolish but wise in their conceits jump to the conclusion: If the Law does not justify, it is good for nothing. How about that? Because money does not justify, would you say that money is good for nothing?

Because the eyes do not justify, would you have them taken out? Because the Law does not justify it does not follow that the Law is without value. We must find and define the proper purpose of the Law. We do not offhand condemn the Law because we say it does not justify.

We say with Paul that the Law is good if it is used properly. Within its proper sphere the Law is an excellent thing. But if we ascribe to the Law functions for which it was never intended, we pervert not only the Law but also the Gospel.

It is the universal impression that righteousness is obtained through the deeds of the Law. This impression is instinctive and therefore doubly dangerous. Gross sins and vices may be recognized or else repressed by the threat of punishment. But this sin, this opinion of man's own righteousness refuses to be classified as sin. It wants to be esteemed as high-class religion. Hence, it constitutes the mighty influence of the devil over the entire world. In order to point out the true office of the Law, and thus to stamp out that false impression of the righteousness of 126the Law, Paul answers the question: "Wherefore then serveth the Law?" with the words:

Verse 19. It was added because of transgressions.

All things differ. Let everything serve its unique purpose. Let the sun shine by day, the moon and the stars by night. Let the sea furnish fish, the earth grain, the woods trees, etc. Let the Law also serve its unique purpose. It must not step out of character and take the place of anything else. What is the function of the Law? "Transgression," answers the Apostle.

The Twofold Purpose of the Law

The Law has a twofold purpose. One purpose is civil. God has ordained civil laws to punish crime. Every law is given to restrain sin. Does it not then make men righteous? No. In refraining from murder, adultery, theft, or other sins, I do so under compulsion because I fear the jail, the noose, the electric chair. These restrain me as iron bars restrain a lion and a bear. Otherwise they would tear everything to pieces. Such forceful restraint cannot be regarded as righteousness, rather as an indication of unrighteousness. As a wild beast is tied to keep it from running amuck, so the Law bridles mad and furious man to keep him from running wild. The need for restraint shows plainly enough that those who need the Law are not righteous, but wicked men who are fit to be tied. No, the Law does not justify.

The first purpose of the Law, accordingly, is to restrain the wicked. The devil gets people into all kinds of scrapes. Therefore God instituted governments, parents, laws, restrictions, and civil ordinances. At least they help to tie the devil's hands so that he does not rage up and down the earth. This civil restraint by the Law is intended by God for the preservation of all things, particularly for the good of the Gospel that it should not be hindered too much by the tumult of the wicked. But Paul is not now treating of this civil use and function of the Law.

The second purpose of the Law is spiritual and divine. Paul describes this spiritual purpose of the Law in the words, "Because of transgressions," i.e., to reveal to a person his sin, blindness, misery, his ignorance, hatred, and contempt of God, his death, hell, and condemnation.

This is the principal purpose of the Law and its most valuable contribution. As long as a person is not a murderer, adulterer, thief, he would swear that he is righteous. How is God going to humble such a person except by the Law? The Law is the hammer of death, the thunder of hell, and the lightning of God's wrath to bring down the proud and shameless hypocrites. When the Law was instituted on Mount Sinai it was accompanied by lightning, by storms, by the sound of trumpets, to tear to pieces that monster called self-righteousness. As long as a person thinks he is right he is going to be incomprehensibly proud and presumptuous. He is going to hate God, despise His grace and mercy, and ignore the promises in Christ. The Gospel of the free forgiveness of sins through Christ will never appeal to the self-righteous.

This monster of self-righteousness, this stiff-necked beast, needs a big axe. And that is what the Law is, a big axe. Accordingly, the proper use and function of the Law is to threaten until the conscience is scared stiff.

The awful spectacle at Mount Sinai portrayed the proper use of the Law.

When the children of Israel came out of Egypt a feeling of singular holiness possessed them. They boasted: "We are the people of God. All that the Lord hath spoken we will do" (Ex. 19:8). This feeling of holiness was heightened when Moses ordered them to wash their clothes, to refrain from their wives, and to prepare themselves all around. The third day came and Moses led the people out of their tents to the foot of the mountain into the presence of the Lord. What happened? When the children of Israel saw the whole mountain burning and smoking, the black clouds rent by fierce lightning flashing up and down in the inky darkness, when they heard the sound of the trumpet blowing louder and longer, shattered by the roll of thunder, they were so frightened that they begged Moses: "Speak thou with us, and we will hear: but let not God speak with us, lest we die" (Ex. 20:19). I ask you, what good did their scrubbing, their snow-white clothes, and their continence do them? No good at all. Not a single one could stand in the presence of the glorious Lord. Stricken by the terror of God, they fled back into their tents, as if the devil were after them.

The Law is meant to produce the same effect today which it produced at Mount Sinai long ago. I want to encourage all who fear God, especially those who intend to become ministers of the Gospel, to learn from the Apostle the proper use of the Law. I fear that after our time the right handling of the Law will become a lost art. Even now, although we continually explain the separate functions of the Law and the Gospel, we have those among us who do not understand how the Law should be used. What will it be like when we are dead and gone?

We want it understood that we do not reject the Law as our opponents claim. On the contrary, we uphold the Law. We say the Law is good if it is used for the purposes for which it was designed, to check civil transgression, and to magnify spiritual transgressions. The Law is also a light like the Gospel. But instead of revealing the grace of God, righteousness, and life, the Law brings sin, death, and the wrath of God to light. This is the business of the Law, and here the business of the Law ends, and should go no further.

The business of the Gospel, on the other hand, is to quicken, to comfort, to raise the fallen. The Gospel carries the news that God for Christ's sake is merciful to the most unworthy sinners, if they will only believe that Christ by His death has delivered them from sin and everlasting death unto grace, forgiveness, and everlasting life. By keeping in mind the difference between the Law and the Gospel we let each perform its special task. Of this difference between the Law and the Gospel nothing can be discovered in the writings of the monks or scholastics, nor for that matter in the writings of the ancient fathers. Augustine understood the difference somewhat. Jerome and others knew nothing of it. The silence in the Church concerning the difference between the Law and the Gospel has resulted in untold harm. Unless a sharp distinction is maintained between the purpose and function of the Law and the Gospel, the Christian doctrine cannot be kept free from error.

Verse 19. It was added because of transgressions.

In other words, that transgressions might be recognized as such and thus increased. When sin, death, and the wrath of God are revealed to a person by the Law, he grows impatient, complains against God, and rebels. Before that he was a very holy man; he worshipped and praised God; he bowed his knees before God and gave thanks, like the Pharisee. But now that sin and death are revealed to him by the Law he wishes there were no God. The Law inspires hatred of God. Thus sin is not only revealed by the Law; sin is actually increased and magnified by the Law.

The Law is a mirror to show a person what he is like, a sinner who is guilty of death, and worthy of everlasting punishment. What is this bruising and beating by the hand of the Law to accomplish? This, that we may find the way to grace. The Law is an usher to lead the way to grace. God is the God of the humble, the miserable, the afflicted. It is His nature to exalt the humble, to comfort the sorrowing, to heal the broken-hearted, to justify the sinners, and to save the condemned. The fatuous idea that a person can be holy by himself denies God the pleasure of saving sinners. God must therefore first take the sledge-hammer of the Law in His fists and smash the beast of self-righteousness and its brood of self-confidence, self-wisdom, self-righteousness, and self-help. When the conscience has been thoroughly frightened by the Law it welcomes the Gospel of grace with its message of a Savior who came into the world, not to break the bruised reed, nor to quench the smoking flax, but to preach glad tidings to the poor, to heal the broken-hearted, and to grant forgiveness of sins to all the captives.

Man's folly, however, is so prodigious that instead of embracing the message of grace with its guarantee of the forgiveness of sin for Christ's sake, man finds himself more laws to satisfy his conscience. "If I live," says he, "I will mend my life. I will do this, I will do that." Man, if you don't do the very opposite, if you don't send Moses with the Law back to Mount Sinai and take the hand of Christ, pierced for your sins, you will never be saved.

When the Law drives you to the point of despair, let it drive you a little farther, let it drive you straight into the arms of Jesus who says: "Come unto me, all ye that labour and are heavy laden, and I will give you rest."

Verse 19. Till the seed should come to whom the promise was made.

The Law is not to have its say indefinitely. We must know how long the Law is to put in its licks. If it hammers away too long, no person would and could be saved. The Law has a boundary beyond which it must not go. How long ought the Law to hold sway? "Till the seed should come to whom the promise was made."

That may be taken literally to mean until the time of the Gospel. "From the days of John the Baptist," says Jesus, "until now the kingdom of heaven suffereth violence, and the violent take it by force. For all the prophets and the law prophesied until John" (Matthew 11:12, 13). When Christ came the Law and the ceremonies of Moses ceased.

Spiritually, it means that the Law is not to operate on a person after he has been humbled and frightened by the exposure of his sins and the wrath of God. We must then say to the Law: "Mister Law, lay off him. He has had enough. You scared him good and proper." Now it is the Gospel's turn. Now let Christ with His gracious lips talk to him of better things, grace, peace, forgiveness of sins, and eternal life.

Verse 19. And it was ordained by angels in the hand of a mediator.

The Apostle digresses a little from his immediate theme. Something occurred to him and he throws it in by the way. It occurred to him that the Law differs from the Gospel in another respect, in respect to authorship. The Law was delivered by the angels, but the Gospel by the Lord Himself. Hence, the Gospel is superior to the Law, as the word of a lord is superior to the word of his servant.

The Law was handed down by a being even inferior to the angels, by a middleman named Moses. Paul wants us to understand that Christ is the mediator of a better testament than mediator Moses of the Law. Moses led the people out of their tents to meet God. But they ran away. That is how good a mediator Moses was.

Paul says: "How can the Law justify when that whole sanctified people of Israel and even mediator Moses trembled at the voice of God? What kind of righteousness do you call that when people run away from it and hate it the worst way? If the Law could justify, people would love the Law. But look at the children of Israel running away from it."

The flight of the children of Israel from Mount Sinai indicates how people feel about the Law. They don't like it. If this were the only argument to prove that salvation is not by the Law, this one Bible history would do the work. What kind of righteousness is this law-righteousness when at the commencement exercises of the Law Moses and the scrubbed people run away from it so fast that an iron mountain, the Red Sea even, could not have stopped them until they were back in Egypt once again? If they could not hear the Law, how could they ever hope to perform the Law?

If all the world had stood at the mountain, all the world would have hated the Law and fled from it as the children of Israel did. The whole world is an enemy of the Law. How, then, can anyone be justified by the Law when everybody hates the Law and its divine author?

All this goes to show how little the scholastics know about the Law. They do not consider its spiritual effect and purpose, which is not to justify or to pacify afflicted consciences, but to increase sin, to terrify the conscience, and to produce wrath. In their ignorance the papists spout about man's good will and right judgment, and man's capacity to perform the Law of God. Ask the people of Israel who were present at the presentation of the Law on Mount Sinai whether what the scholastics say is true. Ask David, who often complains in the Psalms that he was cast away from God and in hell, that he was frantic about his sin, and sick at the thought of the wrath and judgment of God. No, the Law does not justify

Verse 20. Now a mediator is not a mediator of one.

Here the Apostle briefly compares the two mediators: Moses and Christ. "A mediator," says Paul, "is not a mediator of one." He is necessarily a mediator of two: The offender and the offended. Moses was such a mediator between the Law and the people who were offended at the Law. They were offended at the Law because they did not understand its purpose. That was the veil which Moses put over his face. The people were also offended at the Law because they could not look at the bare face of Moses. It shone with the glory of God. When Moses addressed the people he had to cover his face with that veil of his. They could not listen to their mediator Moses without another mediator, the veil. The Law had to change its face and voice. In other words, the Law had to be made tolerable to the people.

Thus covered, the Law no longer spoke to the people in its undisguised majesty. It became more tolerable to the conscience. This explains why men fail to understand the Law properly, with the result that they become secure and presumptuous hypocrites. One of two things has to be done: Either the Law must be covered with a veil and then it loses its full effectiveness, or it must be unveiled and then the full blast of its force kills. Man cannot stand the Law without a veil over it. Hence, we are forced either to look beyond the Law to Christ, or we go through life as shameless hypocrites and secure sinners.

Paul says: "A mediator is not a mediator of one." Moses could not be a mediator of God only, for God needs no mediator. Again, Moses could not be a mediator of the people only. He was a mediator between God and the people. It is the office of a mediator to conciliate the party that is offended and to placate the party that is the offender. However, Moses' mediation consisted only in changing the tone of the Law to make it more tolerable to the people. Moses was merely a mediator of the veil. He could not supply the ability to perform the Law.

What do you suppose would have happened if the Law had been given without a mediator and the people had been denied the services of a go-between? The people would have perished, or in case they had escaped they would have required the services of another mediator to preserve them alive and to keep the Law in force. Moses came along and he was made the mediator. He covered his face with a veil. But that is as much as he could do. He could not deliver men's consciences from the terror of the Law. The sinner needs a better mediator.

That better mediator is Jesus Christ. He does not change the voice of the Law, nor does He hide the Law with a veil. He takes the full blast of the wrath of the Law and fulfills its demands most meticulously.

Of this better Mediator Paul says: "A mediator is not a mediator of one." We are the offending party; God is the party offended. The offense is of such a nature that God cannot pardon it. Neither can we render adequate 134satisfaction for our offenses. There is discord between God and us. Could not God revoke His Law? No. How about running away from God? It cannot be done. It took Christ to come between us and God and to reconcile God to us. How did Christ do it? "Blotting out the handwriting of ordinances that was against us, which was contrary to us, and took it out of the way, nailing it to his cross" (Col. 2:14).

This one word, "mediator," is proof enough that the Law cannot justify. Otherwise we should not need a mediator.

In Christian theology the Law does not justify. In fact it has the contrary effect. The Law alarms us, it magnifies our sins until we begin to hate the Law and its divine Author. Would you call this being justified by the Law?

Can you imagine a more arrant outrage than to hate God and to abhor His Law? What an excellent Law it is. Listen: "I am the Lord thy God, which have brought thee out of the land of Egypt, out of the house of bondage. Thou shalt have no other gods . . . showing mercy unto thousands . . . honor thy father and thy mother: that thy days may be long upon the land . . . " (Ex. 20:2, 3, 6, 12). Are these not excellent laws, perfect wisdom? "Let not God speak with us, lest we die," cried the children of Israel. Is it not amazing that a person should refuse to hear things that are good for him? Any person would be glad to hear, I should think, that he has a gracious God who shows mercy unto thousands. Is it not amazing that people hate the Law that promotes their safety and welfare, e.g., "Thou shalt not kill; thou shalt not commit adultery; thou shalt not steal"?

The Law can do nothing for us except to arouse the conscience. Before the Law comes to me I feel no sin. But when the Law comes, sin, death, and hell are revealed to me. You would not call this being made righteous. You would call it being condemned to death and hell-fire.

Verse 20. But God is one.

God does not offend anybody, therefore He needs no mediator. But we offend God, therefore we need a mediator. And we need a better mediator than Moses. We need Christ.

Verse 21. Is the law then against the promises of God?

Before he digressed Paul stated that the Law does not justify. Shall we then discard the Law? No, no. It supplies a certain need. It supplies men with a needed realization of their sinfulness. Now arises another question: If the Law does no more than to reveal sin, does it not oppose the promises of God? The Jews believed that by the restraint and discipline of the Law the promises of God would be hastened, in fact earned by them.

Paul answers: "Not so. On the contrary, if we pay too much attention to the Law the promises of God will be slowed up. How can God fulfill His promises to a people that hates the Law?"

Verse 21. God forbid.

God never said to Abraham: "In thee shall all the nations of the earth be blessed because thou hast kept the Law." When Abraham was still uncircumcised and without the Law or any law, indeed, when he was still an idol worshiper, God said to him: "Get thee out of thy country, etc.; I am thy shield, etc.; In thy seed shall all the nations of the earth be blessed." These are unconditional promises which God freely made to Abraham without respect to works.

This is aimed especially at the Jews who think that the promises of God are impeded by their sins. Paul says: "The Lord is not slack concerning His promises because of our sins, or hastens His promises because of any merit on our part." God's promises are not influenced by our attitudes. They rest in His goodness and mercy.

Just because the Law increases sin, it does not therefore obstruct the promises of God. The Law confirms the promises, in that it prepares a person to look for the fulfillment of the promises of God in Christ.

The proverb has it that Hunger is the best cook. The Law makes afflicted consciences hungry for Christ. Christ tastes good to them. Hungry hearts appreciate Christ. Thirsty souls are what Christ wants. He invites them: "Come unto me, all ye that labour and are heavy laden, and I will give you rest." Christ's benefits are so precious that He will dispense them only to those who need them and really desire them.

Verse 21. For if there had been a law given which could have given life, verily righteousness should have been by the law.

The Law cannot give life. It kills. The Law does not justify a person before God; it increases sin. The Law does not secure righteousness; it hinders righteousness. The Apostle declares emphatically that the Law of itself cannot save.

Despite the intelligibility of Paul's statement, our enemies fail to grasp it. Otherwise they would not emphasize free will, natural strength, the works of supererogation, etc. To escape the charge of forgery they always have their convenient annotation handy, that Paul is referring only to the ceremonial and not to the moral law. But Paul includes all laws. He expressly says: "If there had been a law given."

There is no law by which righteousness may be obtained, not a single one. Why not?

Verse 22. But the Scripture hath concluded all under sin.

Where? First in the promises concerning Christ in Genesis 3:15 and in

Genesis 22:18, which speak of the seed of the woman and the seed of Abraham. The fact that these promises were made unto the fathers concerning Christ implies that the fathers were subject to the curse of sin and eternal death. Otherwise why the need of promises?

Next, Holy Writ "concludes" all under sin in this passage from Paul: "For as many as are of the works of the law are under the curse." Again, in the passage which the Apostle quotes from Deuteronomy 27:26, "Cursed is every one that continueth not in all things which are written in the book of the law to do them." This passage clearly submits all men to the curse, not only those who sin openly against the Law, but also those who sincerely endeavor to perform the Law, inclusive of monks, friars, hermits, etc.

The conclusion is inevitable: Faith alone justified without works. If the Law itself cannot justify, much less can imperfect performance of the Law or the works of the Law, justify.

Verse 22. That the promise by faith of Jesus Christ might be given to them that believe.

The Apostle stated before that "the Scripture hath concluded all under sin." Forever? No, only until the promise should be fulfilled. The promise, you will recall, is the inheritance itself or the blessing promised to Abraham, deliverance from the Law, sin, death, and the devil, and the free gift of grace, righteousness, salvation, and eternal life. This promise, says Paul, is not obtained by any merit, by any law, or by any work. This promise is given. To whom? To those who believe. In whom? In Jesus Christ.

Verse 23. But before faith came.

The Apostle proceeds to explain the service which the Law is to render. Previously Paul had said that the Law was given to reveal the wrath and death of God upon all sinners. Although the Law kills, God brings good out of evil. He uses the Law to bring life. God saw that the universal illusion of self-righteousness could not be put down in any other way but by the Law. The Law dispels all self-illusions. It puts the fear of God in a man. Without this fear there can be no thirst for God's mercy. God accordingly uses the Law for a hammer to break up the illusion of self-righteousness, that we should despair of our own strength and efforts at self-justification.

Verse 23. But before faith came, we were kept under the law, shut up unto the faith which should afterwards be revealed.

The Law is a prison to those who have not as yet obtained grace. No prisoner enjoys the confinement. He hates it. If he could he would smash the prison and find his freedom at all cost. As long as he stays in prison he refrains from evil deeds. Not because he wants to, but because he has to. The bars and the chains restrain him. He does not regret the crime that put him in jail. On the contrary, he is mighty sore that he cannot rob and kill as before. If he could escape he would go right back to robbing and killing.

The Law enforces good behavior, at least outwardly. We obey the Law because if we don't we will be punished. Our obedience is inspired by fear. We obey under duress and we do it resentfully. Now what kind of righteousness is this when we refrain from evil out of fear of punishment? Hence, the righteousness of the Law is at bottom nothing but love of sin and hatred of righteousness.

All the same, the Law accomplishes this much, that it will outwardly at least and to a certain extent repress vice and crime.

But the Law is also a spiritual prison, a veritable hell. When the Law begins to threaten a person with death and the eternal wrath of God, a man just cannot find any comfort at all. He cannot shake off at will the nightmare of terror which the Law stirs up in his conscience. Of this terror of the Law the Psalms furnish many glimpses.

The Law is a civil and a spiritual prison. And such it should be. For that the Law is intended. Only the confinement in the prison of the Law must not be unduly prolonged. It must come to an end. The freedom of faith must succeed the imprisonment of the Law.

Happy the person who knows how to utilize the Law so that it serves the purposes of grace and of faith. Unbelievers are ignorant of this happy knowledge. When Cain was first shut up in the prison of the Law he felt no pang at the fratricide he had committed. He thought he could pass it off as an incident with a shrug of the shoulder. "Am I my brother's keeper?" he answered God flippantly. But when he heard the ominous words, "What hast thou done? the voice of thy brother's blood crieth unto me from the ground," Cain began to feel his imprisonment. Did he know how to get out of prison? No. He failed to call the Gospel to his aid. He said: "My punishment is greater than I can bear." He could only think of the prison. He forgot that he was brought face to face with his crime so that he should hurry to God for mercy and for pardon. Cain remained in the prison of the Law and despaired.

As a stone prison proves a physical handicap, so the spiritual prison of the Law proves a chamber of torture. But this it should only be until faith be revealed. The silly conscience must be educated to this. Talk to your conscience. Say: "Sister, you are now in jail all right. But you don't have to stay there forever. It is written that we are 'shut up unto faith which should afterwards be revealed.' Christ will lead you to freedom. Do not despair like Cain, Saul, or Judas. They might have gone free if they had called Christ to their aid. Just take it easy, Sister Conscience. It's good for you to be locked up for a while. It will teach you to appreciate Christ."

How anybody can say that he by nature loves the Law is beyond me. The Law is a prison to be feared and hated. Any unconverted person who says he loves the Law is a liar. He does not know what he is talking about. We love the Law about as well as a murderer loves his gloomy cell, his straight-jacket, and the iron bars in front of him. How then can the Law justify us?

Verse 23. Shut up unto the faith which should afterwards be revealed.

We know that Paul has reference to the time of Christ's coming. It was then that faith and the object of faith were fully revealed. But we may apply the historical fact to our inner life. When Christ came He abolished the Law and brought liberty and life to light. This He continues to do in the hearts of the believers. The Christian has a body in whose members, as Paul says, sin dwells and wars. I take sin to mean not only the deed but root, tree, fruit, and all. A Christian may perhaps not fall into the gross sins of murder, adultery, theft, but he is not free from impatience, complaints, hatreds, and blasphemy of God. As carnal lust is strong in a young man, in a man of full age the desire for glory, and in an old man covetousness, so impatience, doubt, and hatred of God often prevail in the hearts of sincere Christians. Examples of these sins may be garnered from the Psalms, Job, Jeremiah, and all the Sacred Scriptures.

Accordingly each Christian continues to experience in his heart times of the Law and times of the Gospel. The times of the Law are discernible by heaviness of heart, by a lively sense of sin, and a feeling of despair brought on by the Law. These periods of the Law will come again and again as long as we live. To mention my own case. There are many times when I find fault with God and am impatient with Him. The wrath and the judgment of God displease me, my wrath and impatience displease Him. Then is the season of the Law, when "the flesh lusteth against the Spirit, and the Spirit against the flesh."The time of grace returns when the heart is enlivened by the promise of God's mercy. It soliloquizes: "Why art thou cast down, O my soul? and why art thou disquieted within me? Can you see nothing but law, sin, death, and hell? Is there no grace, no forgiveness, no joy, peace, life, heaven, no Christ and God? Trouble me no more, my soul. Hope in God who has not spared His own dear Son but has given Him into death for thy sins." When the Law carries things too far, say: "Mister Law, you are not the whole show. There are other and better things than you. They tell me to trust in the Lord."

There is a time for the Law and a time for grace. Let us study to be good timekeepers. It is not easy. Law and grace may be miles apart in essence, but in the heart, they are pretty close together. In the heart fear and trust, sin and grace, Law and Gospel cross paths continually.

When reason hears that justification before God is obtained by grace alone, it draws the inference that the Law is without value. The doctrine of the Law must therefore be studied carefully lest we either reject the Law altogether, or are tempted to attribute to the Law a capacity to save. There are three ways in which the Law may be abused. First, by the self-righteous hypocrites who fancy that they can be justified by the Law. Secondly, by those who claim that Christian liberty exempts a Christian from the observance of the Law. "These," says Peter, "use their liberty for a cloak of maliciousness," and bring the name and the Gospel of Christ into ill repute. Thirdly, the Law is abused by those who do not understand that the Law is meant to drive us to Christ. When the Law is properly used its value cannot be too highly appraised. It will take me to Christ every time.

Verse 24. Wherefore the law was our schoolmaster to bring us unto Christ.

This simile of the schoolmaster is striking. Schoolmasters are indispensable. But show me a pupil who loves his schoolmaster. How little love is lost upon them the Jews showed by their attitude toward Moses. They would have been glad to stone Moses to death (Ex. 17:4). You cannot expect anything else. How can a pupil love a teacher who frustrates his desires? And if the pupil disobeys, the schoolmaster whips him, and the pupil has to like it and even kiss the rod with which he was beaten. Do you think the schoolboy feels good about it? As soon as the teacher turns his back, the pupil breaks the rod and throws it into the fire. And if he were stronger than the teacher he would not take the beatings, but beat up the teacher. All the same, teachers are indispensable, otherwise the children would grow up without discipline, instruction, and training.

But how long are the scolding and the whippings of the schoolmaster to continue? Only for a time, until the boy has been trained to be a worthy heir of his father. No father wants his son to be whipped all the time. The discipline is to last until the boy has been trained to be his father's worthy successor.

The Law is such a schoolmaster. Not for always, but until we have been brought to Christ. The Law is not just another schoolmaster. The Law is a specialist to bring us to Christ. What would you think of a schoolmaster who could only torment and beat a child? Yet of such schoolmasters there were plenty in former times, regular bruisers. The Law is not that kind of a schoolmaster. It is not to torment us always. With its lashings it is only too anxious to drive us to Christ. The Law is like the good schoolmaster who trains his children to find pleasure in doing things they formerly detested.

Verse 24. That we might be justified by faith.

The Law is not to teach us another Law. When a person feels the full force of the Law he is likely to think: I have transgressed all the commandments of God; I am guilty of eternal death. If God will spare me I will change and live right from now on. This natural but entirely wrong reaction to the Law has bred the many ceremonies and works devised to earn grace and remission of sins.

The Law means to enlarge my sins, to make me small, so that I may be justified by faith in Christ. Faith is neither law nor word; but confidence in Christ "who is the end of the law." How so is Christ the end of the Law? Not in this way that He replaced the old Law with new laws. Nor is Christ the end of the Law in a way that 143makes Him a hard judge who has to be bribed by works as the papists teach. Christ is the end or finish of the Law to all who believe in Him. The Law can no longer accuse or condemn them.

READER

AUGUSTINE: SELECTIONS FROM CITY OF GOD WRITTEN 413AD

TOP TEN THEOLOGIANS

Chapter 10.—That the Saints Lose Nothing in Losing Temporal Goods.

These are the considerations which one must keep in view, that he may answer the question whether any evil happens to the faithful and godly which cannot be turned to profit. Or shall we say that the question is needless, and that the apostle is vaporing when he says, "We know that all things work together for good to them that love God?"

They lost all they had. Their faith? Their godliness? The possessions of the hidden man of the heart, which in the sight of God are of great price? Did they lose these? For these are the wealth of Christians, to whom the wealthy apostle said, "Godliness with contentment is great gain. For we brought nothing into this world, and it is certain we can carry nothing out. And having food and raiment, let us be therewith content. But they that will be rich fall into temptation and a snare, and into many foolish and hurtful lusts, which drown men in destruction and perdition. For the love of money is the root of all evil; which, while some coveted after, they have erred from the faith, and pierced themselves through with many sorrows."

They, then, who lost their worldly all in the sack of Rome, if they owned their possessions as they had been taught by the apostle, who himself was poor without, but rich within,—that is to say, if they used the world as not using it,—could say in the words of Job, heavily tried, but not overcome: "Naked came I out of my mother's womb, and naked shall I return thither: the Lord gave, and the Lord hath taken away; as it pleased the Lord, so has it come to pass: blessed be the name of the Lord." Like a good servant, Job counted the will of his Lord his great possession, by obedience to which his soul was enriched; nor did it grieve him to lose, while yet living, those goods which he must shortly leave at his death. But as to those feebler spirits who, though they cannot be said to prefer earthly possessions to Christ, do yet cleave to them with a somewhat immoderate attachment, they have discovered by the pain of losing these things how much they were sinning in loving them. For their grief is of their own making; in the words of the apostle quoted above, "they have pierced themselves through with many sorrows." For it was well that they who had so long despised these verbal admonitions should receive the teaching of experience. For when the apostle says, "They that will be rich fall into temptation," and so on, what he blames in riches is not the possession of them, but the desire of them. For elsewhere he says, "Charge them that are rich in this world, that they be not high-minded, nor trust in uncertain riches, but in the living God, who giveth us richly all things to enjoy; that they do good, that they be rich in good works, ready to distribute, willing to communicate; laying up in store for themselves a good foundation against the time to come, that they may lay hold on eternal life." They who were making such a use of their property have been consoled for light losses by great gains, and have had more pleasure in those possessions which they have securely laid past, by freely giving them away, than grief in those which they entirely lost by an anxious and selfish hoarding of them. For nothing could perish on earth save what they would be ashamed to carry away from earth. Our Lord's injunction runs, "Lay not up for yourselves treasures upon earth, where moth and rust doth corrupt, and where thieves break through and steal; but lay up for yourselves treasures in heaven, where neither moth nor rust doth corrupt, and where thieves do not break through nor steal: for where your treasure is, there will your heart be also." And they who have listened to this injunction have proved in the time of tribulation how well they were advised in not despising this most trustworthy teacher, and most faithful and mighty guardian of their treasure. For if many were glad that their treasure was stored in places which the enemy chanced not to light upon, how much better founded was the joy of those who, by the counsel of their God, had fled with their treasure to a citadel which no enemy can possibly reach! Thus our Paulinus, bishop of Nola, who voluntarily abandoned vast wealth and became quite poor, though abundantly rich in holiness, when the barbarians sacked Nola, and took him prisoner, used silently to pray, as he afterwards told me, "O Lord, let me not be troubled for gold and silver, for where all my treasure is Thou knowest." For all his treasure was where he had been taught to hide and store it by Him who had also foretold that these calamities would happen in the world. Consequently those persons who obeyed their Lord when He warned them where and how to lay up treasure, did not lose even their earthly possessions in the invasion of the barbarians; while those who are now repenting that they did not obey Him have learnt the right use of earthly goods, if not by the wisdom which would have prevented their loss, at least by the experience which follows it.

But some good and Christian men have been put to the torture, that they might be forced to deliver up their goods to the enemy. They could indeed neither deliver nor lose that good which made themselves good. If, however, they preferred torture to the surrender of the mammon of iniquity, then I say they were not good men. Rather they should have been reminded that, if they suffered so severely for the sake of money, they should endure all torment, if need be, for Christ's sake; that they might be taught to love Him rather who enriches with eternal felicity all who suffer for Him, and not silver and gold, for which it was pitiable to suffer, whether they preserved it by telling a lie or lost it by telling the truth. For under these tortures no one lost Christ by confessing Him, no one preserved wealth save by denying its existence. So that possibly the torture which taught them that they should set their affections on a possession they could not lose, was more useful than those possessions which, without any useful fruit at all, disquieted and tormented their anxious owners. But then we are reminded that some were tortured who had no wealth to surrender, but who were not believed when they said so. These too, however, had perhaps some craving for wealth, and were not willingly poor with a holy resignation; and to such it had to be made plain, that not the actual possession alone, but also the desire of wealth, deserved such excruciating pains. And even if they were destitute of any hidden stores of gold and silver, because they were living in hopes of a better life,—I know not indeed if any such person was tortured on the supposition that he had wealth; but if so, then certainly in confessing, when put to the question, a holy poverty, he confessed Christ. And though it was scarcely to be expected that the barbarians should believe him, yet no confessor of a holy poverty could be tortured without receiving a heavenly reward.

Again, they say that the long famine laid many a Christian low. But this, too, the faithful turned to good uses by a pious endurance of it. For those whom famine killed outright it rescued from the ills of this life, as a kindly disease would have done; and those who were only hunger-bitten were taught to live more sparingly, and inured to longer fasts.

Chapter 15.—Of the Man Christ Jesus, the Mediator Between God and Men.

But if, as is much more probable and credible, it must needs be that all men, so long as they are mortal, are also miserable, we must seek an intermediate who is not only man, but also God, that, by the interposition of His blessed mortality, He may bring men out of their mortal misery to a blessed immortality. In this intermediate two things are requisite, that He become mortal, and that He do not continue mortal. He did become mortal, not rendering the divinity of the Word infirm, but assuming the infirmity of flesh. Neither did He continue mortal in the flesh, but raised it from the dead; for it is the very fruit of His mediation that those, for the sake of whose redemption He became the Mediator, should not abide eternally in bodily death. Wherefore it became the Mediator between us and God to have both a transient mortality and a permanent blessedness, that by that which is transient He might be assimilated to mortals, and might translate them from mortality to that which is permanent. Good angels, therefore, cannot mediate between miserable mortals and blessed immortals, for they themselves also are both blessed and immortal; but evil angels can mediate, because they are immortal like the one party, miserable like the other. To these is opposed the good Mediator, who, in opposition to their immortality and misery, has chosen to be mortal for a time, and has been able to continue blessed in eternity. It is thus He has destroyed, by the humility of His death and the benignity of His blessedness, those proud immortals and hurtful wretches, and has prevented them from seducing to misery by their boast of immortality those men whose hearts He has cleansed by faith, and whom He has thus freed from their impure dominion.

Man, then, mortal and miserable, and far removed from the immortal and the blessed, what medium shall he choose by which he may be united to immortality and blessedness? The immortality of the demons, which might have some charm for man, is miserable; the mortality of Christ, which might offend man, exists no longer. In the one there is the fear of an eternal misery; in the other, death, which could not be eternal, can no longer be feared, and blessedness, which is eternal, must be loved. For the immortal and miserable mediator interposes himself to prevent us from passing to a blessed immortality, because that which hinders such a passage, namely, misery, continues in him; but the mortal and blessed Mediator interposed Himself, in order that, having passed through mortality, He might of mortals make immortals (showing His power to do this in His own resurrection), and from being miserable to raise them to the blessed company from the number of whom He had Himself never departed. There is, then, a wicked mediator, who separates friends, and a good Mediator, who reconciles enemies. And those who separate are numerous, because the multitude of the blessed are blessed only by their participation in the one God; of which participation the evil angels being deprived, they are wretched, and interpose to hinder rather than to help to this blessedness, and by their very number prevent us from reaching that one beatific good, to obtain which we need not many but one Mediator, the uncreated Word of God, by whom all things were made, and in partaking of whom we are blessed. I do not say that He is Mediator because He is the Word, for as the Word He is supremely blessed and supremely immortal, and therefore far from miserable mortals; but He is Mediator as He is man, for by His humanity He shows us that, in order to obtain that blessed and beatific good, we need not seek other mediators to lead us through the successive steps of this attainment, but that the blessed and beatific God, having Himself become a partaker of our humanity, has afforded us ready access to the participation of His divinity. For in delivering us from our mortality and misery, He does not lead us to the immortal and blessed angels, so that we should become immortal and blessed by participating in their nature, but He leads us straight to that Trinity, by participating in which the angels themselves are blessed. Therefore, when He chose to be in the form of a servant, and lower than the angels, that He might be our Mediator, He remained higher than the angels, in the form of God,—Himself at once the way of life on earth and life itself in heaven.

Plough Boy

ploughboy.org

60972072R00169

Made in the USA
Lexington, KY
24 February 2017